Early Praise for *Advanced Hands-on Rust: Level Up Your Coding Skills*

In *Advanced Hands-on Rust: Level Up Your Coding Skills*, Herbert Wolverson offers a pragmatic dive into game development with the Bevy Game Engine in Rust, utilizing engaging examples, such as Flappy and Mars One. These hands-on projects guide readers through advanced topics, including reusability, benchmarking, optimization, multithreading, and asynchronous programming. It's an invaluable resource for developers eager to master cutting-edge Rust techniques through fun and practical examples.

➤ **Tim Janus**
  Rust Meetup Organizer, Dortmund

This book is good reading for non-programmers interested in Rust also. My interest in Rust was solely picked up because of Herbert and his great work on LibreQoS, which utilizes it heavily.

➤ **Frantisek Borsik**
  Community Manager, LibreQoS

Advanced Hands-on Rust

Level Up Your Coding Skills

Herbert Wolverson

The Pragmatic Bookshelf

Dallas, Texas

Pragmatic Bookshelf

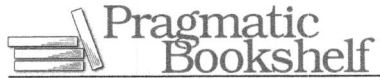

See our complete catalog of hands-on, practical,
and Pragmatic content for software developers:
https://pragprog.com

Sales, volume licensing, and support:
support@pragprog.com

Derivative works, AI training and testing,
international translations, and other rights:
rights@pragprog.com

The team that produced this book includes:

Publisher:	Dave Thomas
COO:	Janet Furlow
Executive Editor:	Susannah Davidson
Development Editor:	Tammy Coron
Copy Editor:	Corina Lebegioara
Indexing:	Potomac Indexing, LLC

ISBN-13: 979-8-88865-072-1
Book version: P1.0—October 2025

Contents

Part III — Flappy Dragon Flies Again

Part IV — Mars Base One

Part V — Library Curation

Acknowledgments

First of all, I'd like to thank the lovely Mel Wolverson for her patience and help while this book was put together. Our daughter joined us shortly after work commenced on *Advanced Hands-on Rust: Level Up Your Coding Skills*, and she's been doing her best to help too.

This book wouldn't have been completed without the assistance of Tim Janus, Vladyslav Batyrenko, Robert Chacon, Frantisek Borsik, and Dave Taht. They provided valuable feedback as the book developed and helped me keep abreast of the Bevy Engine's evolution.

Finally, my various employers: Ardan Labs, LibreQoS, and iZones. All have provided encouragement and support and made this book possible.

Dave Taht deserves a special mention. He passed away before the book was completed, but throughout its development, he was always encouraging, supportive, and a good friend.

Preface

Are you ready to accelerate your Rust development?

This book uses game development to make learning intermediate-to-advanced Rust concepts fun. Each chapter includes hands-on, practical development, creating tools to help you unleash your creativity and quickly build your own games.

As you work through this book, you'll achieve the following:

- Create reusable libraries and improve your code with testing, benchmarking, and optimization.

- Discover how to unlock the power of Rust's trait and generic metaprogramming systems to create code that adapts to fit your needs.

- Customize libraries with feature flags and language syntax with macros.

- Master concurrency with threads and asynchronous programming.

- Find out how to structure your games with reusable state management, menus, user interface elements, and asset management.

- Learn how to quickly build games with simple, reusable physics and collision detection.

- Make your games pop with animations, particles, and rendering tricks, including parallax layering.

- Build a REST client and server for high scores.

- Understand the responsibilities of long-term maintenance, and how to handle licensing and distribution with Cargo.

Each topic improves your game and gives you real-world Rust skills ready for use in any Rust project.

Who Should Read This Book?

This book is for Rust developers who want to move beyond the basics. If you've just finished *Hands-on Rust [Wol21]*, this book is the next step. However, you don't need to have read that book to benefit from this one. If you've mastered Rust's syntax and ownership ideas and want to build reusable libraries, work with generics and macros, optimize performance, and structure real-world projects, this book is for you.

What's in This Book?

This book teaches about library design, gradually introducing you to intermediate and advanced Rust concepts. Each chapter contains hands-on, practical examples of the concepts you're learning, and you get to have fun by using them to build and improve games.

This book does *not* aim to teach you how to work with a specific version of the Bevy Engine. Doing so would be futile; Bevy updates regularly, and the book would be out of date by the time it was printed. The book is about learning intermediate-to-advanced level Rust and the concepts that accompany it. Bevy—and games—are the vehicle to help you learn these concepts. The code examples in this book are based on Bevy 0.16.0, but the concepts will remain relevant as Bevy continues to evolve.

In Chapter 1, Set Up Rust and the Bevy Engine, on page 3, you'll ensure that you have a working Rust setup, and set up the Bevy Engine.[1] You'll build a basic example—moving a character around the screen—and become familiar with the basic concepts that make the Bevy Engine tick.

In Chapter 2, Create and Test Your First Library, on page 19, you'll create your first Rust library. Starting with "hello, library world," you'll build up to generating random numbers as a library service. You'll unit test your library functions, and integration test your systems by building a simple dice game. This builds up to your first interaction with generic functions: adapting your random number generation to fit the type of data requested by the function caller.

Moving on to Chapter 3, Optimize and Benchmark Your Library, on page 49, you'll use Rust and Criterion to benchmark your random number generation library. Benchmarking allows you to prove that your optimizations helped and is an important part of software development. Once you've established baseline performance, you'll use feature flags to offer different random number generation

---

1. https://bevyengine.org/

algorithms to the library consumer and will benchmark each one. Once you've selected an appropriate default—the fastest algorithm—you'll wrap your random number generator in a Bevy plugin and offer different scheduling and mutability characteristics with the use of interior locking. Once again, you'll unit test and integration test your library with the Pig dice game.

In Chapter 4, Document Your Library, on page 73, you'll focus on another important aspect of library development: documentation. Rust includes tools to make documenting libraries easier—even unit-testing your documentation examples. If you're ever going to share your library, good documentation is essential.

Chapter 5, Build Reusable Game State Management, on page 85, starts by creating a Bevy version of Flappy Dragon. Since most arcade-style games require a main menu and game over screen, this chapter walks you through creating a generic system for loading menus and applying them to games you create. State management can quickly become complicated, with states requiring substates to track progress through more complicated games. Because even the generic state-management syntax is becoming complicated, you'll create macros to create a more usable syntax. You'll then apply what you've learned to both Flappy Dragon and Pig.

Chapter 6, Manage Your Game Assets, on page 111, continues the theme of automating common tasks with library code by tackling game assets. You'll build an asset manager that lets you specify which sprites and sounds to load up-front and provides clear error messages if an asset is unavailable. Bevy loads assets asynchronously in the background. This can be wonderful for large titles, but it can also lead to embarrassing pauses as your game finishes loading a sprite and it suddenly appears on the screen. This chapter will teach you how to avoid this by wrapping your asset loading in a loading screen, showing progress as assets load—and not running the game before everything is ready.

In Chapter 7, Teach Your Dragon to Fly, on page 135, you'll flesh out Flappy Dragon. You'll combine your asset system with per-frame animation and timers to provide smoothly rendered animations to the game. The chapter will teach you a few "tricks," such as layering sprites and scrolling graphics at different speeds and scales to provide a "parallax" effect—giving the player an impression of forward movement. Simple movement will be replaced with the beginnings of a time-independent physics simulation, ensuring that your game runs the same on old or new computers. These are all useful techniques, so they'll be wrapped in library code and made available for all of your future games.

Chapter 8, Build Obstacles and Collision Detection, on page 163, continues the physics theme. Instead of hard-coding collision logic, you'll build a generic collision detection system that allows you to create events whenever entities of different types overlap, allowing you to expand Flappy Dragon's gameplay and easily provide collision detection in your games. Simply comparing each entity's position and "hit box" with every other entity can be time-consuming; this chapter will explore different ways to optimize the process.

Changing gears a bit, Chapter 10, Welcome to Mars Base One, on page 209, introduces a new game: Mars Base One. Mars Base One is a physics-based game in which you fly a spaceship around a colony on Mars, as you try to avoid crashing into walls and rescue colonists. You'll stress test your random number generator by procedurally generating a colony, guaranteeing different gameplay each time, and using "seeds" to allow you to use a fixed design while debugging.

In Chapter 11, Build a Mining Outpost on Mars, on page 219, you'll optimize both your library and Mars Base One. Level creation takes some time, so rather than "hitch" the game during level generation, you'll spin level-generation off to a thread and use synchronization primitives to start the game once the level is available.

Rendering thousands of wall pieces is slow, so in Chapter 12, Optimize Mars Base One, on page 243, you'll apply some optimization techniques to combine the walls into a single render mesh, rendering the level thousands of times faster.

Chapter 13, Add Miners and Energy Shields, on page 261, will flesh out Mars Base One and teach you some more rendering tricks. You'll add colonists to rescue, particle effects to convey a greater sense of motion and activity, and a Heads-Up Display (HUD) to better convey progress and game status. Your ship will gain a shield, so you don't die so quickly. At the end of the chapter, Mars Base One is a complete game.

In Chapter 14, Build a High Score Server, on page 279, you'll integrate your game with the Internet. You'll build a high-score server, accepting scores from people who play your game, and providing a list of high scores to display on the main menu. In the process, you'll build full round-trip serialization and deserialization and work with TCP sockets to safely transmit and receive data from other computers. You'll also practice some safe error-handling techniques; the server isn't always available, and random people might send you malicious data.

Chapter 15, Share Your Library, on page 305, focuses on sharing your library with others. Learn about licensing, publishing—or sharing via GitHub—and gain a good idea of what's required to maintain an open source library.

What's Not in This Book?

This book doesn't include the basics of getting started with Rust. If you need to start at the beginning, *Hands-on Rust* is a great start. This book also doesn't contain very advanced Rust—you won't learn the intricacies of directly managing memory, transmuting types, or working with cutting-edge features such as Generic Associated Types (GATs).

If you're an experienced Rust developer and want to learn more about structuring games or using the Bevy Engine, this book can still help you.

How to Read This Book

If you're coming from *Hands-on Rust*, you'll want to read this book in order. If you're an experienced Rust developer, you'll probably want to skim some of the more introductory sections and focus on the areas you need to learn.

Tutorials are as much about the journey as the destination. Working through this book should give you ideas and inspire you to create other games and programs. Building generic library toolkits is a great way to accelerate your development. Whenever you have a new idea, you no longer need to spend a lot of time writing boilerplate; you can reuse your previous work without resorting to copy and paste.

Conventions Used in This Book

The code accompanying this book is wrapped in a Rust *workspace*. Workspaces allow you to combine several projects into a single codebase, and when you compile an example, the resulting build reuses dependencies. Without a workspace, every project would require its own copy of Bevy and all of its dependencies, which can lead to using a huge amount of disk space.

The code is divided into directories as follows:

```
root
  /example_name (e.g. FirstLibraryCreate)
     /src        --- the source code for this example
     /assets     --- game assets required for this example
     Cargo.toml  --- build information for this example
  /src           --- a simple root program that reminds you to run an
                     example, rather than the workspace as a whole.
  Cargo.toml --- the master workspace control, listing all projects.
```

You can run code examples by navigating to example_name and typing cargo run for programs and cargo test for libraries.

Rust doesn't permit multiple projects of the same name to exist within a workspace. Because of this restriction, you'll find that some projects have a slightly different name inside their Cargo.toml descriptions. As you work through each stage of building my_library, the example code will change the name from my_library to my_library_benchmark. You *don't* need to change the names in your source code unless you explicitly want to match the example code.

When a file was created in a previous part of the book and a later example makes changes, changes have been highlighted with an arrow. For example:

```
fn do_something() {
➤    add_this_function();
}
```

When a file has changed and requires that you remove an entry, a comment is added:

```
fn do_something() {
➤    // remove: add_this_function();
}
```

Source Code for This Book

The source code accompanying this book is available from the Pragmatic Bookshelf's website.[2] The Bevy Engine updates frequently—the code in this book is based on Bevy 0.16.0. Bevy updates sometimes break things—so updated code is available on the author's GitHub page.[3]

Online Resources

Here are some online resources that can help you:

- *Rust By Example* provides a good, example-driven introduction to the Rust language.[4]
- The Rust Programming Language provides in-depth concepts and tutorials to learn the finer details of Rust. It's also available online.[5]

2.   https://pragprog.com/titles/hwmrust/advanced-hands-on-rust/
3.   https://github.com/thebracket/AdvancedHandsOnRust
4.   https://doc.rust-lang.org/rust-by-example/
5.   https://doc.rust-lang.org/book/

- *The Rust Standard Library* documentation provides detailed descriptions of everything found in Rust's std library. It's a great reference when you can't remember how something works.[6]
- *The Unofficial Bevy Cheat Book* is a great help when working with the Bevy engine.[7]
- *Bevy - The Quick-Start Guide* provides a lot of great documentation for the Bevy engine.[8]

Wrapping Up

Whether you've just finished *Hands-on Rust* and want to continue your journey or have mastered some of the basics of the Rust programming language and are ready to move to more advanced concepts, this book can help. It's exciting to build a new game and see your hard work come to fruition. It's even more exciting when you've created a toolkit that helps you avoid repeating yourself in every new project. Let's get started by setting up Rust and Bevy.

6.   https://doc.rust-lang.org/std/index.html
7.   https://bevy-cheatbook.github.io/
8.   https://bevyengine.org/learn/book/introduction/

Part I

Getting Started

CHAPTER 1

Set Up Rust and the Bevy Engine

In this book, you're going to make some cool games using the Rust language and the Bevy engine. You'll build a support library to get you up and running with game development quickly. The library will help with random number generation, asset management, animation, physics, game menu structure, user interface elements, and even networked high-score tables. The games themselves are only a small part of the picture; this book is all about learning intermediate-to-advanced Rust. You'll learn about library creation, generics, traits, and declarative macros. You'll use multiple threads and touch a little on asynchronous Rust. As in the previous book, *Hands-on Rust*, game development makes learning fun.

Before you dive into learning some advanced Rust, let's verify that your Rust setup is up to date and in working order. Once you're sure that Rust is working on your computer, you'll take a quick tour of the *Bevy* game engine since you'll be using it throughout this book.

Checking Your Rust Version

First, let's make sure you have Rust installed on your system. Open the command prompt or terminal and type rustup --version. Assuming you have Rust installed, you'll see something like this:

```
rustup 1.27.1 (54dd3d00f 2024-04-24)
info: This is the version for the rustup toolchain manager, not the rustc
compiler.
info: The currently active rustc version is
rustc 1.83.0 (90b35a623 2024-11-26)
```

In this example, the version of Rust is 1.83.0. Your version is likely different. However, to make sure you're using the most current version of Rust—and to update Rust if you're not—type rustup update. The "rustup" system installs your updated compilers, libraries, and toolchains.

What if RustUp Fails?

If rustup fails to run, you may need to install the Rust toolchain. Navigate to the RustUp website and follow the installation instructions.[1]

If you installed Rust through your operating system's package manager (for example, apt or brew), follow that package manager's instructions to update your Rust installation.

That should be all you need to get started. Let's move on to setting up a workspace, which improves your compilation times and reduces disk usage—both of which are helpful when developing complicated applications and libraries.

Setting Up a Workspace

Large Rust programs, and those that have large dependencies, can take a while to compile and often use a lot of disk space. You can mitigate this problem by using *workspaces*, which are managed by Rust's build tool, Cargo.

Workspaces offer the following advantages:

- They're designed to group different components of a project together, making it easy to work on libraries and applications together. For example, a workspace might contain a library, a second library (supporting the first one), and applications that use the two libraries.

- They share compiled dependencies between projects within the same workspace, so you only pay once for compilation time and disk space.

- Cleaning a workspace (with cargo clean) removes all of the workspace's compiled target data at once, which makes it much easier to free up disk space when you're done with a project.

Now that you know the benefits of using a workspace, it's time to create one so that you can use it while working on the projects in this book.

---

1.   https://rustup.rs/

Sample Code Workspace

The sample code for this book is contained within a workspace. Cargo doesn't allow multiple subprojects with the same name to reside within a workspace. For that reason, the project names in Cargo.toml have been changed for successive iterations of each project. You can use this same trick if you'd like to store iterations, or you can keep updating the same projects.

Creating Your First Workspace

Navigate to the directory in which you want to store your Rust projects (for example, /home/my_name/rust).

Create a new top-level project by typing cargo new more_hands. This command creates a basic Rust application project with the following files contained within it:

```
more_hands/          # Your workspace root
  Cargo.toml         # Your workspace configuration/manifest file
  src/               # Your source code directory
    main.rs          # Default "Hello, World!" source code
```

The directory contains a default Rust project.

Accidentally Running the Top Level of a Workspace

It's relatively easy to change your current directory to the workspace and issue cargo run—running the root workspace project, rather than the subproject you intended to run. A quick way to reduce surprises is to edit more_hands/src/main.rs and change the output message to something helpful. For example, you could change it to read, "You probably intended to run a workspace member."

Navigate to your workspace root folder by typing cd more_hands. Create a *second* new project in this directory by typing cargo new hello_world.

Cargo creates the same structure, but it does so inside more_hands/_world.

Let's create a workspace that contains the new project. Edit more_hands/Cargo.toml as follows:

```
[workspace]
members = [ "_world" ]
```

Adding a [workspace] and listing the members is all it takes to create a workspace. Let's try it out.

Change the directory to more_hands/_world and type cargo run. You'll be greeted with the default "Hello, World!" message.

Before moving on, look at the more_hands directory structure:

```
more_hands/          # Your workspace root
  Cargo.toml         # Your workspace configuration/manifest file
  src/               # Workspace source code directory
    main.rs          # Default "Hello, World!" source code
  hello_world/       # Your first sub-project
    Cargo.toml       # Sub-project configuration/manifest file
    src/             # Sub-project source code directory
      main.rs        # Default "Hello, World!" source code
  target/            # Shared build output
```

Notice that hello_world doesn't contain a target directory—your hello_world binary is located in more-hands/target/debug/. This setup indicates that you're sharing compilation resources within the workspace.

Adding Subprojects

Whenever you add a new project to the workspace, add it to your "members" array in more_hands/Cargo.toml. Recent versions of Cargo do this for you—but it's worth checking that the file is in the members list, and you may have to reformat your Cargo.toml file for clarity.

You cannot nest workspaces—that is, you can't put a workspace inside another workspace.

Setting up a workspace is relatively straightforward and keeps all of your compiled code together. This makes a big difference when you're working with large dependencies. Speaking of which, let's dive into Bevy—a very large dependency.

Bootstrapping Bevy

Bevy is a popular game engine for Rust.[2] It's an excellent choice for game development, combining fast execution with a relatively simple interface and a first-class Entity Component System (ECS) core. Bevy takes the ECS model to the extreme. Not only do entities and components represent your game's data model, but by using Bevy-supplied components, such as Transform and Sprite, you can directly tell Bevy to render your entities, with no need for intermediate render() functions.

---

2.   https://bevyengine.org/

Why Not Legion?

Hands-on Rust readers may be wondering why this book doesn't use Legion. Legion remains a capable ECS, but it's being eclipsed by Bevy in both popularity and development. Bevy's ECS is actually based on HECS, which set out to be "Legion, simplified." Bevy has improved upon Legion's extremely high performance and added comfortable ergonomics.

Before we get too far into the code, let's quickly cover how ECS engines work.

Reviewing the Entity Component System

Entity Component Systems are fast in-game databases of a game's state. Rather than build a structure for everything and anything that might exist in your game—including everything that entity needs to function—ECS encourages *composition.*

Let's look at the parts that make up an ECS:

- An Entity is a little more than an identification number. Entities have one or more Components that describe them.

- A Component is designed for reuse. For example, a Position component that describes a character's location on a game map may be reused by everything that needs to be placed on the map.

- Systems query the ECS database and perform logic based on the results. Systems are designed to be easy to parallelize, taking advantage of the full potential of multicore computers.

- Messages may be passed between systems, allowing one system to depend on the results of another.

- Resources act as globally shared data for your program.

The relationship between these parts of an ECS is shown at the top of the next page.

If you're familiar with *Hands-on Rust*, this is the same ECS concept used in that book. Bevy is another implementation of the same method of managing your game state. Don't worry if this concept is new to you—you'll pick it up quickly in the next few chapters as you make use of it.

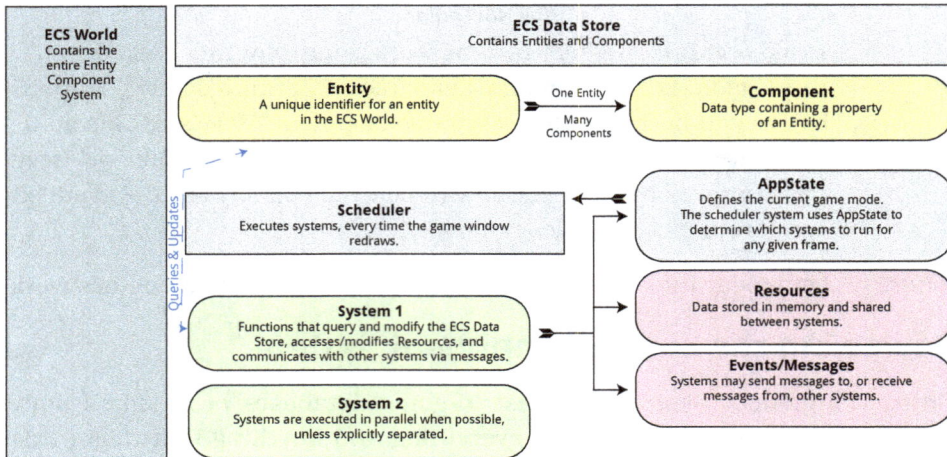

ECS World Contains the entire Entity Component System

ECS Data Store Contains Entities and Components

Entity A unique identifier for an entity in the ECS World.

One Entity
Many Components

Component Data type containing a property of an Entity.

Queries & Updates

Scheduler Executes systems, every time the game window redraws.

AppState Defines the current game mode. The scheduler system uses AppState to determine which systems to run for any given frame.

System 1 Functions that query and modify the ECS Data Store, accesses/modifies Resources, and communicates with other systems via messages.

Resources Data stored in memory and shared between systems.

Events/Messages Systems may send messages to, or receive messages from, other systems.

System 2 Systems are executed in parallel when possible, unless explicitly separated.

Message/Event Terminology

Bevy refers to messages passed between systems as Events. The Unity engine refers to them as Messages. Unreal Engine splits the difference by having an EventMessagingSystem. Other engines regularly use both terms interchangeably. This book prefers "messaging" for historical reasons.

Early object-oriented languages modeled communication between objects—systems—as "messages." SmallTalk, Objective-C, and others focused firmly on passing data between objects in the form of messages. Actor models—from Erland to Akka, Rust to Scala—all use the same terminology. In many ways, a system is an actor—it operates on data in isolation and communicates with other systems by passing messages.

Conversely, many operating systems explicitly refer to messages passed to applications as "events." For example, Windows and Mac OS both require that an application's "event loop" remain active throughout the life of the program. You can expect to run into both terms.

Let's take Bevy for a quick spin.

Saying Hello to Bevy

"Hello, World!" is traditionally the first program you write in a new language, so why break tradition, right? Let's create "Hello Bevy" to get you started with the Bevy engine.

Linux Dependencies

If you're using Bevy on Linux, please refer to Bevy's Linux Dependencies page[3] and install the dependencies listed there. At the time of printing, you can install the basic dependencies on Ubuntu-family distros with the following command: `sudo apt-get install g++ pkg-config libx11-dev libasound2-dev libudev-dev`.

If you're using Wayland as your rendering engine, you'll also need to install the following: `sudo apt-get install libwayland-dev libxkbcommon-dev`.

You'll need a project to hold your first Bevy program. Putting it inside your more_hands workspace allows you to share the Bevy library between projects as you work.

Navigate to the main directory of your more_hands workspace.

Create a new project with `cargo new hello_bevy`. Older versions of Rust required you to manually add the new project to your workspace. Newer versions detect if you already have workspaces and add them for you. If you do need to add the project to your workspace, open up more_hands/Cargo.toml and add hello_bevy to your workspace membership list:

```
[workspace]
members = [ "hello_world", "hello_bevy" ]
```

Next, you need to tell hello_bevy to use the Bevy engine. Open hello_bevy/Cargo.toml and adjust the dependencies:

```
BootstrapBevy/blank_window/Cargo.toml
[dependencies]
bevy = { workspace = true }
```

Workspace Dependencies

Workspaces offer an additional benefit: you can share dependencies between projects within the workspace. If you add a dependency to the workspace to level Cargo.toml, all subprojects can use that dependency. In the child-project's Cargo.toml, you can refer to the dependency as bevy.workspace = true or bevy = { workspace = true }.

Compilation artefacts will be shared between the projects—so you only pay once for compilation time and disk space—and you can update Bevy in one place, rather than in every subproject.

3. https://github.com/bevyengine/bevy/blob/main/docs/linux_dependencies.md

Open hello_bevy/src/main.rs and replace the contents with the following minimal Bevy application:

```
BootstrapBevy/blank_window/src/main.rs
❶ use bevy::prelude::*;

fn main() {
❷   App::new()
❸     .add_plugins(DefaultPlugins)
❹     .run();
}
```

❶ Import the bevy::prelude namespace into your project.

❷ Bevy uses the builder pattern to construct a Bevy application. Start with new() and keep adding instructions.

❸ Ask Bevy to load its default plugin list. This provides 2D and 3D graphics, audio, and input.

❹ After you've finished building Bevy's build instructions, start the application with run().

You now have everything you need to test Bevy. Enter the following commands to run your hello_bevy program:

```
⇒   cd hello_bevy
⇒   cargo run
```

After waiting while Bevy downloads and builds—don't worry, now that Bevy is in your workspace, you won't have to wait this long again—you're greeted with a blank window:

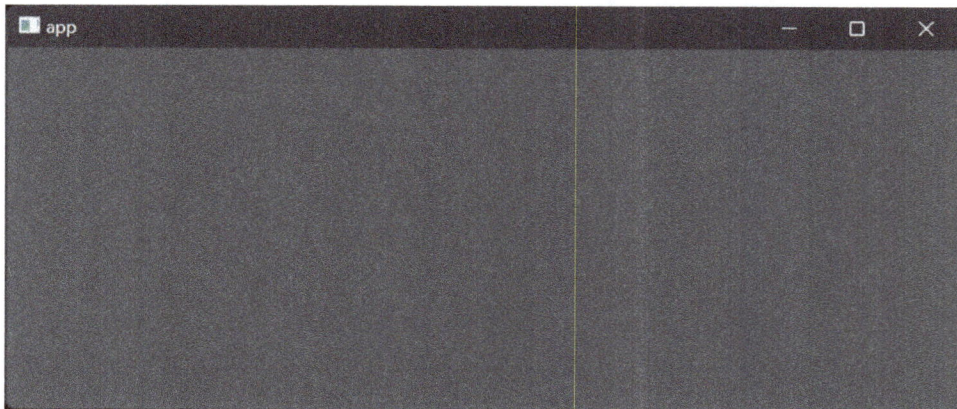

Time to add a little functionality to your Bevy demo and get acquainted with the Bevy way of working.

Bevy Compatibility

The Bevy engine does a good job of working with most configurations. Occasionally, you'll run into trouble.

If you're using Windows, Bevy works well with Rust installed on Windows. If you're using Windows Services for Linux (WSL), you may need to tell Bevy to use Vulkan rather than DirectX for rendering; DirectX is a Windows-only system and doesn't work properly inside WSL. You can do this by setting the WGPU_BACKEND environment variable to vulkan before running your Bevy application. You can do this with export WGPU_BACKEND=vulkan in your terminal before running your Bevy application.

If you're on Linux and using Wayland rather than X11, you may need to add the wayland feature to Bevy (it usually detects this automatically). In your dependencies, change bevy = "0.15.1" to bevy = { version = "0.15.1", features = ["wayland"] }.

Displaying a Graphic with Bevy

Almost every game requires graphics. Fortunately, Bevy includes an *asset server* system that takes care of most of what you need.

First, you need a graphic to load. In the hello_bevy directory, create a new directory and name it assets. This directory is where you'll store all of the graphics and audio for your game.

We'll display a picture of a dragon and move it around. Download dragon.png from the book's source code and place the file in the assets directory.[4]

4. The image is derived from a public domain piece of vector art, tweaked in Adobe Illustrator: https://publicdomainvectors.org/en/free-clipart/Blue-dragon/52592.html

Your subproject's directory structure will now look like this:

```
hello_bevy/         # Your Bevy project
  Cargo.toml        # Your project configuration/manifest file
  src/              # Your source code directory
    main.rs         # Your source code
  assets/           # Your asset directory
    dragon.png      # Your dragon graphic
```

Now you need to teach the program to load and display your dragon. First, you'll add a component type to identify that the dragon is, in fact, your dragon—and not another sprite in the game. Add the following code to your hello_bevy/main.rs file:

```
BootstrapBevy/moving_dragon/src/main.rs
#[derive(Component)]
struct Dragon;
```

Bevy components are relatively simple; they can be structures or enums, but they must implement the component trait. The code #derive(Component) invokes a procedural macro that adds the appropriate trait code for you. Any type that you decorate with this derive is then available to use in Bevy, so there's no need to maintain a component registration list.

Next, you'll add a function that loads your dragon.png graphic and creates an Entity in the ECS that displays your dragon:

```
BootstrapBevy/moving_dragon/src/main.rs
❶ fn setup(
❷   mut commands: Commands,
❸   asset_server: Res<AssetServer>
) {
❹   commands.spawn(Camera2d::default());
❺   let dragon_image = asset_server.load("dragon.png");
  commands
❻     .spawn(Sprite::from_image(dragon_image))
❼     .insert(Dragon);
}
```

❶ This is your first Bevy system. Systems are regular functions, but they benefit from *dependency injection*. Bevy matches parameters to the types of data it can make available, and it automatically links the appropriate data for you.

❷ Commands structures are used to create or delete entities from the Bevy Entity Component System. Commands are collected and executed at the end of the frame—the new entities will be available in the next frame.

❸ Any type wrapped in a Res type is a resource. Bevy defines several resources to help you work with game assets, such as your dragon. AssetServer is the simplest image-loading resource.

❹ It's common to want to spawn an entity with a number of predefined components attached. Bevy's spawn() function reads a component, and it can specify other components in its require definition. Bevy spawns them together with default values for any component you didn't specifically override. For a Camera2d, Bevy is actually spawning a Camera, a DebandDither, a CameraRenderGraph, a Projection, a Frustrum, and a ToneMapping. In most cases, a default value is specified—but if you want to know exactly what you're spawning, you need to inspect the source of the Camera. Note that this has substantially changed in recent Bevy versions; previous versions used a "bundle" system instead.

Every 2D project that uses Bevy's renderer needs a camera.

❺ Instruct the asset server to load the dragon.png image. Bevy will load the image in the background, making it accessible via a Handle.

❻ Request that Bevy spawn a Sprite, using the image handle you acquired before.

❼ Finally, the insert() method allows you to attach your own components to an entity. You'll mark the dragon, so you can easily access it later.

Now that you have a setup() function, you need to tell Bevy to run it. You only want it to run once. Otherwise, Bevy will continually reload the dragon asset and add more entities to your game. Bevy includes the add_systems() function as part of its builder for this purpose. Adding the Startup parameter indicates that the system runs when the program begins. Adjust your main() function to call your new setup function as follows:

```
fn main() {
  App::new()
    .add_plugins(DefaultPlugins)
➤   .add_systems(Startup, setup)
    .run();
}
```

Run the game, and you'll see the dragon is rendered in the middle of the screen.

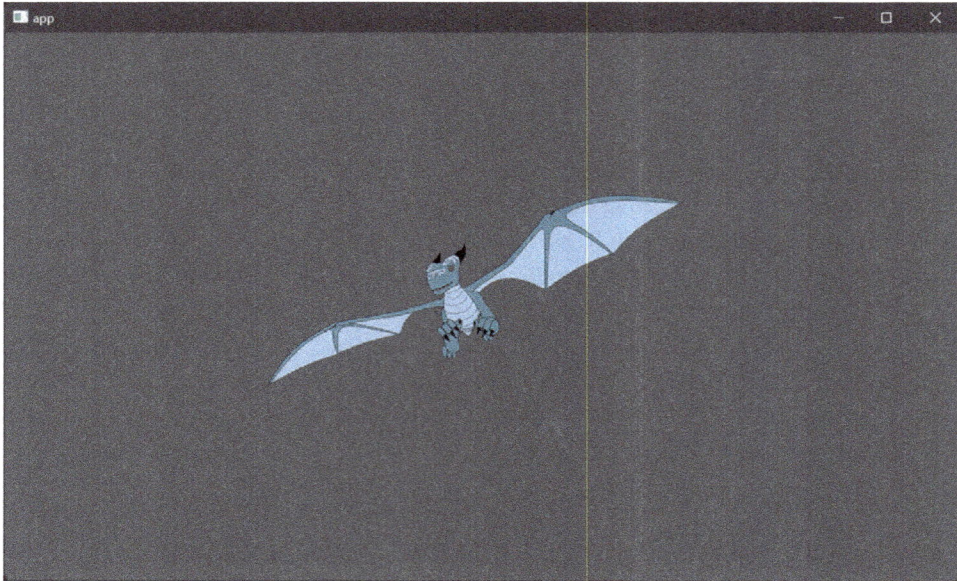

That's cool, but let's make it cooler by making it move.

Moving Entities with Bevy

To make entities move with Bevy, you'll use another system to read keyboard input and modify the dragon's position.

Add the following function to your main.rs file:

BootstrapBevy/moving_dragon/src/main.rs
```
fn movement(
    keyboard: Res<ButtonInput<KeyCode>>,
    mut dragon_query: Query<&mut Transform, With<Dragon>>,
) {
    let delta = if keyboard.pressed(KeyCode::ArrowLeft) {
        Vec2::new(-1.0, 0.0)
    } else if keyboard.pressed(KeyCode::ArrowRight) {
        Vec2::new(1.0, 0.0)
    } else if keyboard.pressed(KeyCode::ArrowDown) {
        Vec2::new(0.0, -1.0)
    } else if keyboard.pressed(KeyCode::ArrowUp) {
        Vec2::new(0.0, 1.0)
    } else {
        Vec2::ZERO
    };

    dragon_query.iter_mut().for_each(|mut transform| {
        transform.translation += delta.extend(0.0);
    });
}
```

❶ Another internal resource offered by Bevy is the ButtonInput type. Combined with KeyCode, you can use this to query the current state of keys on the user's keyboard.

❷ ECS data is accessed with *queries*. Your dragon_query requests writable (mutable) access to the Transform data created with your sprite, and it limits the query to affect only types that have the Dragon component attached. This process is described in more detail in the next steps.

❸ Set the delta variable to a Vec2 (containing x and y values) that indicates the intended direction of travel when a key is pressed or all zeroes when no key is pressed.

❹ iter_mut()() obtains a mutable iterator, and for_each() runs the associated closure for each entity matching the query requirements, passing the values of references components into the included function. Note that this has changed in recent versions of Bevy—you used to have to use for_each_mut().

❺ Add the delta variable to the current *translation* (position on the screen), moving the dragon. The extend function transforms a Vec2 into a Vec3, padding the missing field with the specified number—in this case, 0.

There are a few new concepts here:

• Queries are how you read data from the ECS. Queries have *requirements*—a list of requirements they must match (also known as "predicates" in other formal systems). Required components marked with &mut are read-write. Otherwise, you can read but not write the results. Queries only return entities that have *all* of the listed component types.

• The With type is a special predicate—it requires that query entities have a component type, but it doesn't include the component type in the query results. This reduces the repetitive use of _ in your query handling functions as you studiously ignore unused data types.

• In physics and computer graphics, a vector is a mathematical vector—a collection of coordinates. The name "vector" can be confusing since a Rust vector is a list of items. Bevy defines Vec2 and Vec3 to provide mathematical vectors with (x,y) and (x,y,z) coordinates. So why are you using a Vec3 in a 2D game? The third component is used to sort sprites when they're rendered. Sprites with a higher z value are rendered on top of lower z values. Since you're positioning the dragon in 2D space and don't have other sprites to worry about, you can ignore the z value when thinking about sprite movement. Bevy still expects to find it—you can use the extend function to add the missing z value to a Vec2. Now that you have a movement system in place, let's add it to the Bevy app builder:

BootstrapBevy/moving_dragon/src/main.rs
```
fn main() {
  App::new()
    .add_plugins(DefaultPlugins)
    .add_systems(Startup, setup)
➤   .add_systems(Update, movement)
    .run();
}
```

Run the program with cargo run, and you'll see that you have a movable dragon in a window. (To move the dragon, use the cursor keys.)

Wrapping Up

In this chapter, you verified that you have a working Rust setup, and you took the Bevy engine for a ride by making some simple examples. In the next chapter, you're ready to start diving into more advanced Rust by making your own library.

Part II

Your First Library

CHAPTER 2

Create and Test Your First Library

Now that you're up and running with Rust and the Bevy engine, it's time to create some *libraries*. Libraries let you bundle code together in a reusable format, shared between multiple projects. You've already consumed libraries—every time you make an entry in the [dependencies] section of Cargo.toml, you're making use of the code library provided by the crate you requested. Even "Hello, World!" uses the *standard library* built into Rust.[1]

Grouping code into libraries offers a lot of potential benefits:

- Don't repeat yourself (DRY). Solve a problem or implement an algorithm once, and you can reuse the
- result over and over again in a library. *The Pragmatic Programmer, 20th Anniversary Edition [TH19]* contains excellent guidance about the DRY principle.
- If you find yourself writing the same boilerplate over and over, wrapping it in a function or macro in a library can save you time and energy.
- Libraries are designed to be shared with friends, colleagues, or even the world.

Library Terminology

"Library" and "crate" are often used interchangeably. They're similar concepts, but they're not the same thing. "Library" is a generic term for a package of reusable code, usually supported directly by your operating system. A "crate" is a library, managed by Cargo—the Rust build manager.

A library managed by Cargo is known as a Crate. Rust encourages crate use, and Cargo makes it easy to find and add dependencies. This has the benefit

---

1. https://doc.rust-lang.org/std/

that you aren't reinventing the wheel for every project, and the disadvantage that sometimes you have a large dependency graph. The hello_bevy example from Bootstrapping Bevy, on page 6, installs 595 dependencies in total. This is a good example of how crates can help you: creating a blank window and responding to operating system events is hard work. The Bevy team did some of the hard work, and other teams have created crates that help Bevy run. Your project rests on the shoulders of giants.

Because crates are so important to the Rust ecosystem, Rust includes a lot of tooling to make working with crates easier:

- Crates are developed and built with the same tools as regular Rust programs. The only difference is that instead of a main.rs file (and main() function), you use a lib.rs file. lib.rs doesn't need a main() function.

- You still build your code with cargo build.

- You can't directly execute a library with cargo run: there's no main() function to act as an entry point, indicating where the program should start. Instead, you include a library as a dependency—and use cargo run on the program that depends on your library.

- Unit testing is built into Rust. Executing cargo test on a library will run all of the library's tests.

- Rustdoc is built-in and provides a standardized way to document your library/crate. It can even test that your example code compiles.

- Rust statically links your programs, building libraries into the main program. You don't need to worry about shipping DLL files or shared libraries—everything is included in your program.

It's time to start building your first library.

Hello, Library World

By now, you're familiar with creating new application projects using cargo new. Creating a library project is the same, but it requires you to add --lib to the command line—indicating that you want to make a library. Let's add a new project to the more_hands workspace you created in Creating Your First Workspace, on page 5.

Navigate to your more_hands directory and type cargo new --lib my_library. Newer versions of Cargo will automatically add my_library to your Cargo.toml's workspace; older versions will give you an error message:

```
⇒   cd (path)/more_hands
⇒   cargo new --lib my_library
‹ warning: compiling this new package may not work due to invalid workspace
  configuration

  current package believes it's in a workspace when it's not:
  current:    more_hands\my_library\Cargo.toml
  workspace: more_hands\Cargo.toml

  this may be fixable by adding `my_library` to the `workspace.members`
  array of the manifest located at: (path)
  Alternatively, to keep it out of the workspace, add the package to the
  `workspace.exclude` array, or add an empty `[workspace]` table to the
  package's manifest.
```

The warning says that Rust created your library and detected that it's in your workspace directory structure—but not included in your workspace. You need to open more_hands/Cargo.toml and add my_library to your workspace members:

```
[workspace]
members = [ "hello_world", "hello_bevy", "my_library" ]
```

You now have a my_library project included inside your more_hands workspace.

Cargo has created some placeholder files for your library:

```
more_hands/          # Workspace parent folder
  Cargo.toml         # Workspace configuration file
  src/               # Source code for the workspace
    main.rs          # Main file for the workspace
  my_library/        # my_library project folder
    Cargo.toml       # Library configuration file
    src/             # Source code for the library
      lib.rs         # Library source code with a default unit test
target/              # Shared build directory
```

Cargo.toml is exactly the same as it would be for an executable application. There's no main.rs file because libraries don't need one. Instead, there's a lib.rs file. Cargo has replaced the default "Hello, World!" application with an example unit test. Let's take a quick tour of what it's created; we'll go over the specifics in more detail later in this chapter:

FirstLibraryCreate/default_lib/src/lib.rs
```
❶ #[cfg(test)]
❷ mod tests {
❸   #[test]
    fn it_works() {
      let result = 2 + 2;
❹     assert_eq!(result, 4);
    }
}
```

❶ #[cfg(...)] indicates *conditional compilation.* In this case, the code block following the statement will only be compiled when you're compiling in *test mode*—typically by invoking cargo test. The module won't be included in normal compiles.

❷ mod creates a new *in-line module.* This is the same as creating a file named test.rs and connecting it to your project with mod test—but this keeps the test code inside your file, next to the code it's testing. This also provides the block to which the #[cfg(...)] applies. The module will only be compiled when you're testing your library.

❸ #[test] tells Cargo that the function following this declaration is a unit test and should be executed when you invoke cargo test.

❹ The it_works() function is a normal function. It adds 2 and 2, storing the result in a variable named result. The test then invokes a macro named assert_eq!. The macro takes two parameters and panics—crashing the program—if the parameters aren't equal.

You can't execute your library with cargo run because it has no entry point or main() function. Cargo has ensured that you can still test that your library was created properly. To run your library's unit tests, type cargo test:

```
⇒   cd (path)/more_hands/my_library
⇒   cargo test
❰ running 1 test
  test tests::it_works ... ok
```

Cargo runs the unit test and verifies that 2+2 is still equal to 4. The default unit test isn't useful, other than to remind you that you should write unit tests—and giving you a quick overview of the syntax required to do so.

Let's add some functionality to your new library.

Generating Random Numbers as a Library Service

Computers are deterministic; for the same set of inputs, running a program hundreds of times will give the exact same result. This is the opposite of what you intuitively expect from random numbers—roll a dice 500 times at a casino, and see how long it takes them to show you the door when you roll five hundred sixes.

To overcome this determinism, an entire branch of computer science and math has emerged to create *pseudorandom* numbers. The random number algorithm remains deterministic—you always get the same results from the same starting point (known as a "seed"), but it's difficult to predict what the next random number you generate will be.

Pseudorandom algorithms always represent a trade-off between performance (how quickly you can generate the random number) and quality (how difficult it is to predict the next number). Because of this trade-off, Rust doesn't include a random number generator in its standard library—whichever algorithm the Rust maintainers select will be insufficient for some users' needs. Instead, a variety of random number algorithms are implemented by the rand crate.[2]

Let's add a dependency on rand into my_library.

Depending on Rand

Library dependencies are managed in exactly the same way as application dependencies—you add them to the [dependencies] section of your library's Cargo.toml file. Open my_library/Cargo.toml and add rand as a dependency:

```
[dependencies]
rand = "0.8"
```

my_library now includes rand in its compilation process, and it can access functionality exported by the rand crate in the rand:: namespace.

Let's take a moment to think about visibility. my_library can access rand—but an application using my_library cannot access rand, except through any public functions, types, or modules exported by my_library.

Sometimes, this is exactly what you want: you're shielding your library users from the intricacies of the dependency. In this case, rand offers many useful tools that the user may enjoy. It would be a shame to make the library users jump through the extra hoops of depending on the library to take advantage of any features you haven't exposed in my_library. You can *reexport* a dependency with pub use; wrapping it in pub mod allows you to place it in a child namespace within your crate's namespace.

Let's reexport rand to our library users. Open my_library/src/lib.rs and add the following to the top of the file:

FirstLibraryCreate/my_library/src/lib.rs
```
pub use rand;
```

Consumers of my_library can now access rand through the namespace my_library::rand. Library visibility may be visualized as follows:

2.   https://docs.rs/rand/latest/rand/

Default dependency:

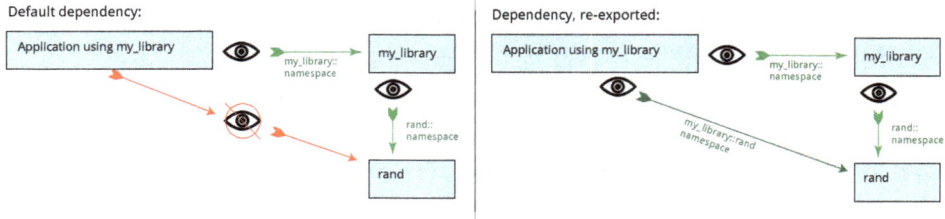

Dependency, re-exported:

Be Careful Exposing Your Privates

C++ has a concept of "friend classes," allowing types to share private data. Rust is more hierarchical and largely prevents this.

- Functions inside a module can access private parts of structures within the same module.

- Functions outside of a module cannot access private parts of anything in another module.

- Adding a pub keyword to a function, structure, or element allows other modules anywhere to access the structure or element. The access is further restricted by structures and modules hierarchically—a public member of a structure is still only public to its parent module.

- Adding pub(crate) allows other modules to access the structure or element, but only within the same crate.

- You can use pub and pub crate on modules and use statements to control access to a module, or part of a module.

This is a common cause of confusion in Rust. You'll refer back to these rules periodically as you implement more library functionality.

Now that my_library can access the rand crate, let's start building a RandomNumberGenerator structure.

Create a Random Number Generator Structure and Constructors

Random numbers are deterministic, generated by an algorithm that starts with a seed (initial value) and updates the current algorithm state each time a random number is generated. This requires the following actions:

- Generating a seed:

  - Either randomly (for an unpredictable result).

  - Or deterministically—generating the same random numbers each time, useful for testing.

- Storing the current random state.

Let's start by telling Rust to include a file named random.rs in the my_library project. Module naming and usage is exactly the same in libraries as it is in applications, so this process should be familiar. Open my_library/src/lib.rs and add the following:

FirstLibraryCreate/my_library/src/lib.rs
```
❶ mod random;
❷ pub use random::*;
```

  ❶ mod random includes the random.rs file as a module named random.

  ❷ pub use random::* publishes every public symbol in the random module, making them available to library consumers.

With that in place, anything you mark with pub in random.rs will be available to library consumers.

Now, create a new file named my_library/src/random.rs. Let's add a new type to random.rs and make the type public:

FirstLibraryCreate/my_library/src/random.rs
```
❶ use rand::{prelude::StdRng, Rng, SeedableRng};
   use std::ops::Range;
❷ pub struct RandomNumberGenerator {
❸    rng: StdRng,
   }
```

  ❶ Libraries use other modules and crates in the same way as other Rust code. We'll include the types we're going to need.

  ❷ Declare a new structure type named RandomNumberGenerator and make it public. The type is now available to library consumers.

  ❸ Declare a member variable named rng. It's private—you can't access it from outside this module. StdRng is a type from the rand crate, the provided "standard" random number generator algorithm offering a balance between quality and performance.

Next, we'll add a couple of constructors to our RandomNumberGenerator:

FirstLibraryCreate/my_library/src/random.rs
```rust
impl RandomNumberGenerator {
  pub fn new() -> Self {
    Self {
      rng: StdRng::from_entropy(),
    }
  }

  pub fn seeded(seed: u64) -> Self {
    Self {
      rng: StdRng::seed_from_u64(seed),
    }
  }
}
```

❶ Our default `new` constructor will try to pick a safe default.

❷ Initializing the random number generator with `from_entropy()` acquires a random number from the operating system's random facilities to use as the random seed. This is often slow, but very random—many operating systems take readings from USB noise, network data, and other unpredictable sources to populate their entropy buffers.

❸ We'll also provide a way to let the caller specify a random seed. This allows us to test that the library is deterministic and allows library consumers to benefit from the determinism.

When you're building a library type, it's good practice to implement the Rust built-in trait, `Default`. If a user isn't sure what constructor to pick, `default()` provides a safe choice. Add the following to random.rs:

FirstLibraryCreate/my_library/src/random.rs
```rust
impl Default for RandomNumberGenerator {
  fn default() -> Self {
    Self::new()
  }
}
```

The default implementation just calls `new()` and returns the result. Your library consumer can now create a random number generator with RandomNumberGenerator::new(), RandomNumberGenerator::seeded(), and RandomNumberGenerator::default().

Next, you'll make the type useful by generating some random numbers. In the impl RandomNumberGenerator block, add the following function to RandomNumberGenerator's implementation block:

FirstLibraryCreate/my_library/src/random.rs
```rust
pub fn range(&mut self, range: Range<u32>) -> u32 {
  self.rng.gen_range(range)
}
```

Library consumers can now use their RandomNumberGenerator instance to generate u32 numbers that fall into a range. For example, rng.range(1..5) will generate a random number between 1 and 4 (an exclusive range).

Now that my_library has some functionality, let's test it to make sure it does what you expect.

Unit Testing Your Random Number Generator

You've created a relatively straightforward interface: the library consumer creates RandomNumberGenerator variables and uses them to create u32 variables that fall within a specified range. The RandomNumberGenerator also carries the implied contract that it's deterministic for a given seed. These are both properties that you can—and should—test.

Code First, or Tests First?

Test-driven development is a popular approach to application development that encourages you to write unit tests first and code later. This process allows you to formalize your interfaces quickly, and tests move from "fail" to "pass" status as you complete your code.

Test-driven development is a great way to implement systems for which you have a good specification. While you're learning to make libraries and tests, it's often easier to write code and then test it.

You should always aim to create a test that would catch a bug you encounter and fix. Rerunning the test whenever you change the library ensures that you avoid *regressions*—those nasty times that bugs sneak back into your code.

Create a Test Module

To get started, let's add the test module back to the end of more_hands/my_library/random.rs:

FirstLibraryCreate/my_library/src/random.rs
```
#[cfg(test)]
mod test {
  use super::*;
```

Including #[cfg(test)] ensures that the test module will *only* be compiled into your library when you're testing—it won't bloat your published library. Importing the parent scope allows you to refer to RandomNumberGenerator directly instead of having to refer to super::RandomNumberGenerator.

Testing Random Ranges

As a first test, you'll verify that random numbers generated within a range fall within that range. Add the following code to your test module scope:

```
FirstLibraryCreate/my_library/src/random.rs
❶ #[test]
fn test_range_bounds() {
  let mut rng = RandomNumberGenerator::new();
❷  for _ in 0..1000 {
    let n = rng.range(1..10);
❸    assert!(n >= 1);
❹    assert!(n < 10);
  }
}
```

❶ Add a #[test] annotation to every function you want to run as a unit test.

❷ Since you're dealing with random numbers, you can't be sure what value will be returned. Repeating the test 1,000 times with a small range should guarantee good coverage of generated numbers.

❸ assert! macros panic—and fail the test—if the condition passed into them evaluates to false. In this case, you want to ensure that your randomly generated number is greater than or equal to 1.

❹ Panic if the generated random number is greater than 9—and therefore outside of the range you specified.

The test_range_bounds test generates 1,000 random numbers in the range 1 through 9 (it's an exclusive range), and it ensures that they all fall within the requested range. With that test written, let's move on to testing determinism.

Testing Random Seed Determinism

Your second test will verify that your random number generator produces reproducible results for a given seed. Add this code to your mod scope:

```
FirstLibraryCreate/my_library/src/random.rs
#[test]
fn test_reproducibility() {
  let mut rng = (
    RandomNumberGenerator::seeded(1),
    RandomNumberGenerator::seeded(1),
❶  );
❷  (0..1000).for_each(|_| {
❸    assert_eq!(
      rng.0.range(u32::MIN..u32::MAX),
      rng.1.range(u32::MIN..u32::MAX),
    );
```

```
    });
}
```

❶ Create a tuple containing two RandomNumberGenerator types, each set to the same seed.

❷ A convenient Rust shorthand (range).for_each converts a range into an iterator and calls the attached closure on each entry. This is the same as for _ in 0..1000.

❸ The assert_eq! panics if its parameters don't contain the same values. By generating a random number from each generator, you should be able to guarantee that the results are the same each time.

The test_reproducibility test creates two RandomNumberGenerator variables with a specified seed (equal to 1). It then generates 1,000 random numbers with each generator and checks that they're the same. If they match, your random number generator is deterministic.

Run the Unit Tests

Run these tests by typing cargo test from the my_library directory:

```
⇒   cargo test
❮ running 2 tests
    test random::test::test_reproducibility ... ok
    test random::test::test_range_bounds ... ok

    test result: ok. 2 passed; 0 failed; 0 ignored; 0 measured; 0 filtered out;
    finished in 0.00s
```

Your library's unit tests worked. You've verified that random numbers fall within the requested range and that your random number generator produces consistently reproducible results. Don't delete the unit tests; as you work on your library, you'll want to periodically run cargo test to ensure that your changes haven't broken any promises your library made to your users.

Integration Testing Your Random Number Generator

You can build and test a library by running unit tests—if you're diligent about testing everything, you can even be pretty sure that it will work. *Integration testing* works by creating a project that uses your library and testing it in the real world. Integration testing is great for finding rough edges in your interfaces as well as actual bugs. You want your library consumer's experience to be as comfortable as possible. For this integration test, you'll create another subproject in our more_hands workspace and build a game known as Pig.

Introducing Pig, a Dice Game

Pig is a simple dice game for two players. With the exception of player choices, the gameplay is entirely random, which makes it a good test of your random number generator's usability.

Here's how it works: in Pig, each player starts with a score of zero. The players take turns, starting with a turn score, also known as a hand score, of zero. A player may either elect to roll the six-sided die or pass. If a player rolls between 2 and 6, the score is added to their current turn or hand score. If they roll a 1, their hand score is zeroed and play passes to the other player. If the player elects to pass, the player's current hand score is added to their total score and play passes to the other player.

Despite its random nature, Pig has been heavily analyzed. There's a great Wikipedia article that describes optimal play.[3] For this example, you'll implement the second player as a simple AI that uses the "hold at 20" stratagem. This AI's strategy is 8% less effective than perfect optimal play, so it should provide a challenge but still be beatable.

Let's get started by creating a project in the workspace. Navigate to your more_hands workspace parent directory and create a new project named pig by running cargo new pig. If necessary, add your new project to more_hands/Cargo.toml:

```
[workspace]
members = [ "hello_world", "hello_bevy", "my_library", "pig" ]
```

Next, you need to make pig depend on my_library and bevy. Open your top-level Cargo.toml and make sure that bevy_egui is included in the dependencies section:

```
[dependencies]
bevy = "0.16"
bevy_egui = "0.34"
```

Open more_hands/pig/Cargo.toml and replace the dependencies as follows:

```
[dependencies]
my_library = { path = "../my_library" }
bevy = { workspace = true }
bevy_egui = { workspace = true }
```

Instead of providing a version number for my_library, you specified a directory path. This forces Cargo to use the local copy of your library.

---

3. https://en.wikipedia.org/wiki/Pig_(dice_game)

What Is Egui?

Bevy's user-interface system is extremely thorough, offering a "flexbox" style display composition system similar to many web pages. It's also overkill for simple applications. egui is a much simpler GUI system, popular for displaying debugging information in games.

egui is an *immediate-mode* user-interface system. Every element is resubmitted on each frame—if you don't submit an element, it won't be rendered. This contrasts with Bevy's UI system, which requires that you submit hierarchies of interface elements to the ECS. Elements in the ECS are then rendered until you remove or hide them. Bevy's system offers a lot more flexibility at the expense of considerable complexity. egui—and the project that inspired it, Dear ImGui—is popular for prototyping, debugging, and quickly creating an interface.

You'll learn to use Bevy's user-interface system in Chapter 6, Manage Your Game Assets, on page 111.

You can run pig by navigating to the more_hands/pig directory and typing cargo run. You'll see your library compile in addition to the executable. You can also change the directory to more_hands/my_library and invoke cargo test to run your unit tests.

Windows Path Separators

Windows uses backslash (\) instead of forward slash (/) for separating directories. More recent versions of Windows quietly allow you to use either—and so does Rust. Stick with the forward-slash version, and your path will work on most operating systems.

Set Up Assets and Framework

You'll need a graphic to represent dice. Create a directory named assets in your more_hands/pig directory. Download dice.png from the book's source folder and place it in the new directory. The dice graphic was created by James White and may be downloaded from OpenGameArt.[4] The image looks like this:

---

4. https://opengameart.org/content/dice-4

Now, open more_hands/pig/src/main.rs and copy in a slightly modified version of the "Hello, Bevy" code Bootstrapping Bevy, on page 6:

FirstLibraryCreate/pig/src/main.rs

```
use bevy::prelude::*;
```
❶
```
use bevy_egui::{egui, EguiContexts, EguiPlugin};
```
❷
```
use my_library::RandomNumberGenerator;
```
❸
```
#[derive(Clone, Copy, PartialEq, Eq, Debug, Hash, Default, States)]
enum GamePhase {
  #[default]
  Player,
  Cpu,
}

fn main() {
  App::new()
    .add_plugins(DefaultPlugins)
    .add_plugins(EguiPlugin{ enable_multipass_for_primary_context: false })
```
❹
```
    .add_systems(Startup, setup)
```
❺
```
    .init_state::<GamePhase>()
```
❻
```
    .add_systems(Update, display_score)
    .add_systems(Update, player.run_if(
```
❼
```
      in_state(GamePhase::Player)))
    .add_systems(Update, cpu.run_if(
```
❽
```
      in_state(GamePhase::Cpu)))
    .run();
}
```

❶ Import egui. EguiPlugin wraps the GUI system in an easy-to-use Bevy plugin. EguiContexts is a helper layer that provides systems with access to the egui system.

❷ Import RandomNumberGenerator from the library you created.

❸ Bevy tracks application state with an enumeration. The game is either in Player mode, choosing to roll or pass, or it's in Cpu mode, where the AI decides on the next move. Deriving Default and annotating the default state lets you tell Bevy in which state the game should start.

❹ Add a start-up system named setup().

❺ Add the GamePhase enumeration you created to the application. This is the *turbofish* syntax—you're attaching the type to the function. The initial state will be inferred from the type's default value.

❻ For any state, call display_score() to display the current AI and player score on the screen.

❼ You can limit a system to only run during a specific state by appending run_if(in_state(STATE)) to the system call. This, in turn, accepts the phase—in this case, Update and the state to match.

❽ Likewise, only run the cpu() system when the application state is set to GamePhase::Cpu.

The preceding code introduces Bevy's approach to *state management*. It's unusual for an application to perform exactly the same steps on each frame—you might need to display a menu, change player turn, or offer in-game settings changes. You'll take a deep dive into state management in Chapter 5, Build Reusable Game State Management, on page 85; for now, follow along and get a feel for how it works.

Next, you need to create structures to represent the elements of the Pig game:

FirstLibraryCreate/pig/src/main.rs
```
#[derive(Resource)]
struct GameAssets {
    image: Handle<Image>,
    layout: Handle<TextureAtlasLayout>,
}

#[derive(Clone, Copy, Resource)]
struct Scores {
    player: usize,
    cpu: usize,
}

#[derive(Component)]
struct HandDie;

#[derive(Resource)]
struct Random(RandomNumberGenerator);

#[derive(Resource)]
struct HandTimer(Timer);
```

❶ Define a structure holding a Handle to a TextureAtlas containing the dice graphics. You'll need access to this handle to add dice to the screen. Handles represent an index to the stored graphic, allowing you to load it once and reuse the image.

❷ Create a structure to store the current score.

❸ Create an empty structure to label—or "tag"—entities as representing dice on the screen.

❹ Wrap RandomNumberGenerator in a Bevy resource.

❺ Wrap Timer in a Bevy resource.

Those are the components you'll need. You're storing the current score and "tagging" entities to indicate their purpose.

Setting Up the Game

Next, let's build the setup() function to initialize the game. Start by defining the function and requesting a resource from Bevy by including them as parameters:

FirstLibraryCreate/pig/src/main.rs

```
fn setup(
①    asset_server: Res<AssetServer>,
②    mut commands: Commands,
③    mut texture_atlas_layouts: ResMut<Assets<TextureAtlasLayout>>,
    ) {
④    commands.spawn(Camera2d::default());

⑤    let texture = asset_server.load("dice.png");
    let layout = TextureAtlasLayout::from_grid(
⑥      UVec2::splat(52), 6, 1, None, None);
⑦    let texture_atlas_layout = texture_atlas_layouts.add(layout);

    commands.insert_resource(
      GameAssets { image: texture, layout: texture_atlas_layout }
⑧    );
⑨    commands.insert_resource(Scores { cpu: 0, player: 0 });
⑩    commands.insert_resource(Random(RandomNumberGenerator::new()));
    commands.insert_resource(HandTimer(Timer::from_seconds
⑪      (0.5, TimerMode::Repeating)));
    }
```

❶ Bevy's primary means of loading assets—images, sounds, 3D models, and so on—is the AssetServer.

❷ Command buffers store a list of instructions for Bevy to execute. You can use commands to add entities and insert resources.

❸ Bevy's list of managed texture atlas layouts can be manipulated through a Bevy-provided resource named Assets<TextureAtlasLayout>.

❹ Every 2D game needs a Camera2d. Without a camera, your game will render a blank screen.

❺ Load the dice image from the assets directory.

❻ Create a TextureAtlasLayout with the from_grid() constructor. Specify that each image is 52 pixels in size, arranged in 6 columns along one row.

❼ TextureAtlasLayouts are reusable and should be stored in a Bevy asset store.

❽ Store the texture atlas handle in a resource named Assets so you can reuse it in other systems.

❽ Store an empty Scores structure representing the starting score.

❿ Create your RandomNumberGenerator and store it as a resource.

⓫ Create a Bevy timer that repeats every half second, and store it as a resource. You'll use it in the AI system.

The setup() system creates everything you need to get started with the actual gameplay: a random number generator, text to display the current and hand scores, and loads of game assets. Now, let's start implementing some gameplay.

Playing Pig

First, you need to display the current score. Add the following function:

FirstLibraryCreate/pig/src/main.rs
```
fn display_score(
  scores: Res<Scores>,
❶  mut egui_context: EguiContexts,
) {
❷  egui::Window::new("Total Scores").show(egui_context.ctx_mut(), |ui| {
❸    ui.label(&format!("Player: {}", scores.player));
    ui.label(&format!("CPU: {}", scores.cpu));
  });
}
```

❶ Interaction with egui requires an EguiContexts. The egui plugin automatically makes the Egui contexts available for inclusion in your systems.

❷ Creating an egui::Window adds a window to the current frame. The window accepts a closure—an in-line function—that renders the window content.

❸ Create an egui label to display the player's current score.

Egui will display the game scores as follows:

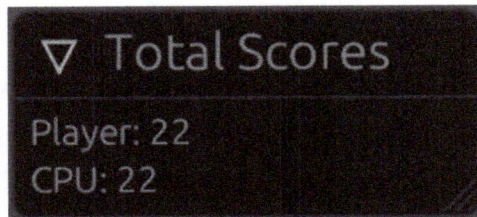

The CPU and human players can choose to roll a die and add to their hand—at the risk of losing the current hand if they score a 1. Both systems share some logic: placing a die on the screen and updating the hand score. Add the following function:

```
FirstLibraryCreate/pig/src/main.rs
fn spawn_die(
❶  hand_query: &Query<(Entity, &Sprite), With<HandDie>>,
   commands: &mut Commands,
   assets: &GameAssets,
   new_roll: usize,
   color: Color,
) {
❷  let rolled_die = hand_query.iter().count() as f32 * 52.0;
❸  let mut sprite = Sprite::from_atlas_image(
❹    assets.image.clone(),
     TextureAtlas {
❺      layout: assets.layout.clone(),
❻      index: new_roll - 1,
     }
   );
❼  sprite.color = color;
❽  commands.spawn((
❾    sprite,
❿    Transform::from_xyz(rolled_die - 400.0, 60.0, 1.0),
⓫    HandDie
     )
   );
}
```

❶ A reference to a Query that requests all entities tagged as a HandDie. Return a reference to the associated sprite. You'll pass this query in from functions that call spawn_die().

❷ Count the number of dice on the screen, and multiply by 52—the size of the die plus some padding. You'll use this to position new dice.

❸ Spawn a Sprite, displaying the newly rolled die on the screen. The from_atlas_image() constructor provides helpers to specify the texture atlas information to use.

❹ Specify the image resource to render.

❺ Specify the atlas layout to use.

❻ Specify the (zero-based) index of the image in the atlas to render.

❼ Specify the tint to apply to the dice image.

❽ Spawn the dice entity. When you want to specify multiple components at once, Bevy lets you wrap them in a tuple (matching parentheses).

❾ Specify that you want to spawn the sprite object you created.

❿ Use the number of dice on the screen to position the new die with a Transform component. If you specify a component, it overrides the default value provided by the Sprite component.

⓫ Tag the new die as a HandDie entity.

You'll learn more about spawning sprites and simplifying asset management in Chapter 6, Manage Your Game Assets, on page 111.

When a hand is complete (because someone rolled a 1), you need to remove all dice from the screen and zero the hand score. Add the following function:

FirstLibraryCreate/pig/src/main.rs
```rust
fn clear_die(
  hand_query: &Query<(Entity, &Sprite), With<HandDie>>,
  commands: &mut Commands,
) {
  hand_query
    .iter()
    .for_each(|(entity, _)| commands.entity(entity).despawn());
}
```

The player controls gameplay with the "Roll" and "Pass" buttons. Let's work through a function to control this:

FirstLibraryCreate/pig/src/main.rs
```rust
fn player(
  hand_query: Query<(Entity, &Sprite), With<HandDie>>,
  mut commands: Commands,
  mut rng: ResMut<Random>,
  assets: Res<GameAssets>,
  mut scores: ResMut<Scores>,
❶  mut state: ResMut<NextState<GamePhase>>,
  mut egui_context: EguiContexts,
) {
  egui::Window::new("Play Options").show(egui_context.ctx_mut(), |ui| {
    let hand_score: usize =
      hand_query.iter().map(|(_, ts)| ts.texture_atlas
❷      .as_ref().unwrap().index + 1).sum();
    ui.label(&format!("Score for this hand: {hand_score}"));
❸    if ui.button("Roll Dice").clicked() {
      let new_roll = rng.0.range(1..7);
      if new_roll == 1 {
        // End turn!
        clear_die(&hand_query, &mut commands);
❹        state.set(GamePhase::Cpu);
      } else {
        spawn_die(
```

```
          &hand_query,
          &mut commands,
          &assets,
          new_roll as usize,
          Color::WHITE,
        );
      }
    }
    if ui.button("Pass - Keep Hand Score").clicked() {
      let hand_total: usize =
        hand_query.iter().map(|(_, ts)| ts.texture_atlas
          .as_ref().unwrap().index + 1).sum();
      scores.player += hand_total;
      clear_die(&hand_query, &mut commands);
      state.set(GamePhase::Cpu);
    }
  });
}
```

❶ You can access the current state with a State type. If you want to change it, you need to use NextState instead.

❷ You can use queries with iterators. In this case, take the displayed sprite index, which ranges from 0 through 5, and add one to it to obtain the die's score. Total these scores with sum() to obtain the current hand score.

❸ Use egui to display a button. If the user presses the button, then clicked() is true and the scope executes.

❹ If the player rolled a 1, clear the displayed hand and transition to the CPU's turn.

The window code in the player() function creates a window with buttons for the player to decide whether to roll or pass:

The computer will try to roll the dice until it achieves a hand score of 20 (or wins the game). Let's implement the logic for this strategy:

FirstLibraryCreate/pig/src/main.rs

```rust
❶ #[allow(clippy::too_many_arguments)]
   fn cpu(
     hand_query: Query<(Entity, &Sprite), With<HandDie>>,
     mut state: ResMut<NextState<GamePhase>>,
     mut scores: ResMut<Scores>,
     mut rng: ResMut<Random>,
     mut commands: Commands,
     assets: Res<GameAssets>,
     mut timer: ResMut<HandTimer>,
     time: Res<Time>,
   ) {
❷   timer.0.tick(time.delta());
❸   if timer.0.just_finished() {
       let hand_total: usize =
         hand_query.iter().map(|(_, ts)| ts.texture_atlas
         .as_ref().unwrap().index + 1).sum();
❹     if hand_total < 20 && scores.cpu + hand_total < 100 {
         let new_roll = rng.0.range(1..7);
         if new_roll == 1 {
           clear_die(&hand_query, &mut commands);
           state.set(GamePhase::Player);
         } else {
           spawn_die(
             &hand_query,
             &mut commands,
             &assets,
             new_roll as usize,
❺           Color::Srgba(Srgba::new(0.0, 0.0, 1.0, 1.0)),
           );
         }
       } else {
❻       scores.cpu += hand_total;
         state.set(GamePhase::Player);
         hand_query
           .iter()
           .for_each(|(entity, _)| commands.entity(entity).despawn());
       }
     }
   }
```

❶ Bevy systems often have a lot of parameters or arguments. Clippy—Rust's linter—will grumble about too many arguments, making your code unclear. This compiler directive asks Clippy to keep quiet.

❷ Bevy timers need to be updated each frame. You'll need this code every time you use a timer.

❸ When you created the timer, you specified an interval of a half second. If the specified time period has just finished—and the timer is running again —run the CPU's logic. Using a timer here lets the player see each die roll, rather than suddenly incrementing the CPU's score.

❹ If the total hand score is less than 20—and the current roll won't win the game—the CPU should roll a die. Much of the logic is similar to the player's turn.

❺ Specifying a color when spawning a die lets you tint the sprite. The CPU's dice will show up in blue.

❻ If the CPU player decides to pass, add the current hand total to their score and transition back to the player's turn.

Playing the Game of Pig

You have a working game of Pig. Run the game (cargo run) and you can compete with a simple AI in a dice game:

Congratulations! You've integration tested your random number generator and proven that it can roll dice. You've also learned how to make sprite sheets in Bevy.

Now that you have unit tests and a working game for integration testing, it's time to look at the friction points you encountered while using your library. The biggest source of friction was that your library could only generate u32 type numbers. Let's use *generics* to make random number generation work with any numeric type.

Creating Generically Typed Random Numbers

The range() function in your RandomNumberGenerator type is strictly limited to u32 types:

FirstLibraryCreate/my_library/src/random.rs
```
pub fn range(&mut self, range: Range<u32>) -> u32 {
```

You could spend some time making range_u32, range_i32, range_f32, and other functions, each of which will accept the specified type. This will work, but it's a lot of redundant typing. Instead, Rust offers *Generics* to alleviate the tedium.

Generic Functions

Let's start with a simpler function named next(). Next returns a single random value of a given type. A u32 version of next would look like this:

```
pub fn next(&mut self) -> u32 { self.rng.gen() }
```

Turning this into a generic function requires some new syntax. You introduce a new generic type named T as part of the function name and then use it as the function's return type:

Declare the generic type

Use the generic type as the function's return type

```
pub fn next<T>(&mut self) -> T {
    self.rng.gen()
}
```

Unfortunately, this still isn't enough to create a working next() function. If you try to compile this function, Rust will inform you:

```
the trait bound `Standard: Distribution<T>` is not satisfied
the trait `Distribution<T>` is not implemented for `Standard`
```

That's a rather opaque error message! Fortunately, Clippy—invoked with cargo clippy—provides a suggestion later in the error message:

```
consider introducing a `where` bound, but there might be an alternative better
way to express this requirement: ` where Standard: Distribution<T>`
```

Standard and Distribution are both traits exported by rand. The gen function requires that the associated variable type be of a type for which rand can use its standard distribution functions. Rust provides an additional clause named *where* that allows you to specify requirements that T must fulfill. Following Clippy's advice, you wind up with a function that looks like the code at the top of the next page.

FirstLibraryGenericType/my_library/src/random.rs
```
pub fn next<T>(&mut self) -> T
where rand::distributions::Standard: rand::prelude::Distribution<T>
{
  self.rng.gen()
}
```

The where clause must be fulfilled by T. rand knows how to distribute random results for most numeric types and implements Distribution for them. Clippy—and this code—use fully qualified types such as rand::prelude::Distribution. Normally, you can simply specify Distribution and add a use statement to the file. The full version has been left in place for clarity—there are a lot of namespaces in the Rand crate! Don't worry too much about the details of how this works yet; you'll build your own traits and use them as generic predicates later in the book. For now, let's add a unit test that illustrates different ways and types of using our generic next() function:

FirstLibraryGenericType/my_library/src/random.rs
```
#[test]
fn test_next_types() {
  let mut rng = RandomNumberGenerator::new();
❶ let _ : i32 = rng.next();
❷ let _ = rng.next::<f32>();
}
```

❶ If the type to be returned from your generic function is clearly specified by the type of the recipient variable, Rust will infer the type of T for you.

❷ If Rust cannot deduce T's type for you, you can use the turbofish construct to specify the desired type as part of the construct.

Run your unit tests with cargo test. The tests succeed; you've created your first generic function.

Generic Ranges

Generic ranges are a little more complicated because Range itself is a generic type. In your range() function, you specify the range as Range<u32>. Rust supports nesting generics; you can use T to specify the type of the range, as well as the function return type. Your function signature becomes:

FirstLibraryGenericType/my_library/src/random.rs
```
pub fn range<T>(&mut self, range: Range<T>) -> T
```

As it turns out, trying to use the where clause from your next() function won't work. rand uses a different trait for range distribution than it does for gen(). You need to use where T: rand::distributions::uniform::SampleUniform + PartialOrd. To generate random ranges, T must fulfill two contracts:

- T must be of a type that supports uniform sampling (the SampleUniform trait).

- T must support at least partial ordering—it must be possible to compare two T values.

The second requirement makes sense if you think about it; you can't check that a number falls within a range if you can't perform a comparison.

The first requirement is a little more convoluted. Creating a random number within a range—with an equal chance of obtaining each value—is not a simple task. The rand crate takes care of the details for you and implements SampleUniform for types for which it can perform this task.

With the where criteria specified, your range function looks like this:

FirstLibraryGenericType/my_library/src/random.rs
```
pub fn range<T>(&mut self, range: Range<T>) -> T
where
T: rand::distributions::uniform::SampleUniform + PartialOrd,
{
  self.rng.gen_range(range)
}
```

Ts Everywhere

If you browse Rust codebases, you'll find a lot of instances of simply naming a generic type T. Generic types can be named whatever you like—the style guide recommends CamelCase for names. Using T is a common abbreviation, particularly when there's only one type specified. It's up to you to balance brevity and readability in your code.

Testing Your Generic Range

Run the unit tests on my_library by invoking cargo test. Your existing unit tests succeed. Your new interface is compatible with the old interface, and your code still works. It would be a good idea to update your tests to include some type-based testing.

Let's test that you really can generate 32-bit floating-point numbers. Open my_library/random.rs and navigate to the end of the unit tests. Insert the following function:

FirstLibraryGenericType/my_library/src/random.rs
```
#[test]
fn test_float() {
  let mut rng = RandomNumberGenerator::new();
  for _ in 0..1000 {
```

```
    let n = rng.range(-5000.0f32..5000.0f32);
    assert!(n.is_finite());
    assert!(n > -5000.0);
    assert!(n < 5000.0);
  }
}
```

This function tests that you can generate a random f32, and that the result is a valid—finite—floating-point number.

Invoke your unit tests again, and they should all succeed:

```
running 4 tests
test random::test::test_next_types ... ok
test random::test::test_float ... ok
test random::test::test_reproducibility ... ok
test random::test::test_range_bounds ... ok

test result: ok. 4 passed; 0 failed; 0 ignored; 0 measured; 0 filtered out;
finished in 0.00s
```

Let's move on to integration testing with our pig application.

Integration Testing Your Generic Range

Navigate to more_hands/pig and invoke cargo run. Your program runs exactly as it did before. Once again, you've changed the signature of the range() function, but the signature remains compatible with all of your old code. You could stop here, but now that you've provided a convenient generic interface to the range() function, it's time to use it to eliminate the unwieldy as casting.

Library Version Numbers

If you're publishing your library, and you break API compatibility with the previous version, you should increment the version number. Rust uses semantic versioning—for example, 1.2.3. The first number is the major version, the second is the minor version, and the third is the patch version. If you break API compatibility, you should increment the major version. If you add new features in a backwards-compatible way, you should increment the minor version. If you fix bugs in a backwards-compatible way, you should increment the patch version. This will be discussed in more detail in Chapter 15, Share Your Library, on page 305.

Open more_hands/pig/src/main.rs. On line 138, you'll see the following code:

```
new_roll as usize,
```

In this code, you generated a random u32 and then converted it to a usize to match the sprite index type. What you wanted was an f32 between 0.1 and 0.9. You can replace this code with a version that takes advantage of range() being generic:

FirstLibraryGenericType/pig/src/main.rs
```
spawn_die(
  &hand_query,
  &mut commands,
  &assets,
➤  new_roll,
  Color::Srgba(Srgba::new(0.0, 0.0, 1.0, 1.0))
);
```

Your program runs as before, but now you've removed some cognitive weight from your library consumers. Your users no longer need to remember to cast random numbers into the types they require. There's one unwieldy bit of code left, so let's take care of it.

Using Inclusive Ranges

The remaining oddity in my_library is that range works with an exclusive range (1..7) but won't compile with an inclusive range (1..=6). Many library consumers find the latter to be more intuitive for specifying a range of numbers.

You've made life easy for your library consumers. They can specify a range in any range-supporting type and receive a random number within that range. The elephant in the room is inclusive types. You used 1..7 to mean "one to six"—but 1..=6 is a more readable way of specifying the same range.

Open more_hands/pig/src/main.rs and change the dice sprite selector to use an inclusive range:

FirstLibraryGenericRange/pig/src/main.rs
```
let hand_total: usize =
  hand_query.iter().map(|(_, ts)|
  ts.texture_atlas.as_ref().unwrap().index + 1).sum();
if hand_total < 20 && scores.cpu + hand_total < 100 {
➤  let new_roll = rng.0.range(1..=6);
```

If you try to run the pig application now, you'll see an error message:

```
mismatched types
expected struct `std::ops::Range<_>`
   found struct `RangeInclusive<{integer}>`
```

Your current range() function expects a Range type, but an inclusive range uses the RangeInclusive type. You could change the function to require a RangeInclusive, but then it wouldn't work with exclusive ranges. You could also implement two functions, one for each type of range, but that quickly becomes cumbersome.

Fortunately, the rand crate has already solved this problem by creating a trait named SampleRange. An obvious first attempt is to change our range() function to use it:

```
pub fn range<T>(&mut self, range: SampleRange<T>) -> T
```

Unfortunately, this doesn't compile. Rust doesn't allow you to receive traits directly as function parameters; they have to be decorated with dyn or impl. What's the difference?

- A dyn trait represents a vtable—and is usually wrapped inside a Box or other pointer. Dynamic traits resolve at runtime, examining the type that *actually* fulfills the trait's contract and calling the correct structure's code.
- An impl requires that a type *implement* a trait. Implementation requirements don't require a wrapping pointer, which in turn requires that the type be known at compile time.

This is one of the rare occasions in which Clippy gets it wrong. The compiler warning suggests using dyn—but a) you know the type at compile time, and b) you don't need the overhead of wrapping all of our ranges in Box variables. In this case, impl is the correct choice.

Checking Crate Source Code for Type Signatures

When you're wrapping a generic function, you often have to look at the signature of the function you're calling. If you have Rust Analyzer installed in your text editor, the text editor can find and display it for you. Otherwise, you can check docs.rs to find the crate's documentation. [5]

Let's modify our range function to use impl SampleRange:

FirstLibraryGenericRange/my_library/src/random.rs
```
pub fn range<T>(&mut self, range: impl SampleRange<T>) -> T
where
  T: SampleUniform + PartialOrd,
{
  self.rng.gen_range(range)
}
```

---

5.   https://docs.rs/rand/latest/rand/trait.Rng.html#method.gen_range

You'll also need to visit the top of random.rs and update your use statements to include the new ranges:

FirstLibraryGenericRange/my_library/src/random.rs
```
use rand::{prelude::StdRng, Rng, SeedableRng,
    distributions::uniform::{SampleRange, SampleUniform}};
```

With this version in place, you can compile and run pig—and make use of inclusive ranges.

So why does this work? rand has declared a trait named SampleRange. In turn, it has implemented the trait for both Range and RangeInclusive. This allows your program to require that a range parameter implement SampleRange—rand has done the implementation for you.

Working with Generic Functions

When you declare a function with a generic type, you're engaging in a form of *metaprogramming* You aren't writing code directly; you're providing Rust with a template to use to generate instances of a function as needed.

The first time you call next() requesting an i32 result, these things happen:

- Rust checks that you haven't previously used next() with an i32.

- You haven't, so Rust checks that i32 fulfills the where clause of your next() function.

- i32 is valid for next(), so Rust generates an entirely new function in the compiled code. It replaces all of your type placeholders (T) with i32 and creates a next i32 function.

Subsequent calls to next() with an i32 type will use the generated function. If you introduce next() with another type, the same process is used to generate a function that supports that type. The generated functions are called "concrete" functions; they're limited to a single type, set in stone.

Wrapping Up

In this chapter, you covered a lot of ground. You created a library, depended on rand, and reexported it for your users' benefit. You created a random number generator and verified its trustworthiness with unit tests. You then used integration testing to try your library in a realistic scenario, identifying many rough edges that could be improved. Using generics and type constraints, you smoothed those rough edges—yielding an easy-to-use random number generation library. Congratulations! You created your first useful library.

Providing a convenient API is only part of the struggle with library creation. In the next chapter, you'll learn to measure the performance of your random number generator and provide library users with a choice of random algorithms.

Too Many Generics Can Slow Compilation

Generics are powerful, and it's tempting to use them everywhere. Compiling a generic function requires more work than compiling a nongeneric function because the Rust compiler has to work through all of the steps previously outlined. Using generic functions everywhere can lead to long compile times.

There's no runtime performance cost for using generics; they compile into regular functions and have the same performance and optimization opportunities as any other function.

CHAPTER 3

Optimize and Benchmark Your Library

In the previous chapter, you built a random number generation library. It's a pretty good library. Generics give the library user type flexibility when determining what type of random number to generate, often transparently. The library is also fast. Games tend to use a *lot* of random numbers, especially when they feature procedurally generated content.

Improving your library's performance requires two concepts:

- *Optimization* seeks to improve the performance of code.

- *Benchmarking* measures the current performance of your code, giving you performance data, which allows you to determine if your optimizations helped.

What About Profiling?

Profiling is a form of benchmarking, but instead of running a function and measuring its performance, you're measuring the performance of your program as it runs. Profiling can give you valuable insights about which parts of your program are a performance bottleneck. Benchmarking focuses on a single, targeted section of your program. You often want to do both: use a profiler to find the bottleneck and benchmarking to help you improve your code's performance.

You'll learn more about profiling when we dive into optimizing game code, in the Mars Base One section on page 219.

Optimizing without benchmarking is a dangerous business; you might have a *hunch* that some of your code is slow, but without benchmarking, you can't be sure. Optimization is a complicated topic, so here are a few tips to help get you started:

- Algorithm choice is often more important than optimizing a specific algorithm. An algorithm designed to solve your specific problem will probably be faster than a generic algorithm.

- Optimization is usually a trade-off. Random number generation algorithms balance the "quality" of random numbers against the speed with which they're generated. A sorting algorithm may be faster for a large or small collection of data. There often isn't a "correct" algorithm in the general sense—you need to find one that suits your specific needs. Sometimes, the only "right answer" is "it's fast enough for my needs."

- The compiler is smart and will perform many "micro-optimizations" for you. On a low level, it's often faster to transform x * 2 into x << 1—at the expense of considerable readability. LLVM will perform many small optimizations like this for you. Unless you can prove that an operation is a bottleneck, it's generally best to stick with the readable version.

The most important rule when optimizing is to measure code performance before and after you try to improve performance. If you've been programming for a while, you probably have a good "gut feeling" as to where the slow parts of your code are. Measuring performance transforms a gut feeling into actionable data.

Rust includes the framework you need to benchmark your code. Let's begin the optimization journey by measuring the performance of your random number generator.

Measuring Random Number Generator Performance

The Rust language provides a framework for benchmarking, and it leaves implementation to libraries. Not every benchmark measures the same data points, and benchmarking methodology is a significant topic of debate. You're going to use a library named criterion.[1] Criterion includes everything you need to benchmark your library: a framework for running measurements, tools to avoid pitfalls, pretty graphs of results, and cross-platform support.

Let's integrate criterion into my_library.

Development Dependencies

Criterion is a large library. To include it in every build would waste a lot of storage space and compilation time. Fortunately, Cargo supports *development dependencies*. Dependencies that are listed in the [dev-depencencies] section of

---

1.   https://docs.rs/criterion/latest/criterion/index.html

Cargo.toml will only be included when you're compiling a unit test or benchmark. Let's add criterion as a development-only dependency.

Open Cargo.toml and add the following code:

FirstLibraryBenchmark/my_library/Cargo.toml
```
[dev-dependencies]
criterion = { version = "0.5.1", features = [ "html_reports"] }
```

Cargo.toml supports two different syntaxes for dependencies: a short version (for example, criterion = "0.5.1") and a longer version that lets you specify additional options. The extended syntax lets you specify more details about the dependency:

- At the time of writing, Criterion version "0.5.1" is current. You can specify "0.5" allows Cargo to select any additional bug fix releases in the "0.5" branch but will avoid upgrading to future versions, which may change the interface.[2]

- Specifying features lets you enable additional options inside a dependency. Specifying html_reports enables building charts of benchmark performance. You'll be implementing your own feature flags later in this chapter.

That's all you need to get started with Criterion, so let's get started making a benchmark.

Set Up a Benchmark Framework

Benchmarks are placed outside of the regular src directory in a directory named benches. Open your my_library directory and create a new directory named benches. In your new benches directory, create a file named random.rs. This file is where you'll benchmark your random number generator. When you're done, your directory tree will now look like this:

```
more_hands/          # Workspace directory
  Cargo.toml         # Workspace configuration file
  src/               # Workspace source directory
    main.rs          # Workspace main program file
  my_library/        # My_library sub-project
    Cargo.toml       # My_library configuration file
    src/             # My_library source directory
      lib.rs         # My_library main source file
      random.rs      # My_library random number generator
    benches/         # My_library benchmark directory
      random.rs      # My_library random number generator benchmark
```

2.   https://doc.rust-lang.org/cargo/reference/specifying-dependencies.html

Open random.rs and let's start by entering some boilerplate code required by criterion:

❶
```
use criterion::{criterion_group, criterion_main, Criterion};
use my_library::*;
```
❷
```
pub fn criterion_benchmark(c: &mut Criterion) {
    // My benchmarks go here
}
```
❸
```
criterion_group!(benches, criterion_benchmark);
```
❹
```
criterion_main!(benches);
```

❶ Import the items you need from Criterion. criterion_group, criterion_main, and Criterion are all required by the framework. You'll use them to tell Criterion where your benchmark tests are located.

❷ Provide a function that will contain your benchmarks. You can use multiple functions if you like—they all have to receive &mut Criterion as a parameter and be listed in the criterion_group! macro call shown in the last step.

❸ Define a group of benchmarks by listing the Criterion functions here. This convenience macro generates code to register your benchmarks with the Criterion framework.

❹ Name your benchmarks and register them with Criterion. You're using the name benches for convenience, which must match the name in the criterion_group! macro.

Finally, you need to open my_library/Cargo.toml and tell Cargo where your benchmark is located. Add the following code to the end of the Cargo.toml file:

FirstLibraryBenchmark/my_library/Cargo.toml
```
[[bench]]
name = "random"
harness = false
```

Now that you have your boilerplate written, take a moment to test that your framework was entered correctly:

```
⇒   cargo bench
❮ running 4 tests
  test result: ok. 0 passed; 0 failed; 4 ignored; 0 measured; 0 filtered out;
  finished in 0.00s

       Running benches\random.rs
  Gnuplot not found, using plotters backend
```

cargo bench runs all registered benchmarks for a project. Since you haven't created any measurements yet, you won't see any useful results. However, it's good to make sure that your framework is working properly. Notice that cargo helpfully read—and then ignored—your unit tests. Regular benchmarking serves as a "sanity check" that your development builds are working properly.

Ignore GnuPlot

Unless you happen to have GNU Plot installed, you'll see messages about GNU Plot when you run your benchmarks. You can safely ignore these messages.

Now that you have a working benchmark framework, it's time to create an actual benchmark.

Your First Benchmark

Open my_library/benches/random.rs again. Let's add some benchmark code to the criterion_benchmark function:

```
FirstLibraryBenchmark/my_library/benches/random.rs
pub fn criterion_benchmark(c: &mut Criterion) {
    // My benchmarks go here
    c.bench_function("random", |b| {
        let mut rng = RandomNumberGenerator::new();
        b.iter(|| {
            rng.range(1.0_f32..10_000_000_f32);
        })
    });
}
```

❶ Each benchmark you create is called by wrapping it inside bench_function. The function passes a Bencher variable into a closure. You use the provided variable to manage your benchmarks.

❷ Create a new RandomNumberGenerator. Notice that you haven't interacted with b in any way. You aren't timing anything yet. Creating your RandomNumberGenerator outside of the test ensures that you're timing the RNG's performance and not the time it takes to instantiate a new random number generator.

❸ Calling iter() on the provided Bencher variable begins the benchmark. Everything inside the iterator scope will be called repeatedly by Criterion and used to gather timing information.

❹ Call rng.range() from your random number generator to generate a number between 1 and 10 million. Notice that you aren't doing anything with the result. This is deliberate, as you want to focus on timing the range() function, not on timing other operations.

Run the benchmark with `cargo bench`. You'll see results similar to these—but you're unlikely to see these exact results, as exact timings depend on the speed of your computer and what else you had running at the time.

```
⇒  cargo bench
❮  running 4 tests
   test result: ok. 0 passed; 0 failed; 4 ignored; 0 measured; 0 filtered out;
   finished in 0.00s

        Running benches\random.rs
   Gnuplot not found, using plotters backend
   random                  time:    [3.4076 ns 3.4595 ns 3.5221 ns]
   Found 13 outliers among 100 measurements (13.00%)
     3 (3.00%) high mild
     10 (10.00%) high severe
```

There are two interesting figures in these benchmark results:

- time: [3.4076 ns 3.4595 ns 3.5221 ns] is telling you:

    - The fastest benchmark took 3.4076 nanoseconds to execute.

    - The average benchmark took 3.4595 nanoseconds to execute.

    - The slowest benchmark took 3.5221 nanoseconds to execute.

- "Found 13 outliers" tells you that of the 100 measurements taken, 13 fell far outside of the normal time range. This may have happened if the computer running the benchmarks scheduled another process, or it may have happened because of an instability in the tested function. The only way to be sure is to rerun the benchmark.

If you execute `cargo bench` again—this time, trying not to run too many other programs at the same time—a new section appears:

```
change: [-2.1131% -0.9728% +0.1588%] (p = 0.11 > 0.05)
No change in performance detected.
```

When you run your benchmarks, Criterion saves the results. Each additional run is compared with the previous run, showing you if you've sped up or slowed down your code with any recent changes. This is useful, as you can test new code and rerun your benchmarks. Regular benchmarking lets you be sure that your optimization work was useful.

Finally, take a look in your more_hands/target/criterion/report directory. Criterion has created a file named index.html. Open this file in a web browser, and you'll notice that it contains a complete performance report for your library:

random

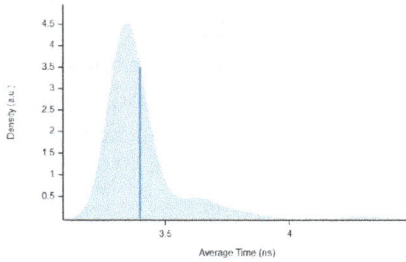

Additional Statistics:

	Lower bound	Estimate	Upper bound
Slope	3.4076 ns	3.4595 ns	3.5221 ns
R²	0.6405232	0.6559101	0.6338296
Mean	3.3750 ns	3.4020 ns	3.4329 ns
Std. Dev.	94.069 ps	148.43 ps	201.78 ps
Median	3.3461 ns	3.3548 ns	3.3648 ns
MAD	40.802 ps	54.290 ps	68.989 ps

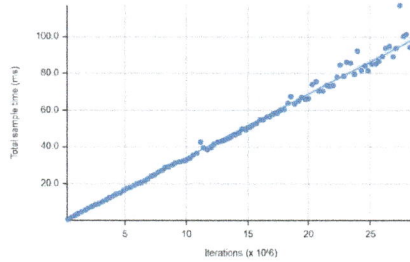

Additional Plots:

- Typical
- Mean
- Std. Dev.
- Median
- MAD
- Slope

Understanding this report:

The plot on the left displays the average time per iteration for this benchmark. The shaded region shows the estimated probability of an iteration taking a certain amount of time, while the line shows the mean. Click on the plot for a larger view showing the outliers.

The plot on the right shows the linear regression calculated from the measurements. Each point represents a sample, though here it shows the total time for the sample rather than time per iteration. The line is the line of best fit for these measurements.

See the documentation for more details on the additional statistics.

Change Since Previous Benchmark

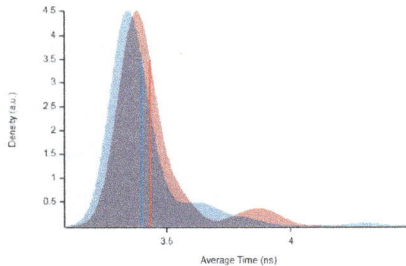

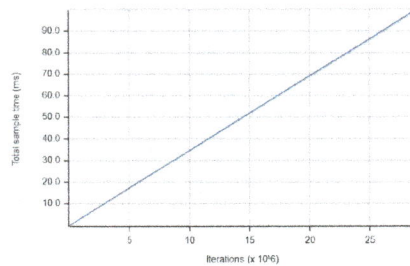

The big takeaway here is that your random number generator is fast. 3.5 nanoseconds per random number is an impressive speed and should be enough for many generation tasks. Since random number generation is often on a program's *critical path*—functions executed most frequently—it's worth spending time further optimizing our random number generator. Let's explore some other random number generation algorithms.

Changing Random Algorithm

There are *many* random number generator algorithms.[3] In game development, two of the more popular algorithms are PCG and XorShift. They were both developed with speed in mind, while trying to minimize quality issues. There's a long and involved academic argument between the creators and proponents of each algorithm. Let's try to avoid the academic fight and make it easy for our library users to switch random algorithms if they so desire.

Why Not StepRng?

Rand's algorithm list includes an algorithm named StepRng. It advertises performance 10 times faster than PCG or Xorshift. It also isn't very random at all—it uses a deterministic step between each random number. You might try benchmarking it for fun—it's extremely fast and relatively predictable.

Be careful when selecting your algorithms, as they may be fast, but not at all what you want.

So, how does RandomNumberGenerator select an algorithm? In my_library/src/random.rs, you're specifying the RNG back end as follows:

```
#[derive(Resource)]
pub struct RandomNumberGenerator {
  rng: StdRng,
}
```

Later on in your RandomNumberGenerator implementation, you refer to functions associated with the StdRng type. For example, StdRng::from_entropy() initializes the standard RNG from an entropy source, and StdRng::seed_from_u64 uses a specified seed. Changing a random core will require replacing StdRng, but you don't want to laboriously change every function that uses it for every possible RNG engine you decide to include in your library.

You can solve the problem by creating a *type alias*. Type aliases allow you to provide an alternative name for a type. Aliases can be particularly useful when you're dealing with long type names. In this case, you'll use it as a placeholder and substitute algorithms by redefining the alias. In my_library/src/random.rs, add the following above your RandomNumberGenerator structure:

```
type RngCore = rand::prelude::StdRng;
```

---

3.   https://rust-random.github.io/book/guide-rngs.html#the-generators

If you still have an import saying use rand::prelude::StdRng in your file without the condition, remove it.

Now, replace every instance of StdRng with RngCore. You have to change the RandomNumberGenerator structure itself, the new() function, and the seeded() function:

```
#[derive(Resource)]
pub struct RandomNumberGenerator {
  rng: RngCore
}

impl RandomNumberGenerator {
  pub fn new() -> Self {
    Self {
      rng: RngCore::from_entropy(),
    }
  }

  pub fn seeded(seed: u64) -> Self {
    Self {
      rng: RngCore::seed_from_u64(seed),
    }
  }
}
// Continues
```

Now that you've replaced the StdRng type with an alias, you can easily substitute it once feature flags are specified. Let's add some random number algorithms.

Feature Flags

StdRng is the "standard" random number generator included in rand. Other generators are available in crates. Searching Cargo for PCG and xorshift locates the following crates:

```
⇒ cargo search pcg
❮ pcg_rand = "0.13.0"          # An implementation of the PCG family of
                                 random number generators in pure Rust

⇒ cargo search xorshift
❮ rand_xorshift = "0.3.0"      # Xorshift random number generator
```

Remember how, when you set up criterion as a dependency in Cargo.toml, you specified a [features] section? Let's make use of Rust's feature flags to allow the user to switch between random number generation algorithms. Open my_library/Cargo.toml and let's add the two crates you found:

FirstLibrarySubstitute/my_library/Cargo.toml
```
[dependencies]
rand = {  workspace = true }
➤ rand_pcg = { workspace = true, optional = true }
➤ rand_xorshift = { workspace = true, optional = true }
```

Notice that you're keeping your dependency on rand itself and adding both generator back ends. Each dependency is marked with optional = true, meaning that Cargo doesn't have to include it in a build—unless it's requested. Let's add another section to Cargo.toml:

FirstLibrarySubstitute/my_library/Cargo.toml
```
[features]
default = [ "pcg" ]
pcg = [ "rand_pcg" ]
xorshift = [ "rand_xorshift" ]
```

The [features] section controls *feature flags*. Each provides a list of crates that are required when a named feature is activated. The default features won't load anything else. Specify pcg or xorshift as features, and the optional dependencies listed will be included in your library build.

Testing XorShift

Now that you have the supporting libraries loaded with feature flags, you need to tell Rust which random algorithm it should use. You can accomplish this with conditional compilation—just like you guard your unit tests against inclusion in release builds.

You can switch out the random number generator algorithm in random.rs by selecting an actual type to alias at compile time. Open random.rs and replace your type alias as follows:

❶
```
#[cfg(feature = "xorshift")]
type RngCore = rand_xorshift::XorShiftRng;
```

❷
```
#[cfg(not(feature = "xorshift"))]
type RngCore = rand::prelude::StdRng;
```

❶ This declaration specifies that the following block will only be compiled when the xorshift feature is active.

❷ If xorshift isn't enabled, you still want to use the default random number generator. You can use not in configuration directives to invert the meaning.

Your library now supports switching between Xorshift and the "standard" random number generator. So how do you use it?

- In Cargo.toml when listing your [dependencies], you can specify: my_library = { path = "../my_library", features = ["xorshift"] }.

- When running benchmarks or tests, append --no-default-features --features xorshift to the command line.

Go ahead and benchmark your new PCG back end. Start by running cargo bench and ignoring the results, which resets the last result to results from the StdRng algorithm—this way, you're sure to be comparing against the standard algorithm. Then, run the test with xorshift:

```
⇒  cargo bench --no-default-features --features xorshift
‹  random        time:    [1.9149 ns 1.9246 ns 1.9367 ns]
                 change: [-43.790% -43.261% -42.746%] (p = 0.00 &lt; 0.05)
                 Performance has improved.
```

That's impressive—Xorshift is 43% faster on average than the standard benchmark system. Let's try the PCG algorithm.

Testing PCG

Let's also support PCG. You've already added it to Cargo.toml, but the conditional compilation logic in random.rs needs revisiting:

FirstLibrarySubstitute/my_library/src/random.rs
```
❶ #[cfg(all(not(feature = "pcg"), not(feature = "xorshift")))]
   type RngCore = rand::prelude::StdRng;

❷ #[cfg(feature = "pcg")]
   type RngCore = rand_pcg::Pcg64Mcg;

   #[cfg(feature = "xorshift")]
❸ type RngCore = rand_xorshift::XorShiftRng;
```

❶ You want to select the StdRng only if neither the pcg nor xorshift features are active. You accomplish this by wrapping the features in an all statement —all of the included criteria must be true for the following code block to compile.

❷ If the pcg feature flag is enabled, compile the PCG back end.

❸ If the xorshift feature flag is enabled, compile the Xorshift back end.

That's the only change you need to make. You could repeat the process for any of the other algorithms supported by rand simply by adding feature flags, dependencies, and updating the conditional compilation of the RngCore type.

Let's test PCG:

```
⇒   cargo bench
‹  (ignore the baseline)
⇒   cargo bench --no-default-features --features pcg
‹  random      time:   [1.8182 ns 1.8272 ns 1.8373 ns]
              change: [-46.190% -45.783% -45.394%] (p = 0.00 &lt; 0.05)
              Performance has improved.
```

PCG is even faster than xorshift—at least on my computer. Your results should be similar but will vary slightly depending on your computer's speed and any other processes you were running when you performed the benchmark.

Typing --no-default-features --features ... is a lot of cognitive effort just to speed up the random number generator. Let's make it easy for the library consumer by selecting a fast default.

Selecting a Default Generator

Let's compare the algorithm selection results side by side. The following table includes both the time (in nanoseconds) required to generate a random floating-point number and the number of floating-point numbers each algorithm can generate per second:

	Default	XorShift	PCG
Average Time (nanoseconds)	3.4595	1.9246	1.8272
Million Random Ranges per Second	289.1	519.6	547.2

Visualizing tabular data as a graph often helps get a better "feel" for relative performance:

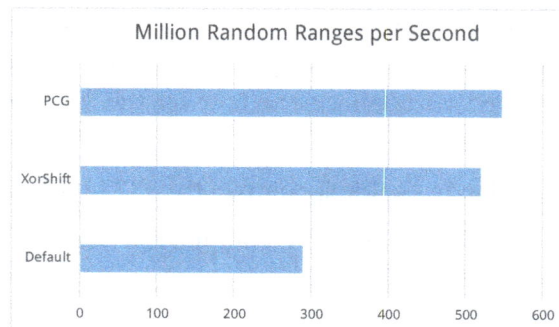

As you can see, both Xorshift and PCG significantly outperform rand's default random number generation algorithm. PCG is slightly faster, so let's make it the default.

Selecting Defaults Is Important

When you're writing a library, it's easy to tell yourself, "I've set up these feature flags; the library user can make the right decision"—especially when you expect to be the primary library user. Despite this, it's always worth taking the time to think about offering good default choices.

Imagine that you've signed up for a game jam, and you only have a few hours to crank out a game. Your caffeine-fueled brain is focused on your great game idea and doesn't want to remember your meticulous benchmarking of random number generator algorithms. Because your focus is making a game, you just import my_library and go with the default values. It would be helpful if the default values were generally the best choice.

With the feature flags added, let's test my_library to make sure nothing's broken.

Testing Your Feature Flags

Now that your library supports replacing the core random number generator, it's time to perform both unit and integration testing to ensure that your library works.

Test Often

Whenever you make a change to your library, you should run your unit tests. Even the most innocuous-looking change might have accidentally broken something—and as a library maintainer, it's your responsibility not to break everyone else's code.

Per-Feature Unit Testing

You can use Cargo to test each feature flag with the same syntax you used for cargo bench. Let's start by testing your new default feature set. In the more_hands/my_library directory, issue the following command:

```
cargo test --no-default-features
running 4 tests
test random::test::test_reproducibility ... ok
test random::test::test_range_bounds ... ok
test random::test::test_float ... ok
test random::test::test_inclusive_range_bounds ... ok

test result: ok. 4 passed; 0 failed; 0 ignored; 0 measured;
0 filtered out; finished in 0.00s
```

Excellent, your default settings passed unit testing. Let's test xorshift:

```
⇒   cargo test --no-default-features --features xorshift
❮ running 4 tests
  test random::test::test_reproducibility ... ok
  test random::test::test_float ... ok
  test random::test::test_inclusive_range_bounds ... ok
  test random::test::test_range_bounds ... ok

  test result: ok. 4 passed; 0 failed; 0 ignored; 0 measured;
  0 filtered out; finished in 0.00s
```

The xorshift feature passes your tests. Finally, let's test that StdRng still works:

```
⇒   cargo test --no-default-features --features pcg
❮ running 4 tests
  test random::test::test_reproducibility ... ok
  test random::test::test_float ... ok
  test random::test::test_inclusive_range_bounds ... ok
  test random::test::test_range_bounds ... ok

  test result: ok. 4 passed; 0 failed; 0 ignored; 0 measured;
  0 filtered out; finished in 0.00s
```

Congratulations! All of your feature flags are passing their unit tests.

Script Your Tests

It's cumbersome to remember to test all of your feature flags, particularly as you add more and more. You can set up a shell script or batch file—depending on your operating system—that includes all of your tests.

For example, on UNIX-style operating systems, the following shell script will run all of your tests for you:

```
❮ #!/bin/bash
  cd (base path)/more_hands/my_library
  cargo test
  cargo test --no-default-features --features xorshift
  cargo test --no-default-features --features pcg
```

Integration Testing

Navigate to more_hands/pig. Make sure you don't change anything—you want to continue using the default settings for my_library. Type cargo run. Your program works exactly as it did before.

Optimizing for Bevy

You've successfully increased random number generation performance by nearly 50% by carefully measuring different algorithms and selecting an appropriate one. That's a large part of the optimization picture and a signifi-cant improvement. Now it's time to consider how my_library and Bevy interact.

In your pig program, manually creating a RandomNumberGenerator and storing it as a resource works, but it isn't ideal. Injecting it via a plugin is cleaner and more in line with the preferred Bevy workflow.

You can solve this problem by using RandomNumberGenerator as a Bevy plugin. Let's be good Bevy citizens and use your library's random number generation in a Bevy-friendly manner.

Random Numbers as a Bevy Plugin

Bevy Plugins let you hide the implementation details of a Bevy extension ini-tialization and functionality. Extensions can access most of the Bevy startup chain and work similarly to the setup in the main() function.

Let's start by adding Bevy as a dependency to my_library. Open more_hands/my_library/Cargo.toml and add the dependency:

```
[dependencies]
rand = "0.8"
rand_pcg = { version = "0.3", optional = true }
rand_xorshift = { version = "0.3", optional = true }
➤ bevy = { workspace = true }
```

my_library requires Bevy because of the Plugin trait, which is used to create plu-gins. Open my_library/src/random.rs and add the following to the end of the file:

```
FirstLibraryMutableRandomPlugin/my_library/src/random.rs
❶ pub struct RandomPlugin;

❷ impl bevy::prelude::Plugin for RandomPlugin {
❸   fn build(&self, app: &mut bevy::prelude::App) {
❹     app.insert_resource(RandomNumberGenerator::new());
   }
}
```

❶ Create a new structure to represent your plugin. It doesn't need any content at all; it exists to hold the Plugin implementation.

❷ Declare that Random implements the Plugin trait from Bevy. This trait requires that you create a build() function. Most Rust IDEs will offer to create it for you.

❸ Implement the build() function. The function's parameters must exactly match those required by the Plugin trait.

❹ The app variable works just like the app builder in your main() function. Insert a RandomNumberGenerator as a resource.

You also need to declare that RandomNumberGenerator is a Bevy *Resource*—a structure that can be shared between systems. In your declaration of Random-NumberGenerator, add the following line:

➤
```
#[derive(bevy::prelude::Resource)]
pub struct RandomNumberGenerator {
  rng: RngCore,
}
```

Using the new plugin requires several changes to pig/src/main.rs:

FirstLibraryMutableRandomPlugin/pig/src/main.rs
```
use bevy::prelude::*;
use bevy_egui::{egui, EguiPlugin, EguiContexts};
```
❶
```
use my_library::{RandomNumberGenerator, RandomPlugin};

#[derive(Clone, Copy, PartialEq, Eq, Debug, Hash, States, Default)]
enum GamePhase {
  #[default]
  Player,
  Cpu,
}

fn main() {
  App::new()
    .add_plugins(DefaultPlugins)
    .add_plugins(EguiPlugin{ enable_multipass_for_primary_context: false })
```
❷
```
    .add_plugins(RandomPlugin)
    .add_systems(Startup, setup)
    .init_state::<GamePhase>()
    .add_systems(Update, display_score)
    .add_systems(Update, player.run_if(
      in_state(GamePhase::Player)))
    .add_systems(Update, cpu.run_if(
      in_state(GamePhase::Cpu)))
    .run();
}
```

❶ You're now using two structures from my_library. You're likely to use more in the future, so use the wildcard (*) to import all public entries from my_library.

❷ Instead of inserting the RandomNumberGenerator resource yourself, add Random as a plugin.

Finally, in the setup() function, remove the following line (around line 58):

```
commands.insert_resource(Random(NumberGenerator::new());
```

Once again, test your program with cargo run. Notice that it runs exactly as before, but my_library is now a canonical Bevy plugin library.

Scheduling and Mutability

Your integration of my_library and Bevy is in great shape. Advanced Bevy users may notice one remaining issue: scheduling. Bevy tries to schedule systems to run in parallel whenever possible. One rule that prevents parallel execution is mutable resource access—two systems cannot safely access a shared mutable resource concurrently. Allowing this would violate Rust's "fearless concurrency" guarantee, because each system might change the shared resource at any time—potentially causing bugs in other concurrent systems.

Suppose you have a large simulation that requires a lot of random numbers. The following diagram illustrates the difference between parallel execution (when resources are immutable) and serial execution (with mutable resources):

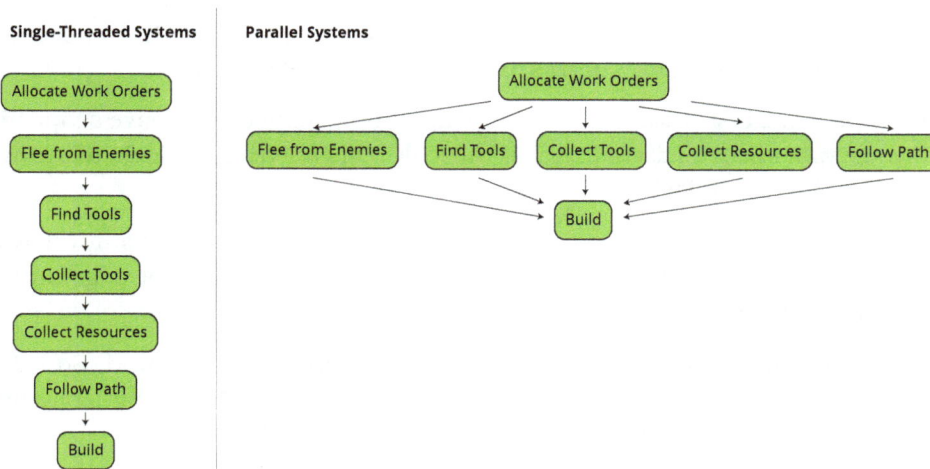

The good news is that you can turn RandomNumberGenerator into an immutable shareable resource by implementing *interior mutability* and *locking*.

Bevy determines if systems can concurrently access a resource by examining how the resource is requested:

- Any number of systems can concurrently access an immutable resource requested via my_resource: Res<MyResource>.

- Only one system can concurrently access a mutable resource requested via mut my_resource: ResMut<MyResource>.

This is checked at compile time. ResMut returns a mutable reference (&mut)—while Res returns a regular, immutable reference (&). If you try to perform an operation that mutates the resource with an immutable reference, the Rust compiler will inform you that you "cannot borrow data as immutable."

Locking with Mutexes

A Mutex is a *locking primitive*. It's often implemented by your operating system, and offers a fast way to ensure that Mutex-protected data isn't concurrently accessed by two threads—allowing the data to be safely shared between threads. When you want to access the data inside a Mutex, you "lock" it. When you request a lock, be aware of the following:

- It checks to see if the structure is currently locked. This is an "atomic" operation and is guaranteed to be accurate even with multiple threads running.

- If the Mutex is locked, the requestor thread pauses and waits until the lock is available.

- If the Mutex is unlocked, the Mutex becomes locked, and the requestor receives a "scope lock", permitting access to the Mutex's data.

- Scope locks last until they're dropped, either because they leave scope or you explicitly call std::mem::drop on the lock. This releases the lock, allowing other threads to lock the Mutex.

Another way to think of a Mutex is as being like a stoplight in that it only allows traffic through one at a time. The diagram at the top og the nect page illustrates the concept.

That's conceptually simple, but difficult to wrap one's head around. So let's implement a locking version of RandomNumberGenerator. Start by copying my_library/src/random.rs to a new file named my_library/src/random_locking.rs.

Open my_library/src/lib.rs, comment out references to the old random module, and add references to the locking version:

```
// mod random;
// pub use random::*;
mod random_locking;
pub use random_locking::*;
```

Making this change keeps the nonlocking version but temporarily disables it. You'll see why later in this section.

Thread #1	Mutex	Thread #2

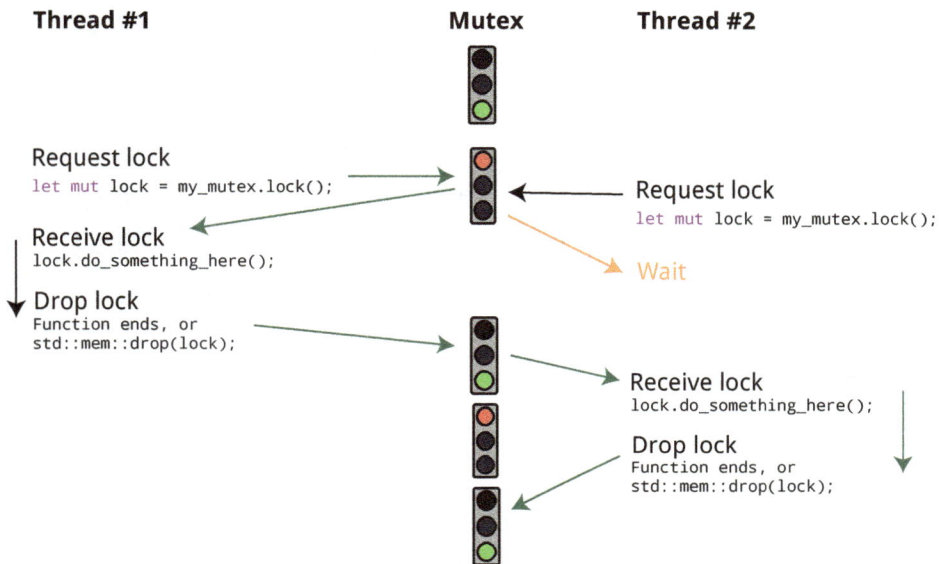

Now, open the random_locking.rs file and add a new use statement at the top:

```rust
use std::sync::Mutex;
```

Next, find the declaration of RandomNumberGenerator and *wrap* the rng variable in a Mutex as follows:

```rust
#[derive(Resource)]
pub struct RandomNumberGenerator {
  rng: Mutex<RngCore>,
}
```

Mutexes are generic and can wrap almost anything. In this case, you're guarding access to rng with a Mutex; you can't access it directly anymore, you have to request a lock. Your random_locking.rs file won't compile until you fix the constructors and data access functions.

Starting with the constructors, you need to wrap RngCore::from_entropy and seed_from_u64 in Mutex structures—to match the declaration:

FirstLibrarySharedRandom/my_library/src/random_locking.rs
```rust
impl RandomNumberGenerator {
  pub fn new() -> Self {
    Self {
      rng: Mutex::new(RngCore::from_entropy()),
    }
  }
```

```
  pub fn seeded(seed: u64) -> Self {
    Self {
➤      rng: Mutex::new(RngCore::seed_from_u64(seed)),
    }
  }
```

Notice that the RngCore syntax is unchanged: you just added a Mutex around it. Next, let's fix the range function to require a Mutex lock:

FirstLibrarySharedRandom/my_library/src/random_locking.rs
```
pub fn next<T>(&self) -> T
where rand::distributions::Standard: rand::prelude::Distribution<T>
{
➤  let mut lock = self.rng.lock().unwrap();
➤  lock.gen()
}

pub fn range<T>(&self, range: impl SampleRange<T>) -> T
where
  T: SampleUniform + PartialOrd,
{
➤  let mut lock = self.rng.lock().unwrap();
➤  lock.gen_range(range)
}
```

The first highlighted line requests a lock. The standard library Mutex returns a Result, so you unwrap it. Once lock is obtained, it has exclusive access to the rng structure. It's guaranteed that no other thread can access it while the lock is valid. Rather than writing directly to rng, you now write to lock—you can treat it just like the wrapped variable. When the function ends, lock falls out of scope, automatically unlocking your Mutex. Rust makes it difficult to accidentally keep a lock forever—potentially "deadlocking" (freezing) your program.

The next() and range() functions no longer require mutable access to themselves. &mut self is replaced with &self. You can also replace ResMut<RandomNumberGenerator> with Res<RandomNumberGenerator>—freeing you from Rust and Bevy's "single mutable access" rule. This allows you to reference RandomNumberGenerator immutably, but the inside can still change. You're using a pattern named "interior mutability": the Mutex structure allows its contents to be mutated, while the outer type remains immutable.

That's all you need to do to implement locking in your RandomNumberGenerator. You've gained "interior mutability": you can share an immutable reference to RandomNumberGenerator, and the structure still updates its state internally.

Testing Locking

Start testing by running your unit tests with cargo test. All of your unit tests work as before.

Now, open pig/src/main.rs and replace all references of ResMut<RandomNumberGenerator> with Res<RandomNumberGenerator>. Run the program, and you'll notice that it works as it did before.

Your locking code is working, and Rust made it surprisingly easy to implement.

Performance Impact of Locking

Sadly, there's no such thing as a free lunch—and locking isn't free. There's a performance impact to enforcing exclusive access, even in a single-threaded environment. Run cargo bench. You should see a significant performance regression:

```
time:   [11.936 ns 11.994 ns 12.059 ns]
```

Locking has increased the random number generation speed from under 2 nanoseconds to almost 12 nanoseconds. That's a large slowdown. It's also typical of the optimization process: almost all optimization is about trade-offs. Sometimes, the slower locking version is worth the performance price—because your total program will be faster with multiple systems running concurrently. This is especially true if they're only lightly using the random number generator. Other times, the slowdown will be unacceptable—and you'd be better off sticking with a mutably shared version.

Locking: Here Be Dragons

Locking is an infamously difficult topic. Rust makes it easier than many other languages, but it still requires careful thought. Here are a few tips and pitfalls to avoid:

- Only lock inside a Bevy system if you absolutely, positively can't avoid doing so. Locks implicitly serialize your code, losing all of the performance benefits of parallel execution.

- Don't "leak" locks outside of functions, especially not as a return value. This makes reasoning about your code much more difficult, and Rust will fight you—with the lifetime system —if you try to do so.

Let's make locking optional, so your library consumer can determine which option works best for their needs.

Optional Locking

You'll start by introducing a new feature. Open my_library/Cargo.toml and add the following feature:

```
FirstLibrarySharedRandom/my_library/Cargo.toml
[features]
default = [ "pcg" ]
pcg = [ "rand_pcg" ]
xorshift = [ "rand_xorshift" ]
➤ locking = []
```

You've added a new feature named locking. It doesn't require any additional dependencies, so the dependency list is empty.

Open my_library/src/lib.rs. Replace your import/export chain as follows:

```
FirstLibrarySharedRandom/my_library/src/lib.rs
#[cfg(not(feature = "locking"))]
mod random;
#[cfg(not(feature = "locking"))]
pub use random::*;

#[cfg(feature = "locking")]
mod random_locking;
#[cfg(feature = "locking")]
pub use random_locking::*;
```

Uses for Conditional Module Loading

A lot of Rust libraries use the conditional module loading idiom to determine behavior. You aren't only limited to feature flags—a lot of possibilities open up with this idiom.

- #[cfg_attr(target_arch = "wasm32", wasm_bindgen)] detects that you're compiling for WebAssembly, and it lets you adjust your library behavior when used in a web browser.

- #[cfg(target_os = "android")] lets you only include or exclude code when building for Android.

There are a lot of possible configuration combinations you might want to detect. The official Rust documentation describes many of them.[4]

Conditionally compiling mod statements works because a file isn't included in your Rust project without a mod statement. Switching between mod random and mod random_locking at compile time—depending on the chosen feature

---

4. https://doc.rust-lang.org/reference/conditional-compilation.html

flag—substitutes the entire data structure at compile time. The as random part renames the random_locking module to random. There will only ever be one random, but the library consumer can decide which one to use.

All that remains is to use the "locking" feature in pig.

```
my_library = { package="my_library", path = "../my_library",
  features = [ "locking" ] }
```

Your pig application can now use RandomNumberGenerator via Res. Changing it back requires removing the feature flag from Cargo.toml and changing your Res<RandomNumberGenerator> statements back to ResMut<RandomNumberGenerator>.

Wrapping Up

You've covered a lot of ground in this chapter. You learned how to measure the performance of parts of your program through benchmarking, and you discovered the ease with which Rust lets you apply locking semantics to support multithreaded applications. You also added a lot of features and options to your library, which leads us to the next chapter: creating library documentation.

Library Names in the Downloadable Source Are Different

If you're following along, keep using my_library. When you look at the code accompanying this book, you'll see that it uses names like my_library_shared_random. This allows the book to provide progressively updated versions of the same code—but without tripping over Cargo's insistence that each package within a workspace has a different name.

CHAPTER 4

Document Your Library

Writing library code is great, and it can save a lot of time for you, your team, and potentially thousands of Internet users. Using a library that you didn't write—or one that you wrote a long time ago—can be tricky and cause you to ask questions, such as, "What exactly does *this* parameter do? Do I need to remember to call functions in a certain order?" That's why documenting your library is an important and necessary step.

When thinking about and writing documentation for your library, know that you should do the following:

- Document every publicly available function and type.

- Provide enough information that library users can quickly get up to speed with your library.

- Include examples that help new library users craft applications that use your library.

Rust includes tools that can help with all of these criteria. By using special comment types, you can include documentation inside your source code. Inline documentation is then included in your development environment, can be baked into a website, and is automatically made available on the docs.rs website when you publish your library. Cargo can even test code examples included in your documentation, and it provides a standardized way to include examples alongside your library.

Documenting Rust Code

You can build a documentation website for your code at any time by running cargo doc. By default, this command will *also* document your library's dependencies, making for some large documentation. You can document only your library by adding --no-deps to the command. You can also instruct Cargo to open your documentation in a web browser when it's finished using --open. For example, run the following command to view the default documentation for your library:

```
⇒ cd my_library
⇒ cargo doc --no-deps --open
‹  Documenting more_hands_on_rust v0.1.0
       Finished dev [unoptimized + debuginfo] target(s) in 3.54s
         Opening target\doc\more_hands_on_rust\index.html
```

A web browser window opens, displaying the autogenerated documentation, which looks something like this:

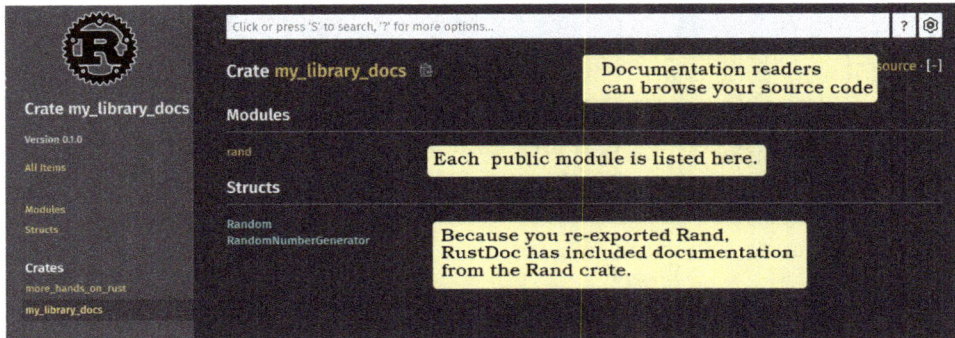

You can find the documentation in target/doc/more_hands_on_rust/index.html.

The documentation that's created is bare-bones, yet complete: all of your functions and types are included. This is a great start, but it'll be more useful after you've added some content.

Now that you have a documentation outline, let's begin documenting my_library.

Describing Your Library and Modules

RustDoc—Rust's documentation system—encourages you to annotate your code with tagged sections containing documentation.[1] Within documentation blocks, you can use *Markdown* to format text.[2] Let's write some top-level documentation for my_library, describing what the library does and the feature flags you've implemented. Add the following code to the top of my_library/src/lib.rs:

FirstLibraryDocs/my_library/src/lib.rs
```
❶ //! `my_library` provides a suite of helpers to create games with Bevy.
   //!
❷ //! ## What's Included?
   //!
```

---

1. https://doc.rust-lang.org/rustdoc/how-to-write-documentation.html
2. https://www.markdownguide.org/

❸ `//! `my_library` includes:`
`//!`
❹ `//! * Random number generation facilities.`
`//!`
`//! ## Feature Flags`
`//!`
`//! The following feature flags are supported: `xorshift`, `pcg`, `locking`.`
`//!`
`//! ### Random Number Generation`
`//!`
`//! * The `locking` feature enables interior mutability inside`
❺ `//! [`RandomNumberGenerator`],`
`//!   allowing it to be used as a resource (`Res<RandomNumberGenerator`)`
`//! rather than requiring mutability (`ResMut<RandomNumberGenerator>`)`
`//! * You can control which random number generation algorithm is used by`
`//! specifying *one* of:`
`//!    * `xorshift` to use the XorShift algorithm.`
`//!    * `pcg` to use the PCG algorithm.`

❶ Lines prefixed with //! are *module-level comments* and will appear at the top of the documentation for the currently displayed module.

❷ Prefix headings with ##.

❸ Adding backticks around a word marks it as a keyword.

❹ You can make bulleted lists by prefixing a line with *.

❺ Wrapping a type in [`my_type`] makes a clickable link to the documentation for the named type.

Run rust doc --no-deps --open again, and you'll see that your description appears on the front page of your crate's documentation:

A nice side effect of adding documentation tags is that most Rust development environments will read them and provide interactive help. Visual Studio Code (with rust-analyzer installed) now shows the following when you hover your cursor over a my_library reference:

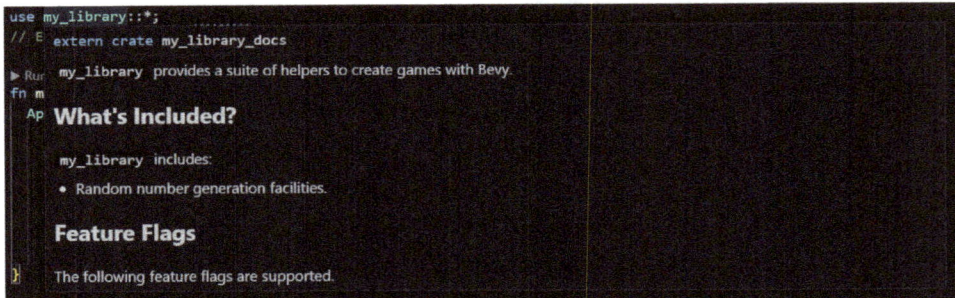

Let's move on to documenting the rest of the program.

Working with Block-Level Documentation

Only pub (public) types need to be included in your Rust documentation. There's no need to document internal types (such as RngCore)—the library user can't access them directly anyway. Rust's linter—Clippy—can help you determine what to document. Add #![warn(missing_docs)] to the top of my_library/src/lib/.rs, and warnings will be added to undocumented types and functions.

The first warning generated indicates that you should document your re-export of rand. Update your module export with the following code:

FirstLibraryDocs/my_library/src/lib.rs
```
/// [`RandomNumberGenerator`] wraps the `rand` crate. The `rand` crate
/// is re-exported for your convenience.
pub use rand;
```

Notice how block-level documentation is prefixed with ///—this attaches your documentation to the subsequent code block.

The next documentation warning asks you to document the RandomNumberGenerator type. This is an important type, so it deserves good documentation. Rust's documentation guide provides a good template:[3]

[short sentence explaining what it is] [more detailed explanation] [at least one code example that users can copy/paste to try it] [even more advanced explanations if necessary]

Add the following documentation to your RandomNumberGenerator structure definition:

---

3. https://doc.rust-lang.org/rustdoc/how-to-write-documentation.html

FirstLibraryDocs/my_library/src/random.rs
```
/// `RandomNumberGenerator` holds random number generation state, and offers
/// random number generation services to your program.
///
/// `RandomNumberGenerator` defaults to using the
❶ /// [PCG](https://crates.io/crates/rand_pcg) algorithm.
/// You can specify `xorshift` as a feature flag to use it instead.
///
/// By default, `RandomNumberGenerator` requires mutability---it
/// is shared in Bevy with `ResMut<RandomNumberGenerator>`. If
/// you prefer interior mutability (and wish to use
/// `Res<RandomNumberGenerator>` instead), specify the `locking`
/// feature flag.
///
❷ /// ## Example
///
/// ```
/// use my_library::RandomNumberGenerator;
/// let mut my_rng = RandomNumberGenerator::new();
/// let random_number = my_rng.range(1..10);
/// println!("{random_number}");
/// ```
```

❶ You can use Markdown-style links to link to other web pages in your documentation.

❷ Great documentation includes example code. You can include code in your comments by wrapping it with ``` markers.

That fits the style guide and introduces some example code. Example code should be short and obvious. Most of the time, you're trying to give a general idea of how to use your library. This introduces a powerful feature: if you run cargo test now, your example code is also tested. This is useful, as it helps you remember to update your examples if your library changes.

You also need to document each of your public functions.

Documenting Functions

Let's add some documentation to RandomNumberGenerator::new():

FirstLibraryDocs/my_library/src/random.rs
```
impl RandomNumberGenerator {
  /// Creates a default `RandomNumberGenerator`, with a randomly
  /// selected starting seed.
  pub fn new() -> Self {
    Self {
      rng: RngCore::from_entropy(),
    }
  }
}
```

This is a simple function, so little documentation is needed. You included an example of using the new function in your structure-level documentation, so there's little need to repeat yourself. Let's look at seeded(), which requires a parameter:

FirstLibraryDocs/my_library/src/random.rs

```
/// Creates a new `RandomNumberGenerator`, with a user-specified random seed.
/// It will produce the same results each time (given the same requests).
///
/// # Arguments
///
/// * `seed` - the random seed to use.
///
/// # Example
///
/// ```
/// use my_library::RandomNumberGenerator;
/// let mut rng1 = RandomNumberGenerator::seeded(1);
/// let mut rng2 = RandomNumberGenerator::seeded(1);
/// let results: (u32, u32) = ( rng1.next(), rng2.next() );
/// assert_eq!(results.0, results.1);
/// ```
pub fn seeded(seed: u64) -> Self {
  Self {
    rng: RngCore::seed_from_u64(seed),
  }
}
```

❶ (on line `/// # Arguments`)

❷ (on line `/// # Example`)

❶ Functions that require arguments/parameters should list each of them in an # Arguments section.

❷ If the consumer isn't intimately familiar with random numbers and seeds, it may not be obvious why they may need to specify a random seed. Example code demonstrating the benefit—repeatability—helps make the purpose of this function clear.

Now that you've written some documentation, you can finish documenting RandomNumberGenerator:

FirstLibraryDocs/my_library/src/random.rs

```
/// Generates a new random number of the requested type.
pub fn next<T>(&mut self) -> T
where rand::distributions::Standard: rand::prelude::Distribution<T>
{
  self.rng.gen()
}

/// Generates a random number within the specified range.
///
/// # Arguments
```

```
///
/// * `range` - the range (inclusive or exclusive) within which to
/// generate a random number.
///
/// # Example
///
/// ```
/// use my_library::RandomNumberGenerator;
/// let mut rng = RandomNumberGenerator::new();
/// let one_to_nine = rng.range(1..10);
/// let one_to_ten = rng.range(1..=10);
/// ```
pub fn range<T>(&mut self, range: impl SampleRange<T>) -> T
where
  T: SampleUniform + PartialOrd,
{
  self.rng.gen_range(range)
}
```

Last, add a little documentation to your Random plugin:

FirstLibraryDocs/my_library/src/random.rs
```
/// `Random` is a Bevy plugin that inserts a `RandomNumberGenerator`
/// resource into your application.
///
/// Once you add the plugin (with `App::new().add_plugin(Random)`),
/// you can access a random number generator in systems with
/// `rng: ResMut<RandomNumberGenerator>`.
pub struct RandomPlugin;
```

Now that all of your types and functions are documented, cargo doc --no-deps -- open results in some very professional-looking documentation, shown on the next page.

Each function appears in tool-tips in your editor, and a newcomer to my_library has a good chance of figuring out how to use it. Let's look at one last way to improve your documentation: complete code examples.

Including Code Examples

Many library consumers start by looking for example code. Reading documentation is great, but nothing beats a good example. Fortunately, Rust includes a robust system for library code examples.

Create a new directory, my_library/examples. In the new directory, create a new file named random_distribution.rs. (The listing starts on the next page.)

Struct my_library_docs::RandomNumberGenerator   source · [–]

```
pub struct RandomNumberGenerator { /* private fields */ }
```

[–] RandomNumberGenerator holds random number generation state, and offers random number generation services to your program.

RandomNumberGenerator defaults to using the PCG algorithm. You can specify xorshift as a feature flag to use it instead.

By default, RandomNumberGenerator requires mutability—it is shared in Bevy with ResMut<RandomNumberGenerator>. If you prefer interior mutability (and wish to use Res<RandomNumberGenerator> instead), specify the locking feature flag.

Example

``` use my_library_docs::RandomNumberGenerator; let mut my_rng = RandomNumberGenerator::new(); let random_number = my_rng.range(1..10); println!("{random_number}"); ```

Implementations

impl RandomNumberGenerator   source

pub fn new() -> Self   source

Creates a default RandomNumberGenerator, with a randomly selected starting seed.

pub fn seeded(seed: u64) -> Self   source

Creates a new RandomNumberGenerator, with a user-specified random seed. It will produce the same results each time (given the same requests).

Arguments

• seed - the random seed to use.

Example

```
use my_library_docs::RandomNumberGenerator;
let mut rng1 = RandomNumberGenerator::seeded(1);
let mut rng2 = RandomNumberGenerator::seeded(1);
let results: (u32, u32) = ( rng1.next(), rng2.next() );
assert_eq!(results.0, results.1);
```

FirstLibraryDocs/my_library/examples/random_distribution.rs
```rust
//! Roll 3d6 repeatedly and graph the resulting distribution.
use my_library_docs::RandomNumberGenerator;

fn main() {
  // Create a random number generator
  let mut rng = RandomNumberGenerator::new();
  // Store the results (minus 3)
  let mut results = vec![0; 16];
  // Roll 1,000 sets of 3d6 and increment results to map distribution
  for _ in 0..1_000 {
    let roll: usize =
      rng.range(1..=6) + rng.range(1..=6) + rng.range(1..=6);
    results[roll - 3] += 1;
  }
  // Print the distribution histogram
  println!("Distribution of 3d6 rolls:");
```
```

```
  for (i, count) in results.iter().enumerate() {
    print!("{: >2} : ", i + 3);
    for _ in 0..*count {
      print! {"#"};
    }
    println!();
  }
}
```

You execute examples by changing directory to the library's folder (cd my_library) and running cargo run --example <name>. Run the example you created with cargo run --example random_distribution, and you'll see a distribution graph of random numbers:

```
Distribution of 3d6 rolls:
 3 : #####
 4 : #############
 5 : ############################
 6 : ####################################################
 7 : ################################################################
 8 : ###############################################################################################
 9 : ###############################################################################################################
10 : ##########################################################################################################
11 : #####################################################################################################################
12 : ####################################################################################################
13 : ####################################################################################
14 : #####################################################
15 : ##########################################
16 : ###########################
17 : ##############
18 : ####
```

Creating example code that uses your library code will get many users up to speed faster than documentation, as many programmers learn better by example.

Wrapping Up

In this part, you've created your first library. The library offers random number generation services, feature flags, and generic types—and integrates into the Bevy engine via a plugin. You've documented your library and provided example code—you're in great shape. In the next part, you'll make a real game and expand the library to ease the creation of future games.

Part III

Flappy Dragon Flies Again

CHAPTER 5

Build Reusable Game State Management

In *Hands-on Rust*, readers built and used the *Flappy Dragon* project as an introductory example to Rust game development. Flappy Dragon is similar to the classic—and popular—game, Flappy Bird. Instead of guiding a bird, players take on the role of a majestic dragon. Despite the character change, the primary objects remain the same: avoid obstacles and don't hit the ground.

Because the game logic and player controls are relatively simple, Flappy-like games are sometimes referred to as the "Hello, World!" of game development. These types of games aren't only fun to build but also extensible: you can add menus, game over screens, track scores, increase difficulty, and best of all, you can add your own visual flair.

Over the next four chapters, you'll build a new, graphical version of Flappy Dragon using both the Bevy engine and the library you built in Part II, Your First Library, on page 17. The initial setup is similar to the example from part one—so let's start with a premade base.

Setting Up Flappy Dragon

You can find the initial implementation of Flappy Dragon in the code/FlappyIntro/flappy_dragon_base/ directory of the accompanying source code. You'll also need my_library in the state it was in at the end of part one of this book. You can find it in the code/FirstLibraryDocs/my_library/ directory.

To get started, you'll need to create a new project for Flappy Dragon. Select a base directory and change the directory to it. Then, create a new project with Cargo:

```
cd (path)
cargo new flappy_dragon
```

Next, copy the source code into the new project structure:

1. Copy flappy_dragon_base (the directory, not just the contents) into the (path)/flappy_dragon directory from code/FlappyIntro/flappy_dragon_base/.
2. Copy my_library (again, the directory) into the code/FirstLibraryDocs/my_library/ directory.

You should now have a directory structure that looks like this:

```
(path)
    flappy_dragon
        flappy_dragon_base
            assets
            src
            Cargo.toml
        my_library
            src
            Cargo.toml
        src
        Cargo.toml
```

Let's add flappy_dragon_base and my_library to the top-level workspace. Open (path)/flappy_dragon/Cargo.toml and add the following lines to the [workspace] section:

```
[workspace]
members = [
    "flappy_dragon_base",
    "my_library"
]
```

It's always a good idea to warn users when they try to run the top-level workspace. Open (path)/flappy_dragon/src/main.rs and change it to warn the user that they're trying to run the top-level workspace:

```
fn main() {
    println!("Please run the flappy_dragon_base project instead.");
}
```

Finally, link the library to the project. Open (path)/flappy_dragon/Cargo.toml and add the my_libary and bevy to the [dependencies] section:

```
[package]
name = "flappy_dragon_base"
version = "0.1.0"
edition = "2021"

[dependencies]
bevy = "0.16"
my_library = { path = "../my_library" }
```

You can now run the project:

```
⇒   cd (path)/flappy_dragon/flappy_dragon_base
⇒   cargo run
```

The game should start and look like this:

Paths in the Downloaded Source Code

The downloadable source code includes multiple versions of both flappy_dragon_base and my_library. The Rust workspace system doesn't like it when projects have the same name inside a workspace, so the downloadable version changes project names in Cargo.toml. As you follow along with the book, update your project and keep the names the same, which will make it easier to follow along.

Understanding the Flappy Dragon Code

This implementation doesn't include anything you haven't already used in the book so far, so there's not much to explain. However, you need to know some things before you get started with the updates.

Flappy Dragon uses two graphics, both located in the assets directory. The dragon graphic is freely available from OpenGameArt.[1] The wall graphic was quickly put together in the Gimp.[2]

Most games follow a similar overall game cycle that includes an optional loading screen, a main menu, playing the game, and finally a game over screen. When players reach the game over screen, they typically either exit the game or play again. You can visualize this game cycle as follows:

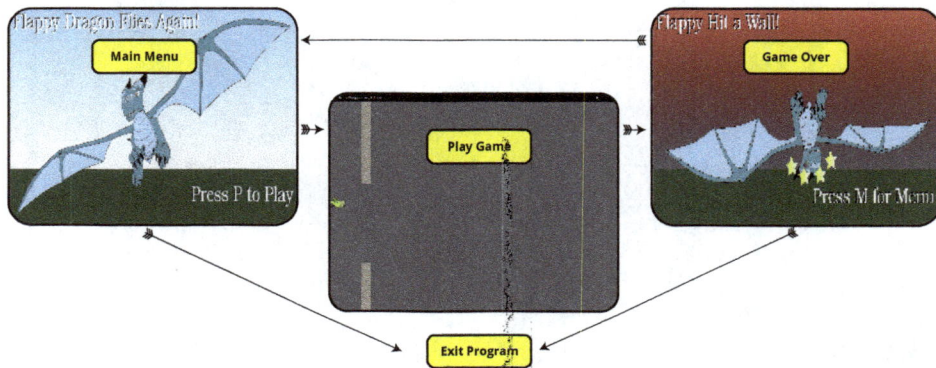

In this chapter, you'll create the main menu and game over screens for Flappy Dragon and Pig. More specifically, you'll build a reusable menu system suitable for inclusion in any game you create, as you'll see when you add these items to Pig (you'll do this near the end of the chapter). As you work through this chapter, you'll learn more about generics, traits, and state management. You'll also learn how to use macros to shorten complicated syntax.

Understanding Bevy and Game States

Before you create your state management system, it's worth taking a moment to study how Bevy handles application state. At the top level, a Bevy game maintains a state variable. State is stored as a resource and can be accessed in systems. And Bevy's scheduler uses the game's state to determine what systems to run.

States operate in phases:

- When a state becomes active, systems attached to its OnEnter phase run.
- With every "tick," the active state's Update systems are executed.
- When a state is deactivated, systems contained in the state's OnExit run.

---

1. https://opengameart.org/content/flappy-dragon-sprite-sheets
2. https://www.gimp.org/

You specify which systems run for each state in your app builder by adding *system sets*. We'll model GameState as an enumeration—it isn't provided by Bevy; you'll have to make one to represent *your* game state. In this example, we've added a PlayMyGame state to illustrate how states can be connected to Bevy systems:

```
// System runs for all states
.add_systems(Update, System1)

// System runs when State becomes active
.add_systems(OnEnter, setup.run_if(in_state(GameState::PlayMyGame)))

// System runs each tick State is active
.add_system(OnUpdate, run.run_if(in_state(GameState::PlayMyGame)))

// System runs when State becomes inactive
.add_system(OnExit, exit.run_if(in_state(GameState::PlayMyGame)))
```

As a rule of thumb, try to make states self-contained.

A state should perform the setup and tag entities as belonging to the state. When the state exits, it should clean up any entities tagged as belonging to that state. This ensures that states can operate independently, which is especially important in a library, since you—the author—have no idea what a library consumer might do in the states you didn't design.

Modeling Game State

Let's start by organizing the code in my_library.

You're building a *framework* to handle game flow, so create a module named bevy_framework. The framework will include multiple modules, so let's put it inside a folder. Create a new directory named my_library/src/bevy_framework. In that folder, create an empty file named mod.rs. Now, include the file in my_library by opening my_library/src/lib.rs and adding the following code:

```
mod bevy_framework;
pub use bevy_framework::*;
```

bevy_framework is now part of my_library, and it exports any public members to library consumers.

Engines vs. Frameworks

A framework is a skeleton organization, while an engine actually does the work. Bevy is an engine: it takes control of your program and requires that you work within its idioms. A framework is more forgiving, offering a suggested approach to a task.

Flappy Dragon is a simple game: you're either playing the game or you're not. Adding in menus, you can model the states as follows:

```
#[derive(Clone, Copy, PartialEq, Eq, Debug, Hash, Default, States)]
enum GamePhase {
➤   MainMenu,
    Flapping,
➤   GameOver,
}
```

Pig is a bit more complicated, with several states that activate while the game is running. Pig's game phase enumeration will need expanding to also include the game menus:

```
#[derive(Clone, Copy, PartialEq, Eq, Debug, Hash, Default, States)]
enum GamePhase {
➤   MainMenu,
    Start,
    Player,
    Cpu,
    End,
➤   GameOver,
}
```

Adding the MainMenu and GameOver items brings a little complexity to your workflow—but don't worry, you're going to automate most of the work of using them in your library. Let's start building a state management plugin for Bevy.

Layered States

Before version 0.11, Bevy supported nesting states inside other states and states with parameters. The Bevy Engine team decided on a simpler state system. It works fine, but you'll have to add generic states into your state enumeration every time.

Building a State Management Plugin

Bevy plugins are represented by a structure that implements the Plugin trait, which is defined by Bevy. Most plugins define their own types, but you need a generic plugin: a plugin that can be customized to your game's state enumeration. In bevy_framework/mod.rs start by defining a generic template for your plugin:

FlappyStatesGeneric/my_library/src/bevy_framework/mod.rs
```
❶ pub struct GameStatePlugin<T> {
❷   menu_state: T,
    game_start_state: T,
    game_end_state: T,
}
```

❶ You're specifying that your plugin will accept a generic type, T. This will contain your game's state enumeration.

❷ You need to store three instances of your state: the state for which the main menu should be rendered, the state for which the game over screen should be rendered, and the state to which the game should transition when the game starts. Each of these is of type T—your game state enumeration.

Notice that you added <T> to the structure definition. The structure is specialized based on the game's playing state. The game_start_state variable stores the game's initial state. Otherwise, the main menu wouldn't know where to send players when they start the game. Plugins don't *have* to define all of their functionality in their build() function; they can use more functions to define it. Let's add a constructor:

FlappyStatesGeneric/my_library/src/bevy_framework/mod.rs
```
❶ impl <T> GameStatePlugin<T>
   {
     #[allow(clippy::new_without_default)]
     pub fn new(menu_state: T, game_start_state: T, game_end_state: T) -> Self
     {
❷      Self { menu_state, game_start_state, game_end_state }
     }
   }
```

❶ You can specialize a trait with your own types using the impl <T> Trait<T> syntax. The syntax is a little unwieldy, but it specifies that you're implementing T for use within Plugin, which uses type T itself.

❷ Store the two menu states and start the game state within the plugin. Calling new() will specify the type to be stored, so the Rust compiler is able to infer the type for the remaining interactions with the plugin.

The new() constructor provides a convenient way to specify which of your game states represent the menus and also specializes your GameStatePlugin to your game's state enumeration. Bevy's Plugin trait requires that you create a build() function that actually applies the plugin to Bevy's internal state. Add the following code to your mod.rs file:

FlappyStatesGeneric/my_library/src/bevy_framework/mod.rs
```
impl<T: States+FromWorld+FreelyMutableState> Plugin for GameStatePlugin<T>
{
  fn build(&self, app: &mut App) {
    app.init_state::<T>();
  }
}
```

You may be asking, "What if I send any type rather than just a game state?" Rust has your back. The init_state function is generic and requires that its state implement Bevy's States trait, so this requirement is transferred to your function. Providing an incompatible type will mean the game doesn't compile. That's a good thing; the Rust type system is powerful and protects you from mistakes.

Let's open Flappy Dragon and make use of the new construct. In the process, we'll walk through what's happening under the hood. Open flappy_dragon_base/src/main.rs and add the following enumeration to your declarations:

```rust
FlappyStatesGeneric/flappy_dragon_base/src/main.rs
#[derive(Clone, PartialEq, Eq, Debug, Hash, Default, States)]
enum GamePhase {
  MainMenu,
  #[default] Flapping,
  GameOver
}
```

Since Flappy Dragon only has one internal state, the enumeration has a single type. It derives Clone, PartialEq, Eq, Debug, Hash, and States. The States trait is defined by Bevy and requires most of the other derivations. A state must be debug-printable and clonable for internal use. PartialEq and Eq specify that Rust must be able to compare two states and determine if they're equal. Hash specifies that Rust can generate a hash representing a specific state. Finally, #[default] indicates the *default* value of the enumeration—if the enumeration is created inside a structure, it will default to the annotated value. oNow, it defaults to Flapping. When menus are implemented, you'll change this to MainMenu.

Next, add a call to load your GameStatePlugin to your setup in main():

```rust
FlappyStatesGeneric/flappy_dragon_base/src/main.rs
App::new()
.add_plugins(DefaultPlugins.set(WindowPlugin {
  primary_window: Some(Window {
  title: "Flappy Dragon - Bevy Edition".to_string(),
  resolution: bevy::window::WindowResolution::new(
    1024.0, 768.0
  ),
  ..default()
}),
  ..default()
}))
  .add_plugins(RandomPlugin)
➤  .add_plugins(GameStatePlugin::<GamePhase>::new(
➤      GamePhase::MainMenu,
➤      GamePhase::Flapping,
➤      GamePhase::GameOver)
➤    )
```

This is where your hard work comes together. One simple line—from the library consumer's perspective—is actually doing a *lot*:

1. Calling GameStatePlugin::new() with your GamePhase validates that GamePhase is a valid source of game state data—it implements all of the requirements of the States trait.
2. GameStatePlugin is initialized and stored in Bevy's builder pattern.
3. The game's starting, ending, and setup states are all stored, ready for the menu system to use them.
4. When Bevy builds the game, GameStatePlugin::build() is called. This sets the game state to use the GameState<GamePhase> type you created and sets the initial game state to Flapping.

Next, you need to make all of the Flappy game self-contained in the Flapping state. Start by defining a tag component to indicate that an entity belongs to the Flapping state:

FlappyStatesGeneric/flappy_dragon_base/src/main.rs
```
#[derive(Component)]
struct FlappyElement;
```

Now update the system specification to wrap Flappy's systems inside the Flapping substate:

FlappyStatesGeneric/flappy_dragon_base/src/main.rs
```
.add_systems(OnEnter(GamePhase::Flapping), setup)
.add_systems(Update, (
  gravity, flap, clamp, move_walls, hit_wall
).run_if(in_state(GamePhase::Flapping)))
.add_systems(OnExit(GamePhase::Flapping), cleanup::<FlappyElement>)
.run();
```

Whenever you spawn an entity, you need to tag it with the FlappyElement type:

FlappyStatesGeneric/flappy_dragon_base/src/main.rs
```
commands.spawn(Camera2d::default())
➤   .insert(FlappyElement);
commands
    .spawn((
      Sprite::from_image(assets.dragon.clone()),
      Transform::from_xyz(-490.0, 0.0, 1.0),
      Flappy { gravity: 0.0 }
  ))
➤   .insert(FlappyElement);
```

FlappyStatesGeneric/flappy_dragon_base/src/main.rs
```
commands
    .spawn((
      Sprite::from_image(wall_sprite.clone()),
```

```
        Transform::from_xyz(512.0, y as f32 * 32.0, 1.0),
        Obstacle,
➤       FlappyElement
    ));
```

Rather than exiting the game when Flappy crashes, let's instead transition to the GameOver state. This change requires that you modify both code locations where you called AppExit:

FlappyStatesGeneric/flappy_dragon_base/src/main.rs
```
fn clamp(
    mut query: Query<&mut Transform, With<Flappy>>,
➤   mut state: ResMut<NextState<GamePhase>>,
) {
    if let Ok(mut transform) = query.single_mut() {
        if transform.translation.y > 384.0 {
            transform.translation.y = 384.0;
        } else if transform.translation.y < -384.0 {
➤           state.set(GamePhase::GameOver);
        }
    }
}
```

FlappyStatesGeneric/flappy_dragon_base/src/main.rs
```
fn hit_wall(
    player: Query<&Transform, With<Flappy>>,
    walls: Query<&Transform, With<Obstacle>>,
➤   mut state: ResMut<NextState<GamePhase>>,
) {
    if let Ok(player) = player.single() {
        for wall in walls.iter() {
            let distance = player.translation.distance(wall.translation);
            if distance < 32.0 {
➤               state.set(GamePhase::GameOver);
            }
        }
    }
}
```

Finally, you referenced a cleanup() function. This is a generic function that despawns all of the entities that have a given component. It's a useful function, so let's make it available in my_library.

Open my_library/src/bevy_framework/mod.rs and add the function:

FlappyStatesGeneric/my_library/src/bevy_framework/mod.rs
```
❶ pub fn cleanup<T>(
❷     query: Query<Entity, With<T>>,
       mut commands: Commands,
   )
❸ where T: Component
```

```
{
  query.iter().for_each(|entity| commands.entity(entity).despawn())
}
```

❶ Systems can be generic, too. The compiler will create a different version of a system for each type parameter, and Bevy will call the fully specified system.

❷ Specifying generic types in a system allows you to use the types in your system's injected parameter declarations. By specifying With<T>, you limit the query to only include entities that have a component of type T.

❸ Queries only work with Component types. Restrict T to only accept components.

Run the game now. Notice that the game runs as before, except that when players fail, they're greeted with a blank screen. You've added a state wrapper, but there are no menus. Let's build the game menus.

Adding Game Menus

Aside from being visually appealing, the main menu and game over screens have specific purposes:

• The main menu screen prevents players from starting a game before they're ready. It's also sometimes used to explain the game's controls and objectives before the game starts.

• The game over screen provides feedback as to how well the game went. It also gives players a way to play another round. Simply terminating a game when it finishes doesn't encourage the player to try again.

Let's get started by adding a main menu to Flappy Dragon. Download main_menu.png and game_over.png from code/FlappyStatesMenu/assets/ and save the images in your flappy_dragon_base/assets/ directory. These are the images you'll use for Flappy's main menu and game over screens:

Now that you have the graphics downloaded, let's add some code to load the graphics and make them available within your plugin. Open my_library/src/bevy_framework/mod.rs and add the following code:

```
FlappyStatesMenu/my_library/src/bevy_framework/mod.rs
#[derive(Resource)]
❶ pub(crate) struct MenuAssets {
  pub(crate) main_menu: Handle<Image>,
  pub(crate) game_over: Handle<Image>,
}

fn setup_menus(mut commands: Commands, asset_server: Res<AssetServer>) {
  let assets = MenuAssets {
    main_menu: asset_server.load("main_menu.png"),
    game_over: asset_server.load("game_over.png"),
  };
  commands.insert_resource(assets);
}
```

❶ You want the MenuAssets type to be available in other modules inside our library, but not published. pub(crate) provides this functionality.

This is similar to code you've worked with in previous chapters, so it should look familiar. You're loading image handles for main_menu.png and game_over.png, and you're storing them in a MenuAssets resource. Notice that MainMenu and set-up_main_menu are *not* public and won't be exported from your library for public use.

Now that the images are loaded, let's build the menu system.

Building Game Menus

Let's start by creating a new (empty) file named my_library/src/bevy_frame-work/game_menus.rs.

Open my_library/src/bevy_framework/mod.rs and add one line:

```
mod game_menus;
```

Next, open my_library/src/bevy_framework/game_menus.rs and add the following use statements:

```
FlappyStatesMenu/my_library/src/bevy_framework/game_menus.rs
use super::{MenuAssets, MenuResource};
use bevy::{app::AppExit, prelude::*};
use bevy::state::state::FreelyMutableState;
```

You're going to follow the same structure as Flappy in that each menu will be self-contained, initializing and cleaning up after itself. Let's facilitate that by making a type that denotes an entity as being part of the menu system:

FlappyStatesMenu/my_library/src/bevy_framework/game_menus.rs

```rust
#[derive(Component)]
pub(crate) struct MenuElement;
```

You're going to handle both the main menu and the game over screen in the same three functions. Let's start with a setup() function that can handle both menu types:

FlappyStatesMenu/my_library/src/bevy_framework/game_menus.rs

```rust
❶ pub(crate) fn setup<T>(
     state: Res<State<T>>,
     mut commands: Commands,
     menu_resource: Res<MenuResource<T>>,
     asset_server: Res<AssetServer>
  ) where
     T: States+FromWorld+FreelyMutableState,
  {
     let menu_assets = MenuAssets {
       main_menu: asset_server.load("main_menu.png"),
       game_over: asset_server.load("game_over.png"),
     };
❷   let current_state = state.get();
     let menu_graphic = {
       if menu_resource.menu_state == *current_state {
         menu_assets.main_menu.clone()
       } else if menu_resource.game_end_state == *current_state {
         menu_assets.game_over.clone()
       } else {
         panic!("Unknown menu state")
       }
     };

     commands
❸     .spawn(Camera2d::default())
       .insert(MenuElement);
     commands
       .spawn(( Sprite {
           image: menu_graphic,
           ..default()
         },
         Transform::from_xyz(0.0, 0.0, 1.0),
       ))
       .insert(MenuElement);
  }
```

❶ Setup references GameState, which is a generic type. This requires that your system also accept the generic type.

❷ You can fetch the current game state from a state resource with get().

❸ Spawn a 2D camera for the menus. It's a good idea to spawn the camera on setup (and despawn on conclusion) in a game phase; you can't be sure that the library user won't decide to use a 3D camera—or even their own custom camera—later in the program.

The setup() function places one of the menu graphics on the screen. Next, you need to handle user input for each menu:

FlappyStatesMenu/my_library/src/bevy_framework/game_menus.rs
```rust
pub(crate) fn run<T>(
  keyboard: Res<ButtonInput<KeyCode>>,
  mut exit: EventWriter<AppExit>,
  current_state: Res<State<T>>,
  mut state: ResMut<NextState<T>>,
➤ menu_state: Res<MenuResource<T>>,
) where
  T: States+FromWorld+FreelyMutableState,
{
  let current_state = current_state.get().clone();
  if current_state == menu_state.menu_state {
      if keyboard.just_pressed(KeyCode::KeyP) {
        state.set(menu_state.game_start_state.clone());
      } else if keyboard.just_pressed(KeyCode::KeyQ) {
        exit.write(AppExit::Success);
      }
    }
    else if current_state == menu_state.game_end_state {
      if keyboard.just_pressed(KeyCode::KeyM) {
        state.set(menu_state.menu_state.clone());
      } else if keyboard.just_pressed(KeyCode::KeyQ) {
        exit.write(AppExit::Success);
      }
    }
}
```

This is similar to code you've written before. You check the current menu state, and then check the input based on the current game phase—exiting the application or transitioning to another mode as needed. The highlighted lines reference a resource you haven't written yet: MenuResource. You need a way to tell the run() system what state should be used to start the game. Open src/my_library/bevy_framework/mod.rs and add the following code:

FlappyStatesMenu/my_library/src/bevy_framework/mod.rs
```rust
#[derive(Resource)]
pub(crate) struct MenuResource<T> {
  pub(crate) menu_state: T,
  pub(crate) game_start_state: T,
  pub(crate) game_end_state: T,
}
```

Finally, it's time to adjust the GameStatePlugin to use the menu system. Replace the build() function as follows:

```
FlappyStatesMenu/my_library/src/bevy_framework/mod.rs
impl<T> Plugin for GameStatePlugin<T>
where
  T: States+Copy+FromWorld+FreelyMutableState,
{
  fn build(&self, app: &mut App) {
    app.init_state::<T>();
    app.add_systems(Startup, setup_menus);
    let start = MenuResource {
      menu_state: self.menu_state,
      game_start_state: self.game_start_state,
      game_end_state: self.game_end_state,
    };
    app.insert_resource(start);

    app.add_systems(OnEnter(self.menu_state), game_menus::setup::<T>);
    app.add_systems(Update, game_menus::run::<T>
      .run_if(in_state(self.menu_state)));
    app.add_systems(OnExit(self.menu_state),
      cleanup::<game_menus::MenuElement>);

    app.add_systems(OnEnter(self.game_end_state), game_menus::setup::<T>);
    app.add_systems(Update, game_menus::run::<T>
      .run_if(in_state(self.game_end_state)));
    app.add_systems(OnExit(self.game_end_state),
      cleanup::<game_menus::MenuElement>);
  }
}
```

❶ Instead of launching directly into the game, start the game in the main menu. Note the use of the turbofish—it denotes that GameState is a generic type dependent upon type T.

❷ Load the menu graphics when the application starts.

❸ Store the state that begins the game—as specified by the user in the plugin setup—in a resource. This allows the menu systems to determine the destination when the player begins the game.

❹ Call the generic cleanup() system you created earlier to remove all menu entities when the menu terminates.

Run the game, and you have a working main and game over screen:

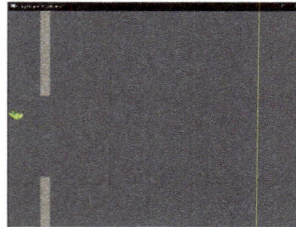

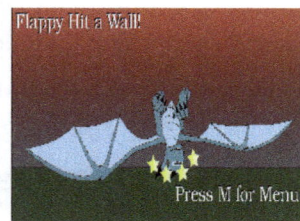

Tidying Unwieldy Syntax with Macros

Bevy's add_systems syntax can get out of hand when you have a lot of systems and complicated game stage logic. Fortunately, Rust offers a mechanism for adjusting language syntax: *macros*.

Should I Use Macros?

Macros are a powerful tool, but they're also a double-edged sword. The famous comic-book line "With great power comes great responsibility" definitely applies here. Macros can make your code more readable and can help avoid boilerplate code. However, they make your code harder to read for anyone who isn't familiar with your macros. They can make debugging more difficult and lead to bizarre compiler errors that refer to code you can't see without performing a macro expansion.

The add_phase! macro is here primarily to teach you how to use macros and how to simplify boilerplate code and unwieldy syntax. If you're working with others—or sharing this code—you may not want to use this macro.

On the upside, this macro has made the author's life a lot easier. The underlying macro has changed three times during the development of this book and has been rewritten once. Bevy loves changing how game states, systems, and system execution predicates work. The macro has made it easy to adapt to these changes and keep up with the continual Bevy engine churn!

If you come from a C or C++ background, you may remember using #define macros. #define directly replaces text in your code and offers little in the way of safety guarantees. A malicious developer might insert #define TRUE FALSE and confuse anyone who reads their code. Rust's macro system protects against this: every macro name must end with an exclamation mark (!) at the end of the name. Macros are also namespaced, so you can't overwrite default language syntax with them.

You've used a lot of Rust macros already. println!(...) is a macro, and so is vec!(...). Both accept a variable number of parameters and variable patterns of parameters. The regular Rust language can't do this, so a macro provides a convenient shorthand for the length of code wrapped inside.

The Rust macro system is intimidating. It implements a complete pattern-matching and expansion system that's different from regular Rust.

Deciding What You Want to Do

The first step for creating any macro is to decide what you'd like to be able to do. In this case, you want to simplify the creation of SystemSet data with a defined setup, run, and exit stage. Wouldn't it be nice if you could replace the enormous chain of .add_systems(OnEnter(GamePhase::Flapping), my_system) and other calls with something clean and easy to read? After much head-scratching, you might come up with something like the following syntax:

```
add_phase!( application, GamePhase, GamePhase::Flapping,
  start => [ setup ],
  run => [ gravity, flap, clamp, move_walls, hit_wall ]
  exit => [ cleanup::<FlappyElement> ]
);
```

That's clean, easy to read, and aligns with Rust's general pattern-matching syntax. Specifying GamePhase twice is a little messy—but it helps to specify the type that represents your game's state as well as the state you're specifying. Let's walk through building a macro that implements the state management design.

Building Your First Macro

Let's build a skeletal macro, describing the pattern we want to implement:

```
#[macro_export]
macro_rules! add_phase {
  (
    $app:expr, $type:ty, $phase:expr,
    start => [   ],
    run => [   ],
    exit => [    ]
  ) => { }
```

Let's break this down:

- #[macro_export] instructs the Rust compiler to make your macro available from outside of the current module. All modules are exported from the *root* of the crate that contains them. So you're exporting my_library::add_phase!.
- add_phase is the name of your macro.

- You then list the three parameters we decided to include: the application, the type containing state data, and the phase in which to execute these systems.
- Finally, you describe the syntax you want by entering it as a template.

This is illustrated as follows:

```
Publish the macro      #[macro_export]         Name the macro
Declare a macro         macro_rules! add_phase {
                           (        Bevy app              State Type        Phase in which to execute
                              $app:expr, $type:ty, $phase:expr,
Name of
each phase, with => []      start => [  ],
matching your chosen        run => [  ],
syntax.                     exit => [  ]
                           ) => {
                        }
```

Notice how all of the parts identified are now macro parameters, denoted with a $? Let's walk through them:

- $app:expr is an *expression*. Expressions can be anything that yields a result. In this case, $app will usually be the app variable, but it could also be a function that returns a variable to use. You mark a parameter as an expression with :expr.
- $type:ty accepts a type. You use this to connect your GamePhase type to the macro. You mark a parameter as a type with :ty.
- $phase:expr is an expression that will accept a GameState. Expressions are like any other expression in Rust—a statement that evaluates to something. It could be a function, some code, or a variable. You mark a parameter as an expression with :expr.

The definition nicely matches the syntax you came up with. The only issue is that it doesn't do anything yet.

Returning to how you add systems to Bevy, OnEnter and OnExit follow the same pattern:

```
app.add_systems(OnEnter(MyPhase), my_system);
app.add_systems(OnExit(MyPhase), second_system);
```

Update follows a slightly different pattern:

```
app.add_systems(Update, tick_system);
```

Let's start by implementing the start section of the macro. We want the library user to be able to specify a list of systems to run on each phase's start-up—or an empty list if there aren't any. The syntax for this is as follows:

```
start => [ $($start:expr),* ],
```

Just like the $app variable, $start is an *expression*. Wrapping it in $(),* means "allow this expression to repeat any number of times, separated by commas." The * means "continue," and the command is part of the pattern to match. For example, "sys1, sys2, sys3" matches the pattern—while "sys1!sys2" doesn't. Each of the "sys1", "sys2" systems will be listed inside a macro variable named $start.

Now, the desired macro call line start => [setup], expands to include setup in the $start macro. So, how do we go about using it? The final {} scope in the macro definition is the macro body. That's where functionality goes. You write it as normal code, with additional macro statements and substituting regular variables with macro variables. The following macro code repeats for every item in $start, adding an add_systems line for each item:

```
$($app.add_systems(
  bevy::prelude::OnEnter::<$type>($phase),
  $start
))*;
```

Let's break this down:

1. $app is replacing the app part of an app.add_systems call. The macro will use the variable you provided in the $app declaration.
2. bevy::prelude::OnEnter::<$type> expands the full type of OnEnter to avoid namespace confusion. It qualifies the OnEnter type with the type specified in $type—the game state type you provided. In the case of Flappy, GamePhase.
3. ($phase), takes the game phase—in Flappy's case, GamePhase::Flapping—and uses it as the parameter to the OnEnter expression.
4. $start represents a single item from the $start list you created.
5. Finally, the whole thing is wrapped in $()*;. This repeats the section over and over for each entry in $start.

You can repeat the same macro pattern for OnExit:

```
$($app.add_systems(
  bevy::prelude::OnExit::<$type>($phase),
  $exit
);)*
```

The code is the same, but with OnExit instead of OnEnter. Update works slightly differently, but you can once again repeat the same principles:

```
$($app.add_systems(
    bevy::prelude::Update, $run.run_if(in_state($phase))
);)*
```

The completed macro looks like this:

FlappyStatesMacro/my_library/src/bevy_framework/mod.rs
```
#[macro_export]
macro_rules! add_phase {
    (
        $app:expr, $type:ty, $phase:expr,
        start => [ $($start:expr),* ],
        run => [ $($run:expr),* ],
        exit => [ $($exit:expr),* ]
    ) => {
        $($app.add_systems(
            bevy::prelude::OnEnter::<$type>($phase),
            $start
        );)*
        $($app.add_systems(
            bevy::prelude::Update, $run.run_if(in_state($phase))
        );)*
        $($app.add_systems(
            bevy::prelude::OnExit::<$type>($phase),
            $exit
        );)*

    };
}
```

That's a great macro. It does everything initially specified. Now it's time to use it. Open flappy_dragon_base/src/main.rs and update the main() function to use your new syntax:

FlappyStatesMacro/flappy_dragon_base/src/main.rs
```
fn main() {
    let mut app = App::new();

    add_phase!(app, GamePhase, GamePhase::Flapping,
        start => [ setup ],
        run => [ gravity, flap, clamp, move_walls, hit_wall ],
        exit => [ cleanup::<FlappyElement> ]
    );

    app.add_plugins(DefaultPlugins.set(WindowPlugin {
        primary_window: Some(Window {
        title: "Flappy Dragon - Bevy Edition".to_string(),
        resolution: bevy::window::WindowResolution::new(
            1024.0, 768.0
        ),
        ..default()
    }),
```

```
    ..default()
  }))
    .add_plugins(RandomPlugin)
    .add_plugins(GameStatePlugin::new(
      GamePhase::MainMenu,
      GamePhase::Flapping,
      GamePhase::GameOver)
    )
    .run();
}
```

You did it: you've replaced the unwieldy Bevy state setup with a concise macro. You've effectively reduced Flappy Dragon to 149 lines of code and added a graphical main menu and game over screen. That's a significant improvement, showcasing the power of libraries, generics, and macros.

Don't Overuse Macros

It can be tempting to define macros to completely change Rust's syntax. This can be helpful for creating domain-specific languages (DSLs), but it comes at a cost: compilation is slower, and your code may confuse users who aren't familiar with your new syntax.

In some languages—notably Lisp derivatives—it's common to start by creating macros to define the language you want to use. You can do this, but it's not recommended.

It's time to update Pig to make use of the new features.

Updating Pig to Use Menus

To get started, download main_menu.png and game_over.png from code/FlappyStates-Macro/pig/assets/ to pig/assets. The pig and dice graphics are freely available, and the scene was designed in Inkscape.[3,4,5] The images look like this:

---

3.   https://freesvg.org/cute-pig
4.   https://freesvg.org/vector-image-of-game-dice-close-up
5.   https://inkscape.org/

Pig has a more complicated game state cycle than Flappy: it alternates between the player's turn and the CPU's turn. You don't want to delete everything whenever the turn switches. Likewise, you don't want to reload everything when the player's turn starts. You can get around this problem by expanding Pig's GamePhase enumeration to include some additional steps:

FlappyStatesMacro/pig/src/main.rs
```
#[derive(Clone, Copy, PartialEq, Eq, Debug, Hash, Default, States)]
enum GamePhase {
➤    #[default]
➤    MainMenu,
     Start,
     Player,
     Cpu,
     End,
➤    GameOver,
}
```

The additional states indicate that the game is beginning or ending.

Just like Flappy Dragon, create a GameElement component to indicate that a component should be cleaned up at the end of the game:

FlappyStatesMacro/pig/src/main.rs
```
#[derive(Component)]
pub struct GameElement;
```

Add insert(GameElement) calls to all of the spawn commands to denote that the entities should be cleaned up at the end of the game.

FlappyStatesMacro/pig/src/main.rs
```
fn setup(
  asset_server: Res<AssetServer>,
  mut texture_atlas_layouts: ResMut<Assets<TextureAtlasLayout>>,
  mut commands: Commands,
) {
➤  commands.spawn(Camera2d::default()).insert(GameElement);
```

FlappyStatesMacro/pig/src/main.rs
```
fn spawn_die(
  hand_query: &Query<(Entity, &Sprite), With<HandDie>>,
  commands: &mut Commands,
  assets: &GameAssets,
  new_roll: usize,
  color: Color,
) {
  let rolled_die = hand_query.iter().count() as f32 * 52.0;
  let mut sprite = Sprite::from_atlas_image(
    assets.image.clone(),
    TextureAtlas {
      layout: assets.layout.clone(),
```

```
        index: new_roll - 1,
    }
);
sprite.color = color;

commands.spawn((
    sprite,
    Transform::from_xyz(rolled_die - 400.0, 60.0, 1.0),
    HandDie,
    GameElement
));
```

You're ready to expand the state management a bit. Start by creating a start_game function:

FlappyStatesMacro/pig/src/main.rs
```
fn start_game(mut state: ResMut<NextState<GamePhase>>) {
    state.set(GamePhase::Player);
}
```

This function is straightforward: it sets the game state to the player's turn. You'll see why this is needed when you put the state map together. The Start phase will *also* load the game assets and initialize the game.

It would be nice to display the final score on the game over screen. Let's make another resource to store the final scores:

FlappyStatesMacro/pig/src/main.rs
```
#[derive(Resource)]
struct FinalScore(Scores);
```

You also need a system to run when the game ends because the End game phase has become active:

FlappyStatesMacro/pig/src/main.rs
```
fn end_game(
    mut state: ResMut<NextState<GamePhase>>,
    scores: Res<Scores>,
    mut commands: Commands,
) {
    commands.insert_resource(FinalScore(*scores));
    state.set(GamePhase::GameOver);
}
```

This system copies the current score and creates a FinalScore resource containing the scores. It then switches the game mode to GameOver.

Pig doesn't currently terminate when someone wins, so let's create a system that determines if the game has ended:

FlappyStatesMacro/pig/src/main.rs
```
fn check_game_over(
  mut state: ResMut<NextState<GamePhase>>,
  scores: Res<Scores>,
) {
  if scores.cpu >= 100 || scores.player >= 100 {
    state.set(GamePhase::End);
  }
}
```

You have the final scores stored, but the GameOver system doesn't display them. You can get around this problem by making another system that displays the score:

FlappyStatesMacro/pig/src/main.rs
```
fn display_final_score(
  scores: Res<FinalScore>,
  mut egui_context: EguiContexts,
) {
  egui::Window::new("Total Scores").show(egui_context.ctx_mut(), |ui| {
    ui.label(&format!("Player: {}", scores.0.player));
    ui.label(&format!("CPU: {}", scores.0.cpu));
    if scores.0.player < scores.0.cpu {
      ui.label("CPU is the winner!");
    } else {
      ui.label("Player is the winnner!");
    }
  });
}
```

You'll attach this to *also* run in the GameOver state in the application builder logic. You can attach as many systems (and entities, components, and so on) to existing game phases as you need. It's a framework, not a straitjacket.

Finally, adjust the main function to make use of the plugin and our new state structure:

FlappyStatesMacro/pig/src/main.rs
```
fn main() {
  let mut app = App::new();
```
❶
```
  add_phase!(app, GamePhase, GamePhase::Start,
    start => [ setup ], run => [ start_game ], exit => [ ]
  );
```
❷
```
  add_phase!(app, GamePhase, GamePhase::Player,
    start => [ ], run => [ player, check_game_over, display_score ]
      ,exit => [ ]
  );
```
❸
```
  add_phase!(app, GamePhase, GamePhase::Cpu,
    start => [ ], run => [ cpu, check_game_over, display_score ]
```

```
            , exit => [ ]
    );
    add_phase!(app, GamePhase, GamePhase::End,
      start => [ ], run => [ end_game ], exit => [ cleanup::<GameElement> ]
    );
    add_phase!(app, GamePhase, GamePhase::GameOver,
      start => [ ], run => [ display_final_score ], exit => [ ]
    );
    app.add_plugins(DefaultPlugins.set(
      WindowPlugin {
        primary_window: Some(Window {
        title: "Pig".to_string(),
        resolution: bevy::window::WindowResolution::new(1024.0, 768.0),
        ..default()
      }),
      ..default()
    }))
    .add_plugins(GameStatePlugin::new(GamePhase::MainMenu, GamePhase::Start,
      GamePhase::GameOver))
    .add_plugins(EguiPlugin{ enable_multipass_for_primary_context: false })
    .add_plugins(RandomPlugin)
    .run();
}
```

❶ When the game starts—following the main menu—start the phase by executing setup(), and then use start_game() to transition to the player's turn.

❷ When it's the player's turn, run the same systems you used in the original Pig for the player's turn. Additionally, check for a game over state, ending the game if the player won.

❸ Likewise, when it's the CPU's turn, execute the systems you used for the CPU's turn in the previous chapter. Also, check if the CPU won the game.

❹ If check_game_over() forwards the game's state machine to End, you run end_game() to store final scores and forward to the game over menu. You also remove all GameElement entities.

❺ If you add system sets to a state that already has system sets, they're appended rather than replaced. This allows you to add more functionality to library-provided systems—in this case, displaying the final score.

Run the game now, and Pig has a full menu system:

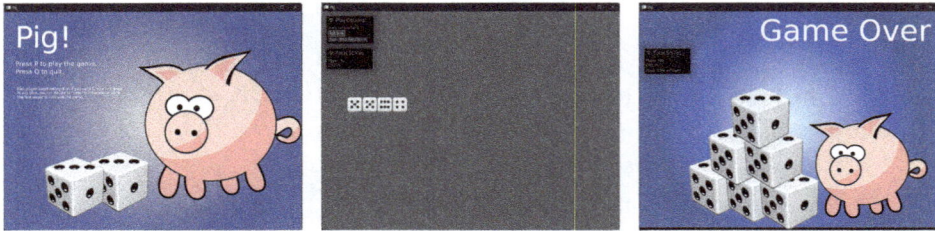

Wrapping Up

Congratulations! You've created a reusable menu and state management system, and you've updated both Flappy Dragon and Pig to use it. Along the way, you've created and worked with generic enumerations—you even created your first macros. These are important building blocks for library creation, both in the game development world and in general development.

In the next chapter, you'll learn more about managing game assets. You'll build a centralized asset manager, a loading screen that ensures your assets are available, and some helpers to make using your assets easier.

CHAPTER 6

Manage Your Game Assets

Assets are important. They include sprites, sprite sheets, video files, music and sound effects, 3D models, and anything your game engine processes and presents to the user. Bevy has a powerful asset management system that you can extend to include almost every format you might need. With a system so powerful, there's bound to be several layers of complexity, such as:

- Loading an asset gives you a handle (pointer) with which you can access the asset later—it's up to you to store the asset somewhere useful until it's needed.

- You need to keep watch on the game log for assets that fail to load. It would be nice if you could mark an asset as "important," and either fail to compile the program, stop the process, or even use an obvious placeholder to better indicate a missing asset.

- Assets are loaded asynchronously in the background. When you load a large image and immediately display that image, you'll often see it "pop" into place and suddenly appear on the screen. This sudden appearance can be disruptive to the overall flow of your program.

- Maintaining a list of your game's assets can be a chore, especially when you're collaborating with other developers and artists. You've seen the gradual accumulation of asset resources in Flappy Dragon and Pig when passing around resources containing asset handles.

In this chapter, you'll build an asset management layer on top of Bevy that provides easy access to the assets in your game systems and a central list of assets to help you keep track of an ever-growing game asset list. You'll then extend your asset system to include audio assets.

Understanding Bevy Assets

Bevy handles assets by loading them with the provided AssetServer, which in turn provides a Handle to uniquely identify each asset. In Flappy Dragon and Pig, you created asset loading code for each project. You then stored the acquired handles in a resource and accessed the resource whenever you needed to spawn an entity that used one of the assets you loaded. Whenever you find yourself repeating similar code over and over again in new projects, it's generally a sign that you could automate the process in a library—and save yourself some boilerplate typing.

The *asset manager* you're building in this chapter will replace the repetitive code with an easy-to-use system that lets you specify assets up front and transform them into an easy-to-access shared resource.

In Flappy Dragon, the following code loads two images:

```
fn setup(
  mut commands: Commands,
  asset_server: Res<AssetServer>,
) {
  let assets = Assets {
    dragon: asset_server.load("flappy_dragon.png"),
    wall: asset_server.load("wall.png"),
  };
}
```

dragon and wall are both variables of the type Handle<Image>.

Handles represent a unique identifier for an asset, whether or not it has been successfully loaded. Handles may not point to anything at all. If an image fails to load, the handle still exists, but it doesn't point to an asset. Likewise, if an image is still loading but hasn't fully loaded, the image's handle is still valid. Using a handle that doesn't (yet) point to anything doesn't trigger any errors. Instead, the asset simply isn't there and, in the case of an image, won't display.

Handles don't represent the asset itself. Instead, they provide a reference-counted pointer to the handle. You can call clone() on an asset handle to make another copy of the handle, and you can keep cloning it as often as you need—the asset itself won't be repeatedly copied in memory. When nothing retains a pointer to the handle, the asset itself is unloaded from memory.

Handles are generically typed. For example, an image has the type Handle<Image>, a sprite sheet has the type Handle<TextureAtlas>, and an audio file might have the type Handle<AudioSource>. With Bevy plugins, you can add more handle types to represent different types of assets.

There are two additional types of asset handles. HandleUntyped can represent any asset type, requiring that you try to cast it into the desired type. A Handle-Untyped may not have been loaded yet. A second untyped Handle is LoadedUntype-dAsset, which represents an asset that has been loaded and has a TypeId attached, specifying the concrete type of the asset. You'll use LoadedUntypedAsset in your asset manager to track assets that are still loading.

Now that you have a better understanding of assets and handles, you're ready to start building an asset manager.

Building an Asset Manager

The objectives are to list game assets up front, tag assets for easy access, and provide a single resource from which asset handles may be obtained. A combined asset manager keeps your asset declarations in one place, making them easier to manage. It also reduces the number of My-Assets resource structures in your program.

Let's start by creating a new module in my_library in which you'll store the asset code. Create a new directory and name it my_library/src/bevy_assets. In that directory, place an empty file named mod.rs. Then, add the module to your file by opening my_library/src/lib.rs and adding the following two lines to the end:

```
mod bevy_assets;
pub use bevy_assets::*;
```

You'll define assets in two stages. In the first stage, you'll define assets using a Bevy plugin that lets the library consumer define their game assets. In the second stage, you'll transform the asset list into a useful resource.

Create a new file named my_library/bevy_assets/asset_manager.rs to hold the first stage. Then, add the following code to my_library/bevy_assets/mod.rs to include the module in your library:

```
mod asset_manager;
pub use asset_manager::AssetManager;
```

Let's flesh out the asset manager plugin.

Requesting Assets

A good place to start is to categorize the assets you want to support. Add an enumeration named AssetType, initially holding only one asset type:

FlappyAssets/my_library/src/bevy_assets/asset_manager.rs
```rust
#[derive(Clone)]
pub enum AssetType {
  Image,
}
```

Next, create a structure that will hold the AssetManager plugin and a list of assets to load:

FlappyAssets/my_library/src/bevy_assets/asset_manager.rs
```rust
❶ #[derive(Resource, Clone)]
  pub struct AssetManager {
❷   asset_list: Vec<(String, String, AssetType)>,
  }
```

> ❶ You're going to insert the AssetManager as a resource, so you need to derive Bevy's Resource type.
>
> ❷ This tuple isn't the final form in which assets are stored, so storing them in an unlabeled tuple is a great way to represent them before they're loaded. The first tuple entry represents the asset tag; the second is the filename, and the final entry is the type of asset.

Time to give AssetManager a constructor:

FlappyAssets/my_library/src/bevy_assets/asset_manager.rs
```rust
impl AssetManager {
  pub fn new() -> Self {
    Self {
      asset_list: Vec::new(),
    }
  }
}
```

The AssetManager constructor creates an empty vector into which you can store assets.

Let's back up a bit for a moment. If your only clue that Bevy failed to load an asset is a log entry, it's very easy to miss the problem. It would be more consistent—and more Rust-like—if failing to load an asset triggered an error, requiring the library consumer to explicitly handle that error.

Rust's error types can quickly lead to an explosion in the number of types you have to create, so many developers like to use the anyhow crate to help.[1] anyhow wraps Rust's built-in Result type and provides an easy way to process errors from different sources by sending readable error messages upstream.

---

1. https://docs.rs/anyhow/latest/anyhow/

Open my_library/Cargo.toml and add the following code to your dependencies:

```
anyhow = "1"
```

anyhow is a useful crate, so let's reexport it for the library consumers. Add the following code to my_library/src/lib.rs:

```
FlappyAssets/my_library/src/lib.rs
pub mod anyhow {
    pub use anyhow::*;
}
```

With anyhow in place, add the following to your AssetManager implementation:

```
FlappyAssets/my_library/src/bevy_assets/asset_manager.rs
❶  pub fn add_image<S: ToString>(
     mut self,
     tag: S,
     filename: S,
❷  ) -> anyhow::Result<Self> {
❸    let filename = filename.to_string();
❹    #[cfg(not(target_arch = "wasm32"))]
     {
❺      let current_directory = std::env::current_dir()?;
❻      let assets = current_directory.join("assets");
       let new_image = assets.join(&filename);
       if !new_image.exists() {
❼        return Err(anyhow::Error::msg(format!(
           "{} not found in assets directory",
           &filename
         )));
       }
     }
❽    self
       .asset_list
       .push((tag.to_string(), filename, AssetType::Image));
❾    Ok(self)
   }
 }
```

❶ Making the user type "flappy.png".to_string() isn't very ergonomic. Requiring that parameters implement ToString allows the user to enter a string literal, a String type, or any other type that can be trivially converted to text by calling to_string().

❷ If successful, the function returns Self. Self—with a capital S—is the type of the parent struct, in this case, AssetManager. Wrapping the return type in anyhow::Result requires that success return Ok(self)—but errors can be returned with the ? operator or explicitly with the Err type.

Returning Self doesn't create a copy unless you've derived copy on your type. Instead, it moves the structure to the returned variable.

❸ Convert filename to a String.

❹ Unlike a lot of platforms, WebAssembly doesn't support direct filesystem access. Skip checking for file existence for WASM.

❺ Obtain the current directory. The ? means that if Rust is unable to determine the current directory, the error returned by the current_dir() function will be returned by your function. If the call succeeded, the result is automatically unwrapped.

❻ The Path type provides a join() function to append paths in a platform-agnostic manner. Add assets to the current directory.

❼ If the asset path doesn't exist, return an error message with anyhow's Error type.

❽ Add the asset to the plugin's asset list.

❾ Everything went well, so return Ok containing the plugin itself.

Your AssetManager can now accept a list of images—using the builder pattern—and verify that they're ready for use. Let's turn AssetManager into a Bevy plugin by adding the following code:

```
impl Plugin for AssetManager {
  fn build(&self, app: &mut bevy::prelude::App) {
    app.insert_resource(self.clone());
    //app.add_systems(Startup, setup);
  }
}
```

The plugin's build() function adds the AssetManager as a resource. In the commented-out line, you called a startup system (that runs when Bevy starts) named setup. You'll write the setup function a little later. For now, open flappy_dragon_base/src/main.rs and make sure the AssetManager works in your existing game framework.

Because you're returning an anyhow::Result type, it's helpful to adjust the main function to also return a Result type. Change fn main as follows:

```
fn main() -> anyhow::Result<()> {
```

At the bottom of the main function, add an expression that returns Ok:

```
  Ok(())
}
```

Returning a Result type from your main function allows you to use the ? operator when calling add_image. If an error occurs, Rust will print the error and terminate the program.

In your main function, you perform a series of add_plugin calls. Let's add the AssetManager to the plugin list, making use of ? to handle errors:

```
FlappyAssets/flappy_dragon_base/src/main.rs
.add_plugins(GameStatePlugin::new(
  GamePhase::MainMenu,
  GamePhase::Flapping,
  GamePhase::GameOver)
)
➤ .add_plugins(AssetManager::new()
➤   .add_image("dragon", "flappy_dragon.png")?
➤   .add_image("wall", "wall.png")?
➤ )
  .run();
```

Change flappy_dragon.png to flappy_dragon2.png and run the program with cargo run. The program refuses to start and displays the following error:

```
Error: flappy_dragon2.png not found in assets directory
```

Restore the name to flappy_dragon.png, and your game works as before; you aren't actually loading any images yet, so let's build an asset store and loader.

Storing and Loading Images

Start by creating an empty file named my_library/src/bevy_assets/asset_store.rs. Then, add this file to your project by adding the following code to my_library/src/bevy_assets/mod.rs:

```
mod asset_store;
pub use asset_store::*;
```

Next, open asset_store.rs and add the following:

```
FlappyAssets/my_library/src/bevy_assets/asset_store.rs
use bevy::{asset::{Asset, LoadedUntypedAsset}, prelude::*,
  platform::collections::HashMap};
```

The use statement imports the prelude and the Asset type from Bevy. It also imports Bevy's HashMap type, which is slightly faster than Rust's default (it uses a faster hashing algorithm). You want to minimize delay when looking up assets, so it makes sense to use Bevy's map type.

You're going to be using some long type names, so let's create some type aliases to make the code more readable:

FlappyAssets/my_library/src/bevy_assets/asset_store.rs

```
pub type LoadedAssets = Assets<LoadedUntypedAsset>;
pub type AssetResource<'w> = Res<'w, LoadedAssets>;
```

The type = declaration sets up an *alias*—the name on the left of the declaration provides a nice name for the type on the right. The types are copied from Bevy's declaration. AssetResource is much easier to type than Res<'w, Assets<LoadedUntypedAsset>>. Type aliases also provide some protection against the underlying types inside Bevy changing—often, you can simply update the type alias to a new type name, and existing code will work. Using a type alias also prevents your library consumer from having to understand too much of Bevy's internals. The LoadedUntypedAsset type isn't included in Bevy's prelude—but by exporting it, you don't require your library user to find the type and import it themselves.

You're ready to define a new type named AssetStore to hold the handles generated by loading assets:

FlappyAssets/my_library/src/bevy_assets/asset_store.rs

```
❶ #[derive(Resource, Clone)]
  pub struct AssetStore {
❷   pub(crate) asset_index: HashMap<String, Handle<LoadedUntypedAsset>>,
  }
```

❶ The AssetStore will be available to systems as a resource, so tag it as such.

❷ A HashMap links keys with values. In this case, it links the name of an asset with an "untyped" handle. Untyped handles are a numerical resource identifier used by Bevy to index resources. Names are much easier to type than the UUIDs that actually identify resources (for example, c7e42177-9461-459f-aae3-270c3af9d24f).

You still need to define a function for accessing stored resources. Since you're storing assets as untyped handles, a little bit of cleverness is required. Let's walk through the process:

FlappyAssets/my_library/src/bevy_assets/asset_store.rs

```
  impl AssetStore {
    pub fn get_handle<T>(&self, index: &str, assets: &LoadedAssets)
❶   -> Option<Handle<T>>
❷   where T: Asset,
    {
❸     if let Some(handle_untyped) = self.asset_index.get(index) {
❹       if let Some(handle) = assets.get(handle_untyped) {
❺         return Some(handle.handle.clone().typed::<T>());
        }
        None
      } else {
```

6   None
      }
    }
  }
}

❶ You want to access assets by name, so the function requires an index string. However, there's no guarantee that the library user typed the name correctly, so the function returns an Option>. Options can contain Some(..) or None, allowing you to indicate if the name was valid or not.

The function becomes a little more complicated because it doesn't know what type of asset you're requesting. You might be requesting a Handle<Image>, a Handle<Texture>, or any other type of resource. Rather than writing a separate function for every possible type of handle, using T to specify a generic type allows the function to work with any handle type.

In most cases, Rust will determine the type you're actually requesting from the type in which you're requesting the handle. In other cases, you can use the turbofish: assets.get_handle::<Image>().

❷ Constrain T to only accept asset types.

❸ If the asset index contains the requested key, process the asset.

❹ We've found the handle in our asset loading map. Now we have to query Bevy to see if this type is available yet, which will allow us to determine the actual handle type. Bevy is unable to determine the type of an asset before it's in memory.

❺ Wrap the result in Some to indicate success. Calling typed() on an Untyped-Handle converts the handle into a handle of the requested type—in this case, the function's generic type T.

❻ If the asset index doesn't contain the requested key, return None.

The AssetStore provides a convenient interface to Bevy assets. Any system can include it by requesting assets: Res<AssetStore> in the system's function signature, and any asset may be obtained with assets.get_handle("my asset"). Let's make the asset store useful by populating it with handles.

In the code on page 116, you commented out the call to setup. Open my_library/src/bevy_assets/asset_manager.rs and uncomment the code:

```
FlappyAssets/my_library/src/bevy_assets/asset_manager.rs
impl Plugin for AssetManager {
  fn build(&self, app: &mut bevy::prelude::App) {
    app.insert_resource(self.clone());
    app.add_systems(Startup, setup);
```

```
    }
}
```

It's time to write the setup function, transforming the builder-pattern asset list into load commands that return a handle you can store:

FlappyAssets/my_library/src/bevy_assets/asset_manager.rs

```
fn setup(
❶  asset_resource: Res<AssetManager>,
   mut commands: Commands,
   asset_server: Res<AssetServer>,
) {
❷  let mut assets = AssetStore {
     asset_index: bevy::platform::collections::HashMap::new(),
   };
   asset_resource.asset_list.iter().for_each(
     |(tag, filename, asset_type)| {
❸       match asset_type {
         _ => {
           // Most asset types don't require a separate loader
           assets
             .asset_index
             .insert(tag.clone(), asset_server.load_untyped(filename));
         }
       }
     },
   );
❹  commands.remove_resource::<AssetManager>();
❺  commands.insert_resource(assets);
}
```

❶ You inserted AssetManager as a resource during plugin building, which retrieves the stored asset manager.

❷ Initialize an empty AssetStore.

❸ You can load most asset types with load_untyped() from Bevy's asset server. Not all asset types can be loaded in this fashion, so including this match expression future-proofs your code.

❹ Now that you've converted tags and filenames into index entries and asset handles, you don't need the AssetManager anymore. Clean it up and save some memory.

❺ In place of the AssetManager, insert your newly created AssetStore.

When the plugin manager runs, it will automatically convert all of the listed assets into handles in the AssetStore resource.

Open flappy_dragon_base/src/main.rs and make use of the new assets system. Delete the Assets structure entirely, as it will be replaced with the AssetStore. You've already added the plugin loading code, so all that remains is to update the two functions that spawn graphics:

```rust
fn setup(
  mut commands: Commands,
  mut rng: ResMut<RandomNumberGenerator>,
  // Remove: asset_server: Res<AssetServer>,
➤ assets: Res<AssetStore>,
➤ loaded_assets: AssetResource,
) {
  commands.spawn(Camera2d::default()).insert(FlappyElement);
commands
    .spawn((
        Sprite::from_image(assets.get_handle("dragon",
          (&loaded_assets)).unwrap()),
        Transform::from_xyz((-490.0), 0.0, 1.0),
    ))
    .insert((Flappy { gravity: 0.0 }))
    .insert(FlappyElement)
➤ build_wall(&mut commands, &assets, rng.range(-5..5), &loaded_assets);
}

fn build_wall(
  commands: &mut Commands,
➤ assets: &AssetStore,
➤ loaded_assets: &LoadedAssets,
  gap_y: i32,
) {
  for y in -12..=12 {
    if y < gap_y - 4 || y > gap_y + 4 {
      commands
        .spawn((
            Sprite::from_image(assets.get_handle("wall",
              (&loaded_assets)).unwrap()),
            Transform::from_xyz(512.0, (y as f32 * 32.0), 1.0),
        ))
        .insert(Obstacle)
        .insert(FlappyElement)
    }
  }
}
```

Changing Assets to AssetStore and calling get_handle isn't a huge win in terms of reducing Flappy's complexity. The asset system is nice and reusable, but the syntax to spawn sprites remains cumbersome.

Simplifying Image Spawning with a Macro

You can make sprite spawning easier with a macro. You learned about using macros in Tidying Unwieldy Syntax with Macros, on page 100. Open src/my_library/src/bevy_assets/mod.rs and build a macro to simplify sprite spawning:

FlappyAssets/my_library/src/bevy_assets/mod.rs
```
#[macro_export]
macro_rules! spawn_image {
  ($assets:expr, $commands:expr, $index:expr, $x:expr, $y:expr, $z:expr,
    $resource:expr,
     $($component:expr),*) =>
{
    $commands.spawn((
        Sprite::from_image($assets.get_handle($index, $resource).unwrap()),
        Transform::from_xyz($x, $y, $z),
    ))
    $(
      .insert($component)
    )*
 };
}
```

The spawn_image! macro uses the same rules you encountered before. The macro accepts your assets and commands variables, an x/y/z position for the image, the name of the image handle to render, and a list of component types to attach to the image entity. It then uses these to reproduce the same commands.spawn syntax you used before.

Using the new macro, you can substantially simplify Flappy's image spawning in flappy_dragon_base/src/main.rs:

FlappyAssets/flappy_dragon_base/src/main.rs
```
fn setup(
  mut commands: Commands,
  mut rng: ResMut<RandomNumberGenerator>,
  assets: Res<AssetStore>,
  loaded_assets: AssetResource,
) {
  commands.spawn(Camera2d::default()).insert(FlappyElement);
  spawn_image!(assets, commands, "dragon", -490.0, 0.0, 1.0, &loaded_assets,
    Flappy { gravity: 0.0 }, FlappyElement);
  build_wall(&mut commands, &assets, rng.range(-5..5), &loaded_assets);
}

fn build_wall(
  commands: &mut Commands,
  assets: &AssetStore,
  gap_y: i32,
  loaded_assets: &LoadedAssets
```

```
) {
  for y in -12..=12 {
    if y < gap_y - 4 || y > gap_y + 4 {
      spawn_image!(assets, commands, "wall", 512.0, y as f32 * 32.0, 1.0,
        &loaded_assets, Obstacle, FlappyElement);
    }
  }
}
```

Congratulations! You've now got a working asset loading system. Next, you'll add a "loading, please wait" screen to Flappy to avoid assets "popping" onto the screen when they finish loading.

Creating a Loading Screen

Bevy loads assets asynchronously in the background. This loading technique is wonderful when managing complex scenes and loading and unloading assets on the fly, as it helps to avoid problems where your game is unresponsive while it waits for files to load. However, it's problematic for simple games: a large menu graphic may take some time to load, and it will suddenly appear some time after the menu itself has begun operating. The solution is to create a loading screen and pause while your assets load—notifying the user of the progress. Your AssetManager and AssetStore have already built a list of all of the assets your game needs. Your loading screen needs to ask Bevy if the assets are available yet and only proceed to the main menu when all of the requested assets are loaded.

Let's start by revisiting some of the code you wrote in Chapter 5, Build Reusable Game State Management, on page 85. Remember the GameState structure? This structure defines the top-level game state, including the main menu and game over screens. You need to add a new Loading state so that Bevy knows when to display your loading screen.

Open flappy_dragon/src/main.rs and add the Loading state to GamePhase:

FlappyAssetsLoadingMenu/flappy_dragon_base/src/main.rs
```
#[derive(Clone, Copy, PartialEq, Eq, Debug, Hash, Default, States)]
enum GamePhase {
➤   #[default] Loading,
    MainMenu,
    Flapping,
    GameOver
}
```

Now that the Loading state exists, you need it to run first. You also need to adjust your menus to load their assets through the asset management system.

Open my_library/src/bevy_framework/mod.rs. In the build() function, delete the line that reads:

```
app.add_systems(Startup, setup_menus);
```

For cleanliness (and to avoid "dead code" warnings), delete the setup_menus function and MenuAssets structure. The second half of making the asset manager handle loading game_over.png and main_menu.png is to automatically add them to the list of assets to be loaded.

Open my_library/src/bevy_assets/asset_manager.rs and replace the asset_list construction:

```
FlappyAssetsLoadingMenu/my_library/src/bevy_assets/asset_manager.rs
impl AssetManager {
  pub fn new() -> Self {
    Self {
➤       asset_list: vec![
➤         ("main_menu".to_string(), "main_menu.png".to_string(),
➤           AssetType::Image),
➤         ("game_over".to_string(), "game_over.png".to_string(),
➤           AssetType::Image),
➤       ],
    }
  }
}
```

Adding the assets to the list automatically has the side effect of causing your program to fail if you forget to create menu graphics.

Why Not Load a Loader Graphic?

A nice background for the loading screen would be pretty, and you could add it here. The problem, however, is that the loading graphic itself has to be loaded, so it, too, will "pop" into existence—precisely the problem you're trying to correct.

Now that the asset loader is loading the menu assets, you can use them when displaying your menus. Open my_library/src/bevy_framework/game_menus.rs. Adjust the use statements at the top of the file to include the asset store, and remove the shared menu resources:

```
FlappyAssetsLoadingMenu/my_library/src/bevy_framework/game_menus.rs
use super::MenuResource;
use bevy::{app::AppExit, prelude::*};
use bevy::state::state::FreelyMutableState;
```

Scroll down to the setup() function and replace the old menu resource with your AssetStore resource. Also, adjust the graphic selection match statement to acquire resource handles from the asset store:

FlappyAssetsLoadingMenu/my_library/src/bevy_framework/game_menus.rs

```rust
pub(crate) fn setup<T>(
  state: Res<State<T>>,
  mut commands: Commands,
➤  menu_resource: Res<MenuResource<T>>,
➤  loaded_assets: crate::AssetResource,
  assets: Res<AssetStore>,
) where
  T: States+FromWorld+FreelyMutableState,
{
  let current_state = state.get();
➤  let menu_graphic = {
➤    if menu_resource.menu_state == *current_state {
➤      assets.get_handle("main_menu", &loaded_assets).unwrap()
➤    } else if menu_resource.game_end_state == *current_state {
➤      assets.get_handle("game_over", &loaded_assets).unwrap()
➤    } else {
➤      panic!("Unknown menu state")
➤    }
➤  };

  commands
    .spawn(Camera2d::default())
    .insert(MenuElement);
  commands
    .spawn((
        Sprite::from_image(menu_graphic.clone()),
          Transform::from_xyz(0.0, 0.0, 1.0),
          MenuElement
        ));
}
```

With your menus adjusted, it's time to build the actual loading screen. You'll want to keep it simple and lightweight; making the user wait for the loading screen to load is self-defeating.

When you were building Pig, you used egui to provide a very lightweight user interface. Egui is perfect for a loading screen because it's lightweight and doesn't require that assets be loaded. Best of all, it doesn't add anything to the Entity Component System, so there's nothing to clean up.

Open my_library/Cargo.toml and add egui to your dependencies:

```toml
[dependencies]
rand = "0.8"
rand_pcg = { version = "0.3", optional = true }
rand_xorshift = { version = "0.3", optional = true }
bevy = "0.16"
anyhow = "1"
➤ bevy_egui = "0.34"
```

Egui is a useful library. You can reexport it from my_library/src/lib.rs so that all of your library users can benefit from using it without having to install it themselves. To do so, add the following code to the end of lib.rs:

FlappyAssetsLoadingMenu/my_library/src/lib.rs
```rust
pub mod egui {
    pub use bevy_egui::*;
}
```

Now that you've put the framework together, you're ready to make the loading screen. Create a new file named my_library/src/bevy_assets/loading_menu.rs (and don't forget to add mod loading_menu to the mod.rs file). Begin the file by building some use statements:

FlappyAssetsLoadingMenu/my_library/src/bevy_assets/loading_menu.rs
```rust
use bevy::{prelude::*, asset::LoadedUntypedAsset};
use bevy::state::state::FreelyMutableState;
use bevy_egui::EguiContexts;
use crate::{AssetStore, egui::egui::Window, MenuResource, AssetManager};
use crate::bevy_assets::setup_asset_store;
```

The use statements load the parts of Bevy you'll need, the EguiContexts type that lets you connect to egui, and the asset system.

Next, you need to give the loading system a list of all the handles that need to be loaded before the main menu executes. Add the following:

FlappyAssetsLoadingMenu/my_library/src/bevy_assets/loading_menu.rs
```rust
#[derive(Resource)]
pub(crate) struct AssetsToLoad(Vec<Handle<LoadedUntypedAsset>>);

pub(crate) fn setup(
    assets: Option<Res<AssetStore>>,
    asset_manager: Option<Res<AssetManager>>,
    asset_server: Res<AssetServer>,
    mut commands: Commands,
) {
    let assets = match assets {
        Some(assets) => assets.into_inner(),
        None => {
            &setup_asset_store(asset_manager.as_ref().unwrap(),
            &mut commands, &asset_server)
        }
    };
    let assets_to_load: Vec<Handle<LoadedUntypedAsset>> = assets
        .asset_index.values().cloned().collect();
    commands.insert_resource(AssetsToLoad(assets_to_load));
}
```

❶ Create a resource structure containing a vector of HandleUntyped entries. This will store the to-be-loaded handles.

❷ Obtain the list of handles from the asset_index. Calling cloned() clones each entry in turn, ensuring that you have ownership of the handle. The handles are then collected into your resource's handle vector.

❸ Insert the AssetsToLoad resource into the game state.

Now that you're storing a list of everything that must be loaded, you can create a run() function to check the status of each handle, display a loading message, and proceed to the main menu when everything is loaded:

FlappyAssetsLoadingMenu/my_library/src/bevy_assets/loading_menu.rs
```
pub(crate) fn run<T>(
    asset_server: Res<AssetServer>,
    mut to_load: ResMut<AssetsToLoad>,
    mut state: ResMut<NextState<T>>,
    mut egui_context: EguiContexts,
    menu_info: Res<MenuResource<T>>,
) where T: States+FromWorld+FreelyMutableState,
{
    to_load.0.retain(|handle| {
        match asset_server.get_load_state(handle.id()) {
            Some(bevy::asset::LoadState::Loaded) => false,
            _ => true,
        }
    });
    if to_load.0.is_empty() {
        state.set(menu_info.menu_state.clone());
    }
    Window::new("Loading, Please Wait").show(
        egui_context.ctx_mut(), |ui| {
            ui.label(
                format!("{} assets remaining", to_load.0.len())
            )
    });
}
```

❶ retain() is a function provided by Rust containers to selectively remove items from the container. retain() calls a function for each entry and removes any entry for which the function returns false.

❷ Bevy's AssetServer provides a function named get_load_state() to determine if an asset has been loaded yet. Calling the function returns a LoadState enumeration.

❸ If the asset's LoadState is equal to Loaded, then the asset is available for use. Return false because you don't wish to retain the handle in the to-load list, now that it has been loaded.

❹ For any other LoadState, return true, and the loader will check again on the next frame.

❺ If the to-load list is empty, proceed to the main menu.

❻ Just as you did in Pig, use egui to display a loading status window.

Finally, when the loading system finishes, you want to clean up after it:

```
FlappyAssetsLoadingMenu/my_library/src/bevy_assets/loading_menu.rs
pub(crate) fn exit(
    mut commands: Commands,
) {
    commands.remove_resource::<AssetsToLoad>();
}
```

The cleanup simply removes the AssetsToLoad resource from Bevy.

All that remains is to tell Bevy to run your loading system. Open my_library/src/bevy_framework/mod.rs and update the build() to load the egui plugin:

```
FlappyAssetsLoadingMenu/my_library/src/bevy_framework/mod.rs
   fn build(&self, app: &mut App) {
     app.init_state::<T>();
➤    app.add_plugins(bevy_egui::EguiPlugin{
➤      enable_multipass_for_primary_context: false });
     let start = MenuResource {
       menu_state: self.menu_state,
       game_start_state: self.game_start_state,
       game_end_state: self.game_end_state,
     };
     app.insert_resource(start);

     app.add_systems(OnEnter(self.menu_state), game_menus::setup::<T>);
     app.add_systems(Update, game_menus::run::<T>
       .run_if(in_state(
       self.menu_state)));
     app.add_systems(OnExit(self.menu_state),
       cleanup::<game_menus::MenuElement>);

     app.add_systems(OnEnter(self.game_end_state), game_menus::setup::<T>);
     app.add_systems(Update, game_menus::run::<T>
       .run_if(in_state(self.game_end_state)));
     app.add_systems(OnExit(self.game_end_state),
       cleanup::<game_menus::MenuElement>);

     app.add_systems(OnEnter(T::default()), crate::bevy_assets::setup);
     app.add_systems(Update, crate::bevy_assets::run::<T>
       .run_if(in_state(T::default())));
```

```
  app.add_systems(OnExit(T::default()), crate::bevy_assets::exit);
}
```

Run Flappy Dragon with cargo run (from the flappy_dragon directory). You'll—very briefly—see a loading screen before the main menu appears:

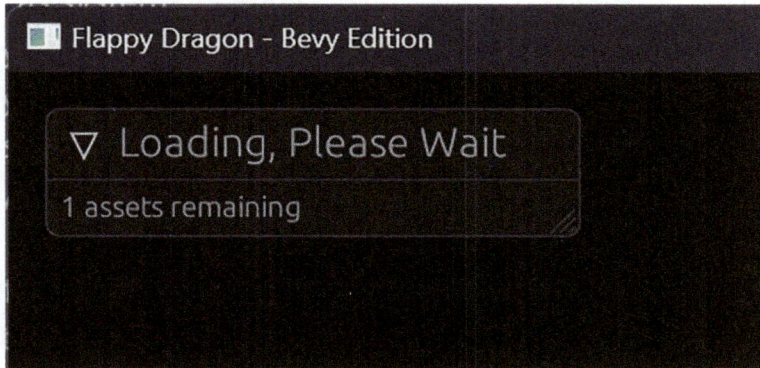

You have a working asset loading system, complete with a "loading, please wait" screen. Let's extend it and add some sounds to Flappy Dragon.

Adding Sound to Flappy Dragon

Sound is a useful feature of games. It provides feedback when something happens and can help set the mood. Building a rich "soundscape" for a game is a skill set in and of itself. For now, let's keep it simple and add a "flapping wings" sound effect and a sound effect that occurs when Flappy hits a wall.

Ogg-Vorbis

By default, Bevy uses the Ogg-Vorbis open source sound format.[2] Ogg is a relatively common sound container in games because it doesn't have any of the licensing restrictions that come with MP3 and other commercially developed formats. Ogg is also not the most common format for sound files on the Internet, so you may have to convert any .wav or .mp3 files you need before you can use them in Bevy.

I find the easiest way to convert audio is to use the VLC program.[3] To convert an audio file into Ogg format, run VLC and open the Media menu. Select Convert/Save and you'll see the the dialog box shown at the top of the next page.

---

2. https://en.wikipedia.org/wiki/Ogg
3. https://www.videolan.org/vlc/

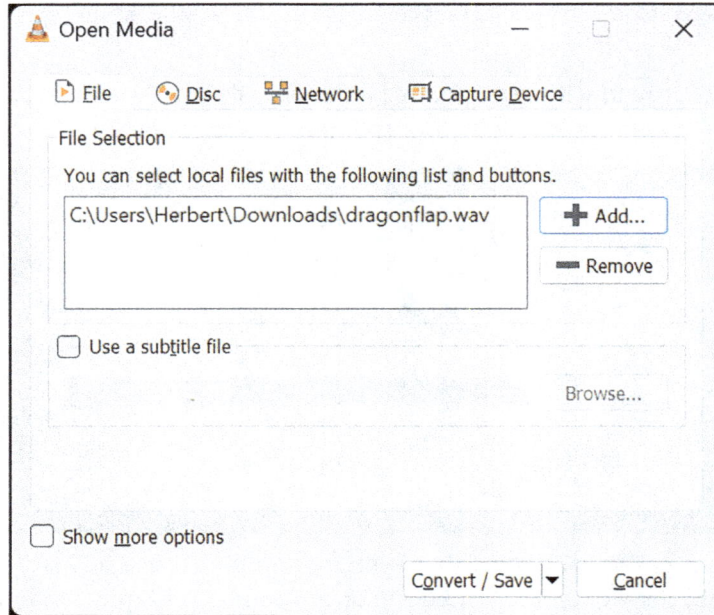

Click the Add button and select the files you wish to convert. Then, click the Convert/Save button at the bottom, and a second dialog box will appear:

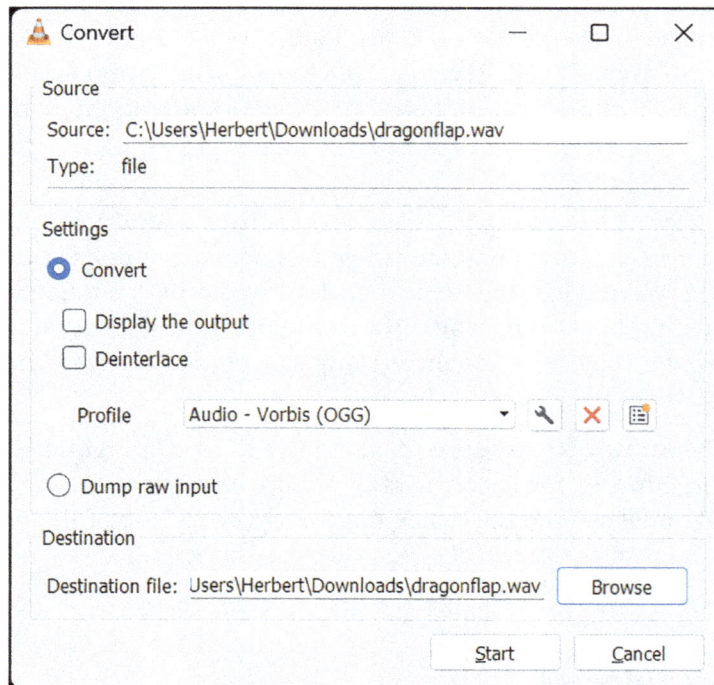

Change the profile to "Audio - Vorbis (OGG)" and select your destination file. Click Start, and in a few moments, your file will be converted.

Audio Asset Support

You're going to use two sound files, dragonflag.ogg and crash.ogg. Both files are included in the downloadable code, in code/FlappyAssetsLoadingMenu/flappy_dragon_base/assets, and are freely available from OpenGameArt.[4,5]

Copy these files to your assets directory.

The first thing you need to do to add sound support is to register audio as a type of asset. Open my_library/src/bevy_assets/asset_manager.rs and add a new entry to the AssetType enumeration:

```
FlappyAssetsLoadingMenu/my_library/src/bevy_assets/asset_manager.rs
#[derive(Clone)]
pub enum AssetType {
  Image,
➤ Sound,
}
```

Next, you need an add_sound function to register audio assets. The new function should check that audio assets exist. You already did this with the add_image function, but duplicating functionality is usually not a great idea. The don't repeat yourself (DRY) principle is one of the most memorable lessons from *The Pragmatic Programmer [TH19]*. So, let's refactor the "does the file exist?" check into a function (inside the AssetManager implementation):

```
FlappyAssetsLoadingMenu/my_library/src/bevy_assets/asset_manager.rs
fn asset_exists(filename: &str) -> anyhow::Result<()> {
  #[cfg(not(target_arch = "wasm32"))]
  {
    let current_directory = std::env::current_dir()?;
    let assets = current_directory.join("assets");
    let new_image = assets.join(filename);
    if !new_image.exists() {
      return Err(anyhow::Error::msg(format!(
        "{} not found in assets directory",
        &filename
      )));
    }
  }
  Ok(())
}
```

4. https://opengameart.org/content/dragon-flap-0
5. https://opengameart.org/content/crash-collision

Now, adjust add_image to use the new function:

FlappyAssetsLoadingMenu/my_library/src/bevy_assets/asset_manager.rs
```
pub fn add_image<S: ToString>(
  mut self,
  tag: S,
  filename: S,
) -> anyhow::Result<Self> {
  let filename = filename.to_string();
➤ AssetManager::asset_exists(&filename)?;
  self
    .asset_list
    .push((tag.to_string(), filename, AssetType::Image));
  Ok(self)
}
```

The new add_sound function is very similar:

FlappyAssetsLoadingMenu/my_library/src/bevy_assets/asset_manager.rs
```
pub fn add_sound<S: ToString>(
  mut self,
  tag: S,
  filename: S,
) -> anyhow::Result<Self> {
  let filename = filename.to_string();
  AssetManager::asset_exists(&filename)?;
  self
    .asset_list
    .push((tag.to_string(), filename, AssetType::Sound));
  Ok(self)
}
```

Next, you need an easy way for games to play the sounds they've loaded. Let's add it to the AssetStore type—that way, playing sounds is similar to using other assets. Add the following function:

FlappyAssetsLoadingMenu/my_library/src/bevy_assets/asset_store.rs
```
pub fn play(&self,
  sound_name: &str,
  commands: &mut Commands,
  assets: &LoadedAssets
) {
  let sound_handle: Handle<AudioSource> = self.get_handle(
    sound_name,
    assets).unwrap();
  commands.spawn((
    AudioPlayer::new(sound_handle.clone()),
  ));
}
```

The penultimate step is to make Flappy Dragon play sounds when the dragon flaps its wings or crashes into a wall. Let's start with the wing-flap sound. Open flappy_dragon/src/main.rs and adjust the flap function:

FlappyAssetsLoadingMenu/flappy_dragon_base/src/main.rs

```rust
fn flap(
  keyboard: Res<ButtonInput<KeyCode>>,
  mut query: Query<&mut Flappy>,
➤ assets: Res<AssetStore>,
➤ loaded: Res<LoadedAssets>,
➤ mut commands: Commands,
)
{
  if keyboard.pressed(KeyCode::Space) {
    if let Ok(mut flappy) = query.single_mut() {
      flappy.gravity = -5.0;
❶     assets.play("flap", &mut commands, &loaded);
    }
  }
}
```

❶ Request that the asset system play the "flap" sound.

Finally, you need to add the sound to the list of assets to be loaded. Open my_library/src/bevy_assets/asset_manager.rs and adjust the new function:

FlappyAssetsLoadingMenu/flappy_dragon_base/src/main.rs

```rust
➤ .add_plugins(AssetManager::new()
➤   .add_image("dragon", "flappy_dragon.png")?
➤   .add_image("wall", "wall.png")?
➤   .add_sound("flap", "dragonflap.ogg")?
➤   .add_sound("crash", "crash.ogg")?
➤ )
```

If you run Flappy Dragon now, you'll hear a flapping sound whenever you press the spacebar. The final change is to add audio feedback when Flappy hits a wall:

FlappyAssetsLoadingMenu/flappy_dragon_base/src/main.rs

```rust
fn hit_wall(
  player: Query<&Transform, With<Flappy>>,
  walls: Query<&Transform, With<Obstacle>>,
  mut state: ResMut<NextState<GamePhase>>,
➤ assets: Res<AssetStore>,
➤ loaded_assets: Res<LoadedAssets>,
➤ mut commands: Commands,
) {
  if let Ok(player) = player.single() {
    for wall in walls.iter() {
      let distance = player.translation.distance(wall.translation);
      if distance < 32.0 {
```

```
➤          assets.play("crash", &mut commands, &loaded_assets);
           state.set(GamePhase::GameOver);
         }
       }
     }
   }
```

Run the game again and hit a wall. BOOM—you hear a crashing sound, as you head to the "game over" menu.

Wrapping Up

In this chapter, you implemented a complete wrapper around Bevy's asset handling system. You can reduce boilerplate code in new projects and easily share asset handles between systems with a shared asset manager resource. The asset manager solves the requirements outlined at the beginning of the chapter:

• An asset that doesn't exist no longer requires you to watch the game log scrolling by—it stops the game from running, with a message telling you what went wrong.
• A loading screen displays asset loading status.
• Assets no longer "pop" into existence because they're loaded ahead of time.
• You have a flexible system that can support images and sound—and can easily be extended to include more types of assets.

Along the way, you learned to use Bevy plugins that transform themselves into game resources—and transform themselves again when they're ready for use. You learned to interact with some of the inner details of Bevy's asset manager, and on a more general level, you built a *facade*—a friendly front-end to a complicated system. On top of all of that, the Flappy Dragon source code is now shorter than when you started.

In the next chapter, you'll extend the assets system to work with sprite sheets and flip-book animations. You'll add some visual niceties that help transform Flappy into a very visually appealing game, and you'll replace the current physics system with a more generic—reusable—system built around realistic velocity calculations.

CHAPTER 7

Teach Your Dragon to Fly

In this chapter, you'll learn two important aspects of 2D games: animation and physics.

Animation brings your game to life by making sprites change over time, providing visual cues as to what's happening in the game. The human eye is sensitive to movement, and static scenes don't attract the same attention as animated scenes. Notice that with most games, almost everything is animated.

Physics also brings games to life. Players intuitively understand physics, and a somewhat accurate modeling of how the world works makes it easier for players to interact with your game.

Physics and animation share a common feature: time. It shouldn't matter how fast your player's PC is running; animations need to remain smooth and consistent. More importantly, running a game on a fast PC shouldn't speed up an entity's movement within a simulation because, in a few years, as computers get faster, your "older" game may run *too fast* to be playable.

Adding Frame-Based Animation

Frame-based animation works similarly to paper flip-books: each page displays a picture, more precisely, a slightly different image on each page. As you flip through the book, you see the characters move. However, each page ("frame") is a static image. Unlike flip-books, frame-based animation can reuse images without adding extra pages.

Frame-based animation can also be tied to instructions, such as "play this sound when this frame appears," and it's a lot easier to switch between animations on a computer than it's in a printed flip-book.

Let's get started by using the full set of animation frames for Flappy the Dragon. Bevoulin (on Open Game Art) includes four animation frames for the dragon:[1]

You can divide these images into frames, where each frame is the same size, essentially making a "digital" page in a flip-book:

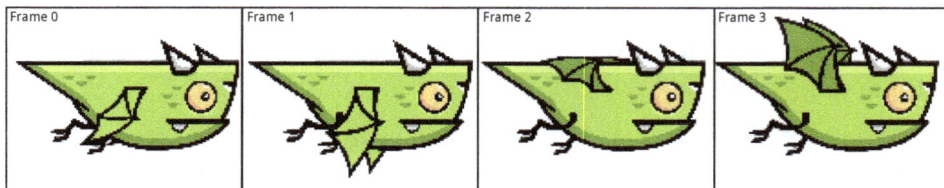

You don't want to simply repeat these frames—if you jump from frame 3 to frame 0, the dragon's wings will go from "all the way up" to "all the way down" with no in-between. Instead, the correct render order is 0, 1, 2, 3, 2, 1 (repeat). This pattern provides a smooth "flapping" cycle, with the wings working their way up and then down again, mimicking a realistic use of wings.

Download code/FlappyAnimation/flappy_dragon_base/flappy_sprite_sheet.png and place the file in the flappy_dragon/src/assets directory. This file has been scaled to match the 1024×768 resolution of your game.

An animation set has multiple logical layers:

- The image itself, containing every frame. Bevy represents this as an Image, just like your other game sprites.
- A grid, placed over the sprite image to provide identically sized sub-images. Bevy names this your SpriteSheet. Each frame in the previous image is a separate sprite sheet entry.
- Animations, which group animations together by name for easy access. You'll create a type for these named PerFrameAnimation.
- Each animation frame, containing the *index* of the sprite to use (from the SpriteSheet), a duration for the frame, and one or more *actions* to perform when the frame is active.

Let's extend the asset manager to handle frame-based animations.

---

1.   https://opengameart.org/content/flappy-dragon-sprite-sheets

Defining Sprite Sheets

The first step is to add SpriteSheet handling to your asset system. You used a SpriteSheet in Playing Pig, on page 35.

Add an entry to the AssetType enum in my_library/src/bevy_assets/asset_manager.rs.

```
FlappyAnimation/my_library/src/bevy_assets/asset_manager.rs
#[derive(Clone)]
pub enum AssetType {
  Image,
  Sound,
➤  SpriteSheet{tile_size: Vec2, sprites_x: usize, sprites_y: usize},
}
```

Bevy needs to know a few things about the sprite sheet, so they're included in this type:

- The size of each frame (in pixels), represented by tile_size—a Vec2 containing an x and y value.
- The number of sprites in the x dimension (columns), sprites_x.
- The number of sprites in the y dimension (rows), sprites_y.

Next, just as with the image and audio asset types, you need to add a function to add a sprite sheet to the requested assets list. Add the new function inside the AssetManager implementation, after add_image():

```
FlappyAnimation/my_library/src/bevy_assets/asset_manager.rs
pub fn add_sprite_sheet<S: ToString>(
  mut self,
  tag: S,
  filename: S,
  sprite_width: f32,
  sprite_height: f32,
  sprites_x: usize,
  sprites_y: usize,
) -> anyhow::Result<Self> {
  let filename = filename.to_string();
  AssetManager::asset_exists(&filename)?;
  self
    .asset_list
    .push((tag.to_string(), filename, AssetType::SpriteSheet{
      tile_size: Vec2::new(
        sprite_width,
        sprite_height),
        sprites_x,
        sprites_y,
    }));
  Ok(self)
}
```

Your library consumer can now request that a sprite sheet be loaded in the same way as other assets. Next, you need to add the code to actually create a Bevy TextureAtlas.

Building Sprite Sheets

Bevy's Sprite Sheet documentation shows that creating a sprite sheet is a two-step operation. The first step loads an image, just like your previous image loading code. The second step creates a TextureAtlas structure, which refers to the image, has a Handle, and won't appear in the list of loaded assets. TextureAtlass is a *meta-asset*. Describing an interaction with physical assets depends on the asset, but they don't actually occupy a slot in the asset manager's data store.

The difficult part with creating a meta-asset is that you have to first load the base asset and then initialize the meta-asset, using it. The meta-asset then gains a Handle, but never has a Handle<LoadedUntypedAsset> because no loading stage was ever invoked. This requires that the asset system load the base image and store everything required to build the texture atlas after it has been loaded.

Start by creating a new FutureAtlas type in my_library/src/bevy_assets/asset_store.rs:

```
FlappyAnimation/my_library/src/bevy_assets/asset_store.rs
#[derive(Clone)]
pub(crate) struct FutureAtlas {
  pub(crate) tag: String,
  pub(crate) texture_tag: String,
  pub(crate) tile_size: Vec2,
  pub(crate) sprites_x: usize,
  pub(crate) sprites_y: usize,
}
```

This type will be used to store atlases that are awaiting creation. Next, extend your AssetStore type to include the list of future atlases and a HashMap to store atlases once they've been created:

```
FlappyAnimation/my_library/src/bevy_assets/asset_store.rs
#[derive(Resource, Clone)]
pub struct AssetStore {
  pub(crate) asset_index: HashMap<String, Handle<LoadedUntypedAsset>>,
➤ pub(crate) atlases_to_build: Vec<FutureAtlas>,
➤ pub(crate) atlases: HashMap<String, (Handle<Image>, Handle<TextureAtlasLayout>)>,
}
```

While you're in the file, add a function to retrieve texture atlases by name. Add the code inside the impl AssetStore block:

FlappyAnimation/my_library/src/bevy_assets/asset_store.rs
```rust
pub fn get_atlas_handle(&self, index: &str)
-> Option<(Handle<Image>, Handle<TextureAtlasLayout>)>
{
  if let Some(handle) = self.atlases.get(index) {
    return Some(handle.clone());
  }
  None
}
```

Now that the AssetStore supports texture atlases, you need to add some logic to create them. Open the asset_manager.rs file, and add the following code above the default option (_ =>):

FlappyAnimation/my_library/src/bevy_assets/asset_manager.rs
```rust
match asset_type {
  AssetType::SpriteSheet { tile_size, sprites_x, sprites_y } => {
    // Sprite Sheets require that we load the image first, and defer
    // sheet creation to the loading menu - after the image has loaded
❶   let image_handle = asset_server.load_untyped(filename);
❷   let base_tag = format!("{tag}_base");
    assets
      .asset_index
❸     .insert(base_tag.clone(), image_handle);

    // Now that its loaded, we store the future atlas in the asset store
❹   assets.atlases_to_build.push(FutureAtlas {
      tag: tag.clone(),
      texture_tag: base_tag,
      tile_size: *tile_size,
      sprites_x: *sprites_x,
      sprites_y: *sprites_y,
    });
  }
```

❶ Load the underlying image, just as you did for images previously.

❷ You want to use a different tag for the underlying image. You can't have duplicate tags in a HashMap.

❸ Insert the base image, identified by the new tag.

❹ Add the atlas's details to the future texture atlases list you created.

The loading menu needs to finish the process—actually building the texture atlases once the underlying image is loaded. Start by creating a new function in loading_menu.rs. (This is shown on the next page.)

FlappyAnimation/my_library/src/bevy_assets/loading_menu.rs

```rust
fn load_atlases(
    store: &mut AssetStore,
    texture_atlases: &mut Assets<TextureAtlasLayout>,
    loaded_assets: &LoadedAssets,
) {
    for new_atlas in store.atlases_to_build.iter() {
        let atlas = TextureAtlasLayout::from_grid(
            new_atlas.tile_size.as_uvec2(),
            new_atlas.sprites_x as u32,
            new_atlas.sprites_y as u32,
            None, None);
        let atlas_handle = texture_atlases.add(atlas);
        let img = store.get_handle(&new_atlas.texture_tag, loaded_assets).unwrap();
        store
            .atlases
            .insert(new_atlas.tag.clone(), (img, atlas_handle));
    }
}
```

The new function iterates through the list of future atlases and builds each one. The last step is to call the function when all asynchronous asset-loading is complete. In the run<T> function, update the loading completion code to call your new function, make the AssetStore mutable, and require the AssetResource and TextureAtlas data as parameters:

FlappyAnimation/my_library/src/bevy_assets/loading_menu.rs

```rust
pub(crate) fn run<T>(
    asset_server: Res<AssetServer>,
    mut to_load: ResMut<AssetsToLoad>,
    mut state: ResMut<NextState<T>>,
    mut egui_context: EguiContexts,
    menu_info: Res<MenuResource<T>>,
➤    mut store: ResMut<AssetStore>,
➤    mut texture_atlases: ResMut<Assets<TextureAtlasLayout>>,
➤    loaded_assets: Res<LoadedAssets>,
) where T: States+FromWorld+FreelyMutableState,
{
    to_load.0.retain(|handle| {
        match asset_server.get_load_state(handle.id()) {
            Some(bevy::asset::LoadState::Loaded) => false,
            _ => true,
        }
    });
    if to_load.0.is_empty() {
➤        load_atlases(&mut store, &mut texture_atlases, &loaded_assets);
        state.set(menu_info.menu_state.clone());
    }
    Window::new("Loading, Please Wait").show(
        egui_context.ctx_mut(), |ui| {
```

```
        ui.label(
            format!("{} assets remaining", to_load.0.len())
        )
    });
}
```

You now have an assets system that supports loading sprite sheets into texture atlases. You also have the foundation for other meta-asset types if you need them in the future.

Defining and Storing Animations

It's a good idea to separate the definition of an animation from the sprite that's using it. You may find yourself with multiple characters needing to reuse animations. Create a new file named src/my_library/bevy_framework/bevy_animation.rs.

In src/my_library/bevy_framework/mod.rs, add the new file to your project:

```
mod bevy_animation;
pub use bevy_animation::*;
```

Now open your new bevy_animation.rs file and add a use statement to the top:

```
use bevy::{prelude::*, log};
use bevy::platform::HashMap;
```

Start building the animation system by thinking about what *actions* you want to occur for any given frame. You're building a state machine, so each animation will run separately, following a script defined by the animation. Add the following enumeration:

FlappyAnimation/my_library/src/bevy_framework/bevy_animation.rs
```
pub enum AnimationOption {
    None,
    NextFrame,
    GoToFrame(usize),
    SwitchToAnimation(String),
    PlaySound(String),
}
```

❶ Do nothing. Don't change frame. The animation freezes.

❷ Move to the next frame in the animation sequence.

❸ Jump to a numbered frame in the animation, allowing you to skip frames or repeat the sequence.

❹ Switch to a different, named animation sequence.

❺ Play a sound. This isn't as out of place as it looks; it's common to want to synchronize animation with sound effects.

If you're thinking "this looks like a miniature scripting language," you're absolutely right. Animations run as a tiny state machine, and scripting options offer a huge amount of flexibility to the users of your library.

Now that you've defined a list of what *can* happen in a frame, let's define the frame itself:

FlappyAnimation/my_library/src/bevy_framework/bevy_animation.rs
```
pub struct AnimationFrame {
    sprite_index: usize,
    delay_ms: u128,
    action: Vec<AnimationOption>,
}

impl AnimationFrame {
    pub fn new(
        sprite_index: usize,
        delay_ms: u128,
        action: Vec<AnimationOption>
    ) -> Self {
        Self { sprite_index, delay_ms, action }
    }
}
```

❶ The SpriteSheet frame index to display while this frame is active. Despite using rows and columns, images are indexed from zero to the total number of sprites available on the sprite sheet.

❷ The time—in milliseconds—to display this frame before executing any options. u128 is surprisingly large—but it's the type Bevy provides for this data.

❸ You might want to do more than one thing with a frame. For example, you might want to play a sound and move to the next frame. A vector of options lets the library user include as many as they need and doesn't require potentially confusing logical leaps, such as "playing a sound also skips to the next frame," which may or may not be what the user wants.

❹ Define a constructor for convenience.

Finally, pull this all together with a structure and a constructor that holds the definition of an animation sequence:

FlappyAnimation/my_library/src/bevy_framework/bevy_animation.rs
```
pub struct PerFrameAnimation {
    pub frames: Vec<AnimationFrame>,
}
```

```
impl PerFrameAnimation {
    pub fn new(frames: Vec<AnimationFrame>) -> Self {
        Self { frames }
    }
}
```

That's enough data to define an animation. Next, you need a Bevy resource structure in which you can store animations, associated with a "tag" to let you call animations by name:

FlappyAnimation/my_library/src/bevy_framework/bevy_animation.rs
```
#[derive(Resource)]
pub struct Animations(HashMap<String, PerFrameAnimation>);

impl Animations {
    pub fn new() -> Self {
        Self(HashMap::new())
    }

    pub fn with_animation<S: ToString>(
        mut self,
        tag: S,
        animation: PerFrameAnimation
    ) -> Self
    {
        self.0.insert(
            tag.to_string(),
            animation
        );
        self
    }
}
```

This code works like your AssetStore: a HashMap indexes animations by name and stores the animation details. A constructor and a with_animation builder function allow for easy addition of animations to your game.

Let's create components and systems through which the library user can attach an animation to an entity.

State Machines Are Powerful

State machines (sometimes known as *finite state machines* are amazingly powerful structures. A state machine stores all state—data needed to operate—and uses the stored data to transfer between states. Your animations don't need to access any external data; they quietly operate on their own. This is a great design pattern, so use it when you can.

Running the Animation State Machine

Each animation runs as an independent state machine—a self-contained set of data storing the current state of the entity's animation, applying rules from the animation definition. An animated entity needs a component to tell Bevy that the attached entity is part of the animation system:

```
FlappyAnimation/my_library/src/bevy_framework/bevy_animation.rs
#[derive(Component)]
pub struct AnimationCycle {
    animation_tag: String,
    current_frame: usize,
    timer: u128,
}

impl AnimationCycle {
    pub fn new<S: ToString>(tag: S) -> Self {
        Self {
            animation_tag: tag.to_string(),
            current_frame: 0,
            timer: 0,
        }
    }

    pub fn switch<S: ToString>(&mut self, new: S) {
        let new = new.to_string();
        if new != self.animation_tag {
            self.animation_tag = new;
            self.current_frame = 0;
            self.timer = 0;
        }
    }
}
```

❶ The tag by which you want to refer to the animation sequence.

❷ Internal state: which frame is currently executing for this animation?

❸ How many microseconds have elapsed since the animation was last rendered? Retaining the timer state separately for each executing animation prevents all of the animations from running in lock-step, which can be a little jarring.

❹ Create a constructor for convenience and to avoid exposing the structure's private members.

❺ A function to instruct an already-running animation to switch to a different animation sequence.

❻ Only change the sequence if the new sequence is different from the previous one.

With the component defined, you need a system that makes use of animation data. Let's start by defining the system function and the data the system needs to import from Bevy:

FlappyAnimation/my_library/src/bevy_framework/bevy_animation.rs

```
pub fn cycle_animations(
①    animations: Res<Animations>,
②    mut animated: Query<(&mut AnimationCycle, &mut Sprite)>,
③    time: Res<Time>,
④    assets: Res<crate::AssetStore>,
     mut commands: Commands,
     loaded_assets: Res<crate::LoadedAssets>,
```

❶ Link to the Animations resource you defined earlier.

❷ Define a query that returns mutable access to all entities with both an AnimationCycle component and a TextureAtlasSprite component.

❸ Retrieve the current time from Bevy.

❹ Link to the AssetStore you created for easy access to asset handles.

Bevy will inject these dependencies into the system call for you. Now, let's use this data to cycle through all active animations, applying the timer and sequence steps to each animated entity:

FlappyAnimation/my_library/src/bevy_framework/bevy_animation.rs

```
①    let ms_since_last_call = time.delta().as_millis();
②    animated.iter_mut().for_each(|(mut animation, mut sprite)| {
③        animation.timer += ms_since_last_call;
④        if let Some(cycle) = animations.0.get(&animation.animation_tag) {
⑤            let current_frame = &cycle.frames[animation.current_frame];
⑥            if animation.timer > current_frame.delay_ms {
⑦                animation.timer = 0;
⑧                for action in current_frame.action.iter() {
                     match action {
                         AnimationOption::None => {},
⑨                        AnimationOption::NextFrame => {
                             animation.current_frame += 1;
                         }
⑩                        AnimationOption::GoToFrame(frame) => {
                             animation.current_frame = *frame;
                         }
⑪                        AnimationOption::SwitchToAnimation(new) => {
                             animation.animation_tag = new.to_string();
                             animation.current_frame = 0;
                         }
⑫                        AnimationOption::PlaySound(tag) => {
                             assets.play(tag, &mut commands, &loaded_assets);
                         }
                     }
```

```
                     if let Some(ta) = &mut sprite.texture_atlas {
                         ta.index = cycle
                           .frames[animation.current_frame]
                           .sprite_index;
                     }
              }
            }
        } else {
            log::warn!("Animation Cycle [{}] not found!",
              animation.animation_tag);
        }
    });
}
```

❶ Get the elapsed time since the previous frame, in milliseconds.

❷ Mutably iterate through the query you defined in the function signature.

❸ Add the elapsed time to the individual animation's clock.

❺ Rather than repeatedly looking up the current frame, store a reference to the current frame for easy access.

❻ If the elapsed time on the entity's clock has exceeded the time for a frame to be displayed, continue with this function. Otherwise, do nothing. This ensures that animations always play at the same speed, but won't miss frames if the PC on which you're running the game is moving slowly.

❼ Reset the entity's clock to zero. You've started the new frame; you don't want to act again on this entity until the frame time completes.

❽ Iterate all of the actions associated with the new frame, and match on each action.

❾ Increment the frame counter, moving to the next frame.

❿ Jump to a specific frame.

⓫ Change the tag defining which animation is playing.

⓬ Play a sound, just like you did in Chapter 6, Manage Your Game Assets, on page 111.

⓭ Change the displayed SpriteIndex in the TextureAtlasSprite component to point to the new frame's index.

Finally, let's put together a macro for easily spawning animated characters:

```
FlappyAnimation/my_library/src/bevy_framework/bevy_animation.rs
#[macro_export]
macro_rules! spawn_animated_sprite {
    ($assets:expr, $commands:expr, $index:expr, $x:expr, $y:expr, $z:expr,
        $animation_name:expr, $($component:expr),*) =>
  {
        let Some((img, atlas)) = $assets.get_atlas_handle($index)
          else { panic!() };
        $commands.spawn((
            Sprite::from_atlas_image(img.clone(), TextureAtlas {
                layout: atlas.clone(),
                index: 0,
            }),
            Transform::from_xyz($x, $y, $z),
            AnimationCycle::new($animation_name),
        ))
        $(
         .insert($component)
        )*;
  }
}
```

You now have everything you need to make it easy for users of your library
to add animations. Let's animate your Dragon.

Animate Your Dragon

Open flappy_dragon_base/src/main.rs.

Your main function starts with the add_phase! macro. In the run section, add
your new system:

```
run => [ gravity, flap, clamp, move_walls, hit_wall, cycle_animations ],
```

In the main function, locate your asset requests and add a request to load the
sprite sheet you added to the assets directory:

```
FlappyAnimation/flappy_dragon_base/src/main.rs
.add_plugins(AssetManager::new()
  .add_image("dragon", "flappy_dragon.png")?
  .add_image("wall", "wall.png")?
  .add_sound("flap", "dragonflap.ogg")?
  .add_sound("crash", "crash.ogg")?
➤ .add_sprite_sheet("flappy", "flappy_sprite_sheet.png",
➤    62.0, 65.0, 4, 1)?
```

Next, insert the Animations resource you created, and define an animation:

```
FlappyAnimation/flappy_dragon_base/src/main.rs
.insert_resource(
  Animations::new()
```

```
  .with_animation("Straight and Level", PerFrameAnimation::new(
    vec![
      AnimationFrame::new(2, 500, vec![AnimationOption::NextFrame]),
      AnimationFrame::new(3, 500, vec![
        AnimationOption::GoToFrame(0)]),
    ]
  ))
```

The "Straight and Level" animation has Flappy barely moving their wings and is designed for normal movement when the player isn't pounding the "flap" control. There's a long delay—500 ms, half a second—between frames and the frames cycle.

Let's add a second animation in which Flappy vigorously flaps their wings:

FlappyAnimation/flappy_dragon_base/src/main.rs
```
.with_animation("Flapping", PerFrameAnimation::new(
  vec![
    AnimationFrame::new(0, 66, vec![AnimationOption::NextFrame,
      AnimationOption::PlaySound("flap".to_string())]),
    AnimationFrame::new(1, 66, vec![AnimationOption::NextFrame]),
    AnimationFrame::new(2, 66, vec![AnimationOption::NextFrame]),
    AnimationFrame::new(3, 66, vec![AnimationOption::NextFrame]),
    AnimationFrame::new(2, 66, vec![AnimationOption::NextFrame]),
    AnimationFrame::new(1, 66, vec![
      AnimationOption::SwitchToAnimation(
        "Straight and Level".to_string())
      ]),
  ]
```

At the start of this animation, you ask the animation system to play the "flap" sound. This makes sense: the sound only plays when Flappy is actively using their wings. Then the animation quickly cycles through a complete wing flap, before switching back to "Straight and Level".

In the setup() function, replace Flappy's spawn_sprite! macro with your new spawn_animated_sprite! macro:

FlappyAnimation/flappy_dragon_base/src/main.rs
```
fn setup(
  mut commands: Commands,
  mut rng: ResMut<RandomNumberGenerator>,
  assets: Res<AssetStore>,
  loaded_assets: Res<LoadedAssets>,
) {
  commands.spawn(Camera2d::default()).insert(FlappyElement);
➤ spawn_animated_sprite!(assets, commands, "flappy", -490.0, 0.0, 10.0,
➤   "Straight and Level", Flappy { gravity: 0.0 }, FlappyElement);
  build_wall(&mut commands, &assets, rng.range(-5..5), &loaded_assets);
```

The flap() function can be simplified a little. Remove the references to audio (since the animation system is now taking care of it for you), and switch to the "Flapping" animation when flapping:

FlappyAnimation/flappy_dragon_base/src/main.rs

```
fn flap(
  keyboard: Res<ButtonInput<KeyCode>>,
  mut query: Query<(&mut Flappy, &mut AnimationCycle)>,
➤  // Remove the audio reference
)
{
  if keyboard.pressed(KeyCode::Space) {
    if let Ok((mut flappy, mut animation)) = query.single_mut() {
      flappy.gravity = -5.0;
➤      animation.switch("Flapping");
    }
  }
}
```

Go ahead and run the game with cargo run. Flappy idly flaps while moving and actively flaps—with sound—when you press the spacebar. The game is looking a lot more polished.

Let's add a bit more polish with an animated background.

Simulating Movement with Parallax Layers

A common trick in 2D games is to use *parallax* rendering. With parallax rendering, different background images move at differing speeds in the background, with the closest visual elements moving fastest and the most distant one moving slowly. This simple trick provides a convincing illusion of forward movement even when your main character is actually static.

Let's use Emcee Flesher's excellent Rocky Desert Landscape pack from OpenGameArt. [2] It provides four layers: a mountain backdrop (static), a distant layer (moving slowly), a midpoint layer (moving less slowly), and a nearby layer (moving quickly). These are shown at the top of the next page.

Let's create a component and system to provide parallax rendering.

Graphical Conveyor Belts

You use a simple "conveyor belt" trick to scroll the background. Other than the nonmoving background, spawn each background graphic *twice*—once filling the screen and once off the screen to the right. Each graphic slowly

---

2. https://opengameart.org/content/rocky-desert-landscape-layered-looping

Layer 1: Static Backdrop

Layer 2: Distant Hills

Layer 3: Mid-point Hills

Layer 4: Nearby Terrain

moves to the left, and when it has completely left the visible area, it moves to the right of the visible area. This gives the illusion of a continual cycle.

FlappyAnimation/my_library/src/bevy_framework/bevy_animation.rs
```
#[derive(Component)]
pub struct ContinualParallax {
    image_width: f32,
    move_every_ms: u128,
    scroll_speed: Vec2,
    timer: u128,
}

impl ContinualParallax {
  pub fn new(image_width: f32, move_every_ms: u128, scroll_speed: Vec2)
  -> Self {
    Self {
      image_width, move_every_ms, scroll_speed, timer: 0
    }
  }
}
```

❶ The width of the image, required to know where to move it when it's no longer visible.

❷ Move the image every x milliseconds.

❸ How far should the image move each tick?

❹ Internal state for the parallax animation's timer.

The conveyor belt is implemented with the continual_parallax() function:

FlappyAnimation/my_library/src/bevy_framework/bevy_animation.rs
```
pub fn continual_parallax(
  mut animated: Query<(&mut ContinualParallax, &mut Transform)>,
  time: Res<Time>,
) {
  let ms_since_last_call = time.delta().as_millis();
  animated.iter_mut().for_each(|(mut parallax, mut transform)| {
    parallax.timer += ms_since_last_call;
    if parallax.timer >= parallax.move_every_ms {
      parallax.timer = 0;
      transform.translation.x -= parallax.scroll_speed.x;
      transform.translation.y -= parallax.scroll_speed.y;
      if transform.translation.x <= (0.0 - parallax.image_width) {
        transform.translation.x = parallax.image_width;
      }
    }
  });
}
```

The continual_parallax() function is quite similar to the timing you used to manage cycling animation: it checks to see if it's time to move the sprite yet, and if it is, it updates the Transform component to perform the movement. Then, if the sprite has left the display to the left, it's moved to the right.

Open flappy_dragon_base/src/main.rs. In the add_phase! macro, add the new system:

```
run => [ gravity, flap, clamp, move_walls, hit_wall, cycle_animations,
  continual_parallax ],
```

Modify the setup() function to place Flappy safely above the background:

FlappyAnimation/flappy_dragon_base/src/main.rs
```
fn setup(
  mut commands: Commands,
  mut rng: ResMut<RandomNumberGenerator>,
  assets: Res<AssetStore>,
  loaded_assets: Res<LoadedAssets>,
) {
  commands.spawn(Camera2d::default()).insert(FlappyElement);
➤ spawn_animated_sprite!(assets, commands, "flappy", -490.0, 0.0, 10.0,
➤   "Straight and Level", Flappy { gravity: 0.0 }, FlappyElement);
  build_wall(&mut commands, &assets, rng.range(-5..5), &loaded_assets);
```

Then, add the following to the setup() function:

FlappyAnimation/flappy_dragon_base/src/main.rs
```
spawn_image!(assets, commands, "bg_static", 0.0, 0.0, 1.0,
  &loaded_assets, FlappyElement);
spawn_image!(assets, commands, "bg_far", 0.0, 0.0, 2.0,
  &loaded_assets, FlappyElement,
ContinualParallax::new(1280.0, 66, Vec2::new(1.0, 0.0)));
```

```
spawn_image!(assets, commands, "bg_far", 1280.0, 0.0, 2.0,
  &loaded_assets, FlappyElement,
ContinualParallax::new(1280.0, 66, Vec2::new(1.0, 0.0)));
spawn_image!(assets, commands, "bg_mid", 0.0, 0.0, 3.0,
  &loaded_assets, FlappyElement,
ContinualParallax::new(1280.0, 33, Vec2::new(1.0, 0.0)));
spawn_image!(assets, commands, "bg_mid", 1280.0, 0.0, 3.0,
  &loaded_assets, FlappyElement,
ContinualParallax::new(1280.0, 33, Vec2::new(1.0, 0.0)));
spawn_image!(assets, commands, "bg_close", 0.0, 0.0, 4.0,
  &loaded_assets, FlappyElement,
ContinualParallax::new(1280.0, 16, Vec2::new(2.0, 0.0)));
spawn_image!(assets, commands, "bg_close", 1280.0, 0.0, 4.0,
  &loaded_assets, FlappyElement,
ContinualParallax::new(1280.0, 16, Vec2::new(2.0, 0.0)));
```

You also need to add the images to load into the main() function:

FlappyAnimation/flappy_dragon_base/src/main.rs
```
fn main() -> anyhow::Result<()> {
  let mut app = App::new();

  add_phase!(app, GamePhase, GamePhase::Flapping,
    start => [ setup ],
    run => [ gravity, flap, clamp, move_walls, hit_wall, cycle_animations,
      continual_parallax ],
    exit => [ cleanup::<FlappyElement> ]
  );

  app.add_plugins(DefaultPlugins.set(WindowPlugin {
    primary_window: Some(Window {
    title: "Flappy Dragon - Bevy Edition".to_string(),
    resolution: bevy::window::WindowResolution::new(
      1024.0, 768.0
    ),
    ..default()
  }),
    ..default()
  }))
    .add_plugins(RandomPlugin)
    .add_plugins(GameStatePlugin::new(
      GamePhase::MainMenu,
      GamePhase::Flapping,
      GamePhase::GameOver)
    )
    .add_plugins(AssetManager::new()
      .add_image("dragon", "flappy_dragon.png")?
      .add_image("wall", "wall.png")?
      .add_sound("flap", "dragonflap.ogg")?
      .add_sound("crash", "crash.ogg")?
      .add_sprite_sheet("flappy", "flappy_sprite_sheet.png",
        62.0, 65.0, 4, 1)?
```

```
    .add_image("bg_static", "rocky-far-mountains.png")?
     .add_image("bg_far", "rocky-nowater-far.png")?
     .add_image("bg_mid", "rocky-nowater-mid.png")?
     .add_image("bg_close", "rocky-nowater-close.png")?
   )
   .insert_resource(
    Animations::new()
      .with_animation("Straight and Level", PerFrameAnimation::new(
        vec![
          AnimationFrame::new(2, 500, vec![AnimationOption::NextFrame]),
          AnimationFrame::new(3, 500, vec![
            AnimationOption::GoToFrame(0)]),
        ]
      ))
      .with_animation("Flapping", PerFrameAnimation::new(
        vec![
          AnimationFrame::new(0, 66, vec![AnimationOption::NextFrame,
            AnimationOption::PlaySound("flap".to_string())]),
          AnimationFrame::new(1, 66, vec![AnimationOption::NextFrame]),
          AnimationFrame::new(2, 66, vec![AnimationOption::NextFrame]),
          AnimationFrame::new(3, 66, vec![AnimationOption::NextFrame]),
          AnimationFrame::new(2, 66, vec![AnimationOption::NextFrame]),
          AnimationFrame::new(1, 66, vec![
            AnimationOption::SwitchToAnimation(
              "Straight and Level".to_string())
            ]),
        ]
      )
    )
    .run();

  Ok(())
}

.add_image("bg_static", "rocky-far-mountains.png")?
  .add_image("bg_far", "rocky-nowater-far.png")?
  .add_image("bg_mid", "rocky-nowater-mid.png")?
  .add_image("bg_close", "rocky-nowater-close.png")?
)
```

Finally, change the wall's z position from 1.0 to 10.0:

```
fn build_wall(
  commands: &mut Commands,
  assets: &AssetStore,
  gap_y: i32,
  loaded_assets: &LoadedAssets,
) {
  for y in -12..=12 {
    if y < gap_y - 4 || y > gap_y + 4 {
      spawn_image!(assets, commands, "wall", 512.0, y as f32 * 32.0, 10.0,
      loaded_assets, Obstacle, FlappyElement);
    }
```

```
    }
}
```

Run the game now, and you have a smooth parallax effect behind the main game, giving a convincing illusion of forward movement, and much more to look at than a grey background.

Creating Consistent Movement with Physics

All of the emphasis on timing in this chapter has been building up to the creation of a physics engine. Rather than hard-coding that "flap" moves up and gravity applies at every turn, an engine should know that. The majority of 2D games use similar physics. Creating a generic physics platform will help with the creation of many different games.

At the heart of every physics engine is a clock. No matter how fast—or slow—a player's computer is running, physics should simulate the world at a consistent pace. Here's a new Bevy concept: *events*.

An event is a message passed between systems. Events are broadcast: sending an event with an EventWriter<MyEvent> causes all systems that subscribe to an EventReader<MyEvent> to receive it. This is perfect for creating a monotonic—periodically firing at a set rate—physics clock.

Create a Monotonic Physics Clock

Create a new file named my_library/bevy_framework/bevy_physics.rs. Don't forget to add it to my_library/src/bevy_framework/mod.rs:

```
mod bevy_physics;
pub use bevy_physics::*;
```

In the new file, let's put together a physics engine clock:

```
FlappyPhysics/my_library/src/bevy_framework/bevy_physics.rs
use bevy::prelude::*;

// How frequently should the physics tick fire (ms)
const PHYSICS_TICK_TIME: u128 = 33;

#[derive(Default)]
pub struct PhysicsTimer(u128);

#[derive(Event)]
pub struct PhysicsTick;
```

You import the Bevy prelude and create a constant indicating how often you want the physics engine to generate a clock message. Then you create a structure named PhysicsTimer containing a u128. You'll use this timer to store the accumulated time between frames. Finally, you create an empty structure named PhysicsTick. PhysicsTick will be the *event message* sent when the clock ticks.

Bevy requires that all messages that will be used are registered when the game starts. Open my_library/src/bevy_framework/mod.rs and register the PhysicsTick message in your plugin builder:

```
fn build(&self, app: &mut App) {
➤   app.add_event::<PhysicsTick>();
```

Bevy can now send and receive PhysicsTick events. Returning to bevy_physics.rs, let's build a system that keeps track of the time and sends PhysicsTick messages periodically:

```
FlappyPhysics/my_library/src/bevy_framework/bevy_physics.rs
pub fn physics_clock(
  mut clock: Local<PhysicsTimer>,
  time: Res<Time>,
  mut on_tick: EventWriter<PhysicsTick>,
) {
  let ms_since_last_call = time.delta().as_millis();
  clock.0 += ms_since_last_call;
  if clock.0 >= PHYSICS_TICK_TIME {
    clock.0 = 0;
    on_tick.write(PhysicsTick);
  }
}
```

This code is a lot like the other timers you've used: it accumulates frame time, and when the accumulated time is greater than or equal to the required interval, it uses the EventWriter to send a message. Other systems can then receive this message and know that it's time to function.

Let's start tackling velocity and impulses.

Applying Velocity and Impulses

Most physics engines track *velocity*—movement over time. You've defined time strictly as 33 ms, so the values in a velocity vector represent how far that item should move in one physics frame. Let's define a Velocity component:

```
FlappyPhysics/my_library/src/bevy_framework/bevy_physics.rs
#[derive(Component)]
pub struct Velocity(pub Vec3);

impl Default for Velocity {
  fn default() -> Self {
    Self(Vec3::ZERO)
  }
}
```

```
impl Velocity {
  pub fn new(x: f32, y: f32, z: f32) -> Self {
    Self(Vec3 { x, y, z })
  }
}
```

Velocity is a Vec3—an x, y, and z value. Velocity represents the *total* movement an entity should perform during a tick. You want to avoid directly writing to an entity's Velocity component to allow other physics entities to interact with it. Instead, you'll apply *impulses* to physics-based entities. An impulse represents the application of force to an object. If you push a ball away from you, you're applying an impulse away from you. If Flappy flaps their wings, an upwards impulse is applied. It's entirely possible for several impulses to be applied to an object during a physics tick period. You want to apply the *sum* of all impulses, giving a total velocity for that physics tick.

You'll once again use an event to indicate the application of an impulse to an entity.

FlappyPhysics/my_library/src/bevy_framework/bevy_physics.rs
```
#[derive(Event)]
pub struct Impulse {
❶   pub target: Entity,
❷   pub amount: Vec3,
❸   pub absolute: bool,
❹   pub source: i32,
}
```

❶ The entity to which the impulse should be applied.

❷ The velocity adjustment to be applied.

❸ Sometimes, you want to override the total velocity rather than sum it. An absolute impulse (set to true) will replace the entity's velocity rather than add to it. This is useful for handling situations such as bouncing off a wall, in which you don't want your reflection to become confused by additional inputs.

❹ A tag indicating the event source. Each possible event source per physics tick should be uniquely identified. This allows you to deduplicate impulses from the same source, preventing multiple impulses being applied to the same entity in a single physics tick from being processed multiple times.

Once again, open my_library/src/bevy_framework/mod.rs and register the Impulse message in your plugin builder:

```
fn build(&self, app: &mut App) {
  app.add_event::<PhysicsTick>();
➤ app.add_event::<Impulse>();
```

Now, any system in your game can send an Impulse event. Velocity is the current velocity (providing continued momentum), optionally reduced by friction. For now, you're going to allow Flappy to fly in a frictionless environment. Each impulse is then added to the velocity—unless it overrides it. This gives you the final velocity for the frame:

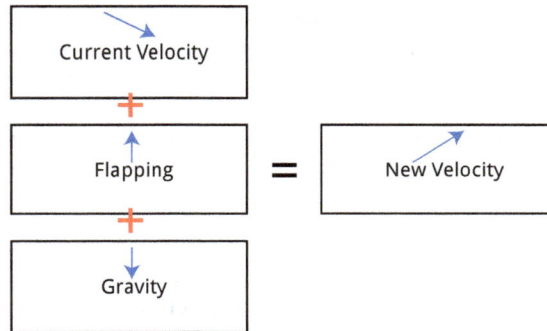

Another system, sum_impulses(), calculates the total forces applied to an entity during a physics tick:

FlappyPhysics/my_library/src/bevy_framework/bevy_physics.rs
```
pub fn sum_impulses(
❶  mut impulses: EventReader<Impulse>,
❷  mut velocities: Query<&mut Velocity>,
) {
❸  let mut dedupe_by_source = std::collections::HashMap::new();
   for impulse in impulses.read() {
     dedupe_by_source.insert(impulse.source, impulse);
   }
❹  let mut absolute = std::collections::HashSet::new();
   for (_, impulse) in dedupe_by_source {
❺    if let Ok(mut velocity) = velocities.get_mut(impulse.target) {
       if absolute.contains(&impulse.target) {
❻        continue;
       }
       if impulse.absolute {
         velocity.0 = impulse.amount;
❼        absolute.insert(impulse.target);
       } else {
         velocity.0 += impulse.amount;
       }
     }
   }
}
```

❶ An EventReader receives messages sent by other EventWriters for the same event type. You can iterate it like other collections.

❷ Create a query giving mutable access to Velocity components.

❸ Iterate the event reader, and deduplicate impulses by entity. This prevents multiple impulses being applied to the same entity in a single physics tick from being processed multiple times.

❹ Create a HashSet of entities with absolute impulses.

❺ You can access an individual entity's components with get_mut(). You have to define a query granting your system access to that component for this to work.

❻ If you've applied an absolute impulse for this entity, stop processing more impulses for this frame and keep the absolute value.

❼ Insert the entity into the absolute set.

Now that you have velocity and impulses, you can apply the summed velocity at the end of each physics tick. Add the following function:

FlappyPhysics/my_library/src/bevy_framework/bevy_physics.rs
```
pub fn apply_velocity(
  mut tick: EventReader<PhysicsTick>,
  mut movement: Query<(&Velocity, &mut Transform)>,
) {
  for _tick in tick.read() {
    movement.iter_mut().for_each(|(velocity, mut transform)| {
      transform.translation += velocity.0;
    });
  }
}
```

This function adds each entity's velocity—if they have one—to the current screen position of the entity.

Let's add one more system: gravity.

Falling Victim to Gravity, Again

Gravity is a special system that fires once every physics tick and applies a downwards impulse to each entity subject to gravity. It's important to provide an escape hatch for applying gravity—if you apply it to everything, then things you *don't* want to fall will plummet off the screen. This is particularly amusing for obstacles—the obstacle will fall off the map before Flappy can reach them, making for an easy game. Add the following code:

FlappyPhysics/my_library/src/bevy_framework/bevy_physics.rs

```
#[derive(Component)]
❶ pub struct ApplyGravity;

pub fn apply_gravity(
  mut tick: EventReader<PhysicsTick>,
  mut gravity: Query<&mut Velocity, With<ApplyGravity>>,
) {
  for _tick in tick.read() {
    gravity.iter_mut().for_each(|mut velocity| {
      velocity.0.y -= 0.75;
    });
  }
}
```

❶ A tag component. Apply this to all entities that should be subject to gravity.

Now that the engine is complete in my_library, it's time to enable it in the Flappy Dragon game.

Apply Physics to Flappy Dragon

The first thing to do is to enable all of the physics systems you've created. In main(), update the systems list for the run phase:

FlappyPhysics/flappy_dragon_base/src/main.rs

```
add_phase!(app, GamePhase, GamePhase::Flapping,
  start => [ setup ],
  run => [ flap, clamp, move_walls, hit_wall, cycle_animations,
    continual_parallax, physics_clock, sum_impulses, apply_gravity,
    apply_velocity],
  exit => [ cleanup::<FlappyElement> ]
);
```

You've removed the gravity system from the game altogether. Go ahead and delete the gravity() function as well. You can also remove the gravity element from the Flappy struct. The engine is now handling that for you.

Next, you need to give Flappy a default velocity and mark the dragon as subject to gravity:

FlappyPhysics/flappy_dragon_base/src/main.rs

```
fn setup(
  mut commands: Commands,
  mut rng: ResMut<RandomNumberGenerator>,
  assets: Res<AssetStore>,
  loaded_assets: Res<LoadedAssets>,
) {
  commands.spawn(Camera2d::default()).insert(FlappyElement);
  spawn_animated_sprite!(assets, commands, "flappy", -490.0, 0.0, 10.0,
```

```
    "Straight and Level", Flappy, FlappyElement,
➤   Velocity::default(), ApplyGravity);
  build_wall(&mut commands, &assets, rng.range(-5..5), &loaded_assets);
```

Next, add a velocity to walls when they're spawned, and *don't* enable gravity—you don't want them falling off the screen:

FlappyPhysics/flappy_dragon_base/src/main.rs
```
fn build_wall(
  commands: &mut Commands,
  assets: &AssetStore,
  gap_y: i32,
  loaded_assets: &LoadedAssets
) {
  for y in -12..=12 {
    if y < gap_y - 4 || y > gap_y + 4 {
      spawn_image!(assets, commands, "wall", 512.0, y as f32 * 32.0, 10.0,
        &loaded_assets, Obstacle, FlappyElement,
        Velocity::new(-4.0, 0.0, 0.0));
    }
  }
}
```

Now you can adjust the Flap function to not directly edit gravity and instead submit an impulse when the player flaps:

FlappyPhysics/flappy_dragon_base/src/main.rs
```
fn flap(
    keyboard: Res<ButtonInput<KeyCode>>,
➤   mut query: Query<(Entity, &mut AnimationCycle)>,
➤   mut impulse: EventWriter<Impulse>
)
{
  if keyboard.pressed(KeyCode::Space) {
    if let Ok((flappy, mut animation)) = query.single_mut() {
➤     //flappy.gravity = -5.0; // <-- Delete
➤     impulse.write(Impulse{
➤       target: flappy, amount: Vec3::Y,
➤       absolute: false
➤     });
      animation.switch("Flapping");
    }
  }
}
```

It's fun to play with "absolute" on this. Setting an absolute impulse gives a consistent boost to Flappy's altitude, while leaving it relative allows for more dramatic maneuvering. Try both to determine which one you prefer.

Finally, you can adjust the move_walls() function to no longer move the walls—the physics system is doing that for you—but instead, look for walls that have exited the screen and replace them.

FlappyPhysics/flappy_dragon_base/src/main.rs
```rust
fn move_walls(
  mut commands: Commands,
  query: Query<&Transform, With<Obstacle>>,
  delete: Query<Entity, With<Obstacle>>,
  assets: Res<AssetStore>,
  mut rng: ResMut<RandomNumberGenerator>,
  loaded_assets: Res<LoadedAssets>,
) {
  let mut rebuild = false;
    for transform in query.iter() {
    //transform.translation.x -= 4.0; // Delete this line
    if transform.translation.x < -530.0 {
      rebuild = true;
    }
  }

  if rebuild {
    for entity in delete.iter() {
      commands.entity(entity).despawn();
    }
    build_wall(&mut commands, &assets, rng.range(-5..5), &loaded_assets);
  }
}
```

Run the game now with cargo run. Notice you have a much more exciting game of Flappy Dragon to play:

Wrapping Up

You've covered a lot in this chapter. You learned to work with time and ensure that parts of your program run at a frame-rate independent speed. Adding frame-based animation, complete with a state machine and a mini-scripting language, has given you both a more visually appealing game and a lot of control over how Flappy renders. Parallax layers have provided a consistent illusion of movement. Using what you learned about time, you've created a monotonic physics clock and used it to consistently apply gravity and impulses, giving you a much better physics approximation and a more natural-feeling movement.

In the next chapter, you'll learn all about collision detection, determining if Flappy hits walls or other entities. A simple distance check between entities is fine when you only have a few entities on the screen. But what if you need to simulate a *lot* of entities? The next chapter will focus on collision detection, precision, and performance.

CHAPTER 8

Build Obstacles and Collision Detection

Many games require *collision detection*—a process of detecting when one object has "hit" another object. For example, in Flappy Dragon, the dragon crashes into walls. In space shooter games, lasers obliterate monsters, and the monsters' weapons damage the player. In physics games, collision detection is used to determine bounce and movement. The list is endless. Collision detection is important, and it's a good service to offer in a game-making library.

At the moment, Flappy Dragon is inefficient in detecting collisions. On each frame, the distance between Flappy and every wall is calculated. If the distance is sufficiently small, a collision has occurred and the game ends. Flappy Dragon can get by with inefficient collision detection because there aren't many potentially colliding objects. However, increasing the game's complexity would lead to a rapid drop in performance.

In this chapter, you'll follow a common journey for the library developer. You'll identify a performance problem and construct a test bed, focused on the particular problem you need to solve. You'll then incrementally test algorithmic improvements, graphing the results. After you have a good solution, you'll convert it into generic library-friendly code and update Flappy Dragon to use it.

Let's get started by building a collision test bed.

Building a Collision-Detection Test Bed

Often, when you're optimizing one element of a game or engine, it's helpful to create a test bed that emphasizes the problem you're trying to optimize. Rather than add thousands of objects to Flappy Dragon and then take them away again, it's easier to build an example designed to stress the feature you're optimizing. You're going to set Flappy to one side for a moment and build a billiards table with an easy way to add more and more balls. The balls collide with one another, and the test bed reports statistics—allowing you to *measure* your optimization progress.

Let's build a billiards table in hyperspace. Balls spawn on the table in a random position, with a random velocity. If balls collide, they're propelled away from the ball with which they collide. The table wraps at the edges—if a ball goes off one side of the screen, it reappears on the opposite side of the screen.

The basic framework of the simulation is similar to the other games you've created, so rather than fill pages with code listings, you can download the code from the accompanying source folder: code/FlappyCollision/bouncy. Some parts of the program differ from what you've written before, so let's look at them before moving on to the next step.

The show_performance() uses Bevy's Diagnostics plugin to obtain performance details:

FlappyCollision/bouncy/src/main.rs
```
fn show_performance(
  mut egui_context: egui::EguiContexts,
❶  diagnostics: Res<DiagnosticsStore>,
  mut collision_time: ResMut<CollisionTime>,
  mut commands: Commands,
  mut rng: ResMut<RandomNumberGenerator>,
  assets: Res<AssetStore>,
  query: Query<&Transform, With<Ball>>,
  loaded_assets: Res<LoadedAssets>,
) {
❷  let n_balls = query.iter().count();
❸  let fps = diagnostics
    .get(&FrameTimeDiagnosticsPlugin::FPS)
    .and_then(|fps| fps.average())
    .unwrap();
  collision_time.fps = fps;
  egui::egui::Window::new("Performance").show(
    egui_context.ctx_mut(),
    |ui| {
❹      let fps_text = format!("FPS: {fps:.1}");
❺      let color = match fps as u32 {
        0..=29 => Color32::RED,
        30..=59 => Color32::GOLD,
        _ => Color32::GREEN,
      };
      ui.colored_label(color, &fps_text);
      ui.colored_label(
        color,
        &format!("Collision Time: {} ms", collision_time.time),
      );
```

```
        ui.label(&format!("Collision Checks: {}", collision_time.checks));
        ui.label(&format!("# Balls: {n_balls}"));
❻      if ui.button("Add Ball").clicked() {
          println!(
            "{n_balls}, {}, {}, {:.0}",
            collision_time.time, collision_time.checks, collision_time.fps
          );
          spawn_bouncies(1, &mut commands, &mut rng, &assets,
            &loaded_assets);
        }
        if ui.button("Add 100 Balls").clicked() {
          println!(
            "{n_balls}, {}, {}, {:.0}",
            collision_time.time, collision_time.checks, collision_time.fps
          );
          spawn_bouncies(100, &mut commands, &mut rng, &assets,
            &loaded_assets);
        }
        if ui.button("Add 1000 Balls").clicked() {
          println!(
            "{n_balls}, {}, {}, {:.0}",
            collision_time.time, collision_time.checks, collision_time.fps
          );
          spawn_bouncies(1000, &mut commands, &mut rng, &assets,
            &loaded_assets);
        }
      }
    },
  );
}
```

❶ Request Bevy's Diagnostics type as a resource.

❷ Count the number of balls being simulated.

❸ Diagnostics provides a number of statistics. You're requesting the frames-per-second count as an average of recent frames. An average is useful because the actual number can fluctuate.

❹ Format the FPS to one decimal place.

❺ Change the FPS color to indicate "good," "warning," or "terrible" using the colors green, gold, and red, respectively.

❻ Add buttons to the user interface to add more balls to the simulation. Provide increments of 1, 100, and 1,000 balls.

bounce_on_collision() is another useful function. When two balls collide, it calculates the vector between them and sends a ball away from the object with which it collided. The function runs for both balls, providing relatively realistic—but not perfect—collision:

FlappyCollision/bouncy/src/main.rs

```
fn bounce_on_collision(
  entity: Entity,
  ball_a: Vec3,
  ball_b: Vec3,
  impulse: &mut EventWriter<Impulse>,
) {
  let a_to_b = (ball_a - ball_b).normalize();
  impulse.write(Impulse {
    target: entity,
    amount: a_to_b / 8.0,
    absolute: false,
    source: 0,
  });
}
```

❶ Bevy's Vec3 type implements the Sub trait, allowing you to subtract one vector from another. Normalizing is an operation that scales the total distance represented by the vector (from zero) to 1.0.

❷ Rather than try to calculate a perfect elastic collision—a topic on which whole books have been written—you're applying a force based on the direction of the collision.

You can illustrate the bounce_on_collision() function's effect like this:

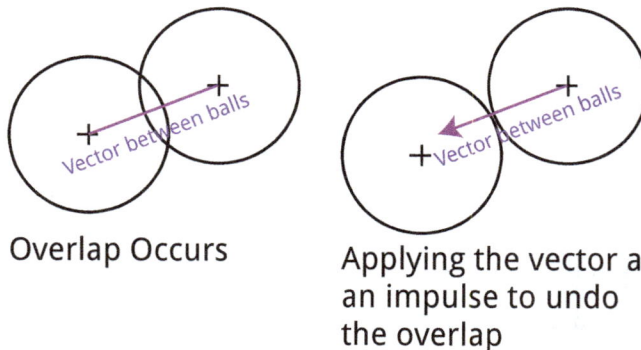

Overlap Occurs

Applying the vector adds
an impulse to undo
the overlap

Since you're applying an *impulse*—not an absolute force—momentum is preserved, and the result is a convincing bounce.

Finally, the collisions() queries each ball against every other ball and detects if they overlap:

FlappyCollision/bouncy/src/main.rs

```
fn collisions(
  mut collision_time: ResMut<CollisionTime>,
  query: Query<(Entity, &Transform), With<Ball>>,
```

```
    mut impulse: EventWriter<Impulse>,
) {
    // Start the clock
    let now = std::time::Instant::now();

    // Naïve Collision
    let mut n = 0;
    for (entity_a, ball_a) in query.iter() {
        query
            .iter()
            .filter(|(entity_b, _)| *entity_b != entity_a)
            .filter(|(_, ball_b)| {
                n += 1; // Count the collision check
                ball_a.translation.distance(ball_b.translation) < 8.0
            })
            .for_each(|(_, ball_b)| {
                bounce_on_collision(
                    entity_a,
                    ball_a.translation,
                    ball_b.translation,
                    &mut impulse,
                );
            });
    }

    // Store the time result
    collision_time.time = now.elapsed().as_millis();
    collision_time.checks = n;
}
```

The collision function is equivalent to the collision detection used in Flappy Dragon. If we run the code wih 5,000 balls, we get the screen shown at the top of the next page

Now that you have a working test bed, you can begin to analyze and optimize the collision detection system.

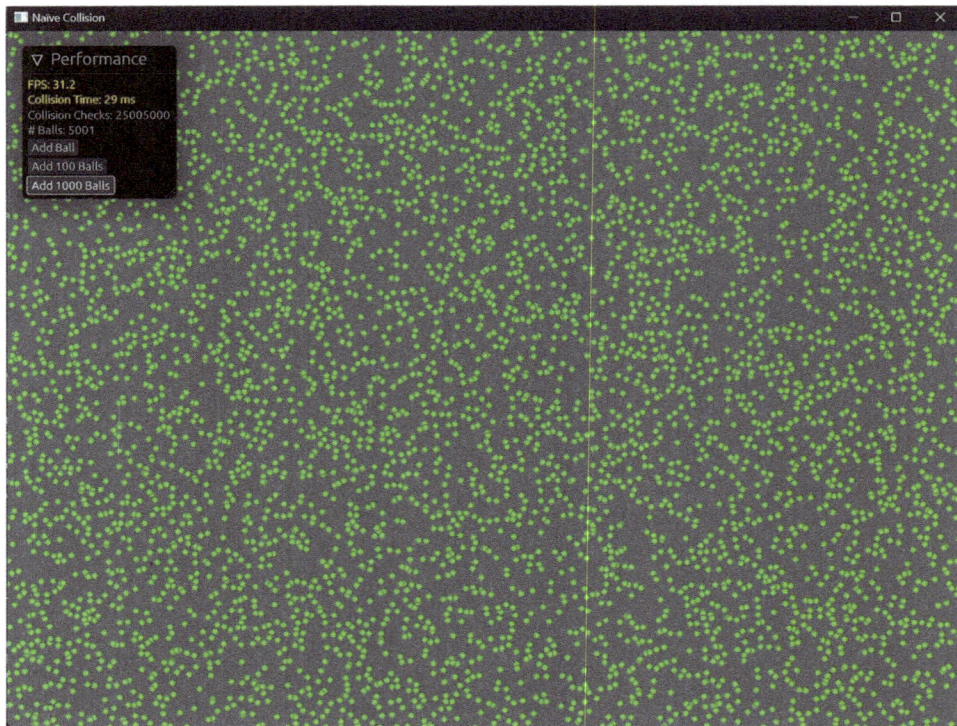

A rather chaotic screenshot of the bouncing balls playground. The grey window is filled with five thousand balls. A Performance window indicates 31.2 frames-per-second, with a collision calculation time of 29 ms. 25,005,000 collision checks have been performed.

Simple Collision Detection

Running the bouncy program on a 12th-generation Intel Core i7 with 12 cores yields the following results in release mode:

# Balls	Time (ms)	# Checks	Frames per Second
1	0	0	60
1001	1	1,001,000	60
2001	5	4,002,000	60
3001	10	9,003,000	60
4001	18	16,004,000	48
5001	30	25,005,000	30
6001	42	36,006,000	22
7001	56	49,007,000	16
8001	75	64,008,000	13
9001	93	81,009,000	10
10001	115	100,010,000	8

The results are a little easier to read as a graph:

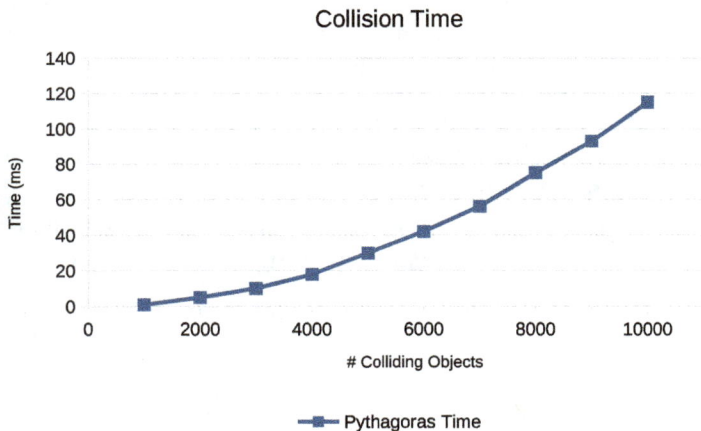

These aren't happy results: the naive collision detection algorithm takes nearly-exponentially—a polynomial curve—longer to execute relative to the number of colliding objects. It's still impressively fast, but it could easily become a bottleneck in a complicated game. Algorithm designers refer to a function with a polynomial worst-case as the dreaded $O(n^2)$.

Let's start trimming some of the performance times.

"Big O" Notation

"Big O" notation describes the worst-case time or space complexity of an algorithm. It typically takes the form O(n). n denotes the number of inputs fed into the algorithm—in this case, the number of entities. It provides a relative estimate of performance between different algorithms that perform the same task, and gives an idea of the complexity of an algorithm and how well it will scale as the number of inputs increases.

O(1) is the simplest form of the Big O notation. Complexity remains constant as the number of inputs increases. Creating a window, for example, is an O(1) operation.

O(log n) means that the algorithm's complexity increases logarithmically as the number of inputs increases. Binary search is an example of an O(log n) algorithm.

O(n) complexity means that the algorithm's complexity increases linearly as the number of inputs increases. A simple search algorithm is an O(n) algorithm.

O(n²) complexity means that the algorithm's complexity increases quadratically as the number of inputs increases. A simple nested loop is an O(n²) algorithm. Higher power numbers indicate algorithms that won't scale well!

You generally want to avoid O(n²) algorithms, especially in games. They can quickly become a bottleneck as the number of entities increases. There are times when this isn't a problem—algorithms that don't impact overall performance or small games that don't need additional complexity or many collision checks.

You can learn more about Big O notation in Wikipedia.[1]

Removing Square Roots from Distance Calculations

If you've read a few older game development books, you'll discover that it's almost a point of faith that calculating square roots is slow. Many books go to great lengths to implement square root approximations and find ways to avoid using square roots altogether. You're calculating the distance between objects using the Pythagoras algorithm. You can elide the need for a square root by working with squared distances:

1.   https://en.wikipedia.org/wiki/Big_O_notation

$$c = \sqrt{(a^2 + b^2)} \qquad\qquad c^2 = a^2 + b^2$$

Pythagoras   Without
Theorum   Square Root

You can test this article of faith by completely removing the square root from the calculation and instead working with distance squared. You can eliminate the square root by changing one line of your code:

```
.filter(|(_, ball_b)| {
  n += 1; // Count the collision check
  ball_a.translation.distance_squared(ball_b.translation) < (8.0 * 8.0)
})
```

Eliminating the square root from your distance calculation yields a small performance improvement:

Collision Time

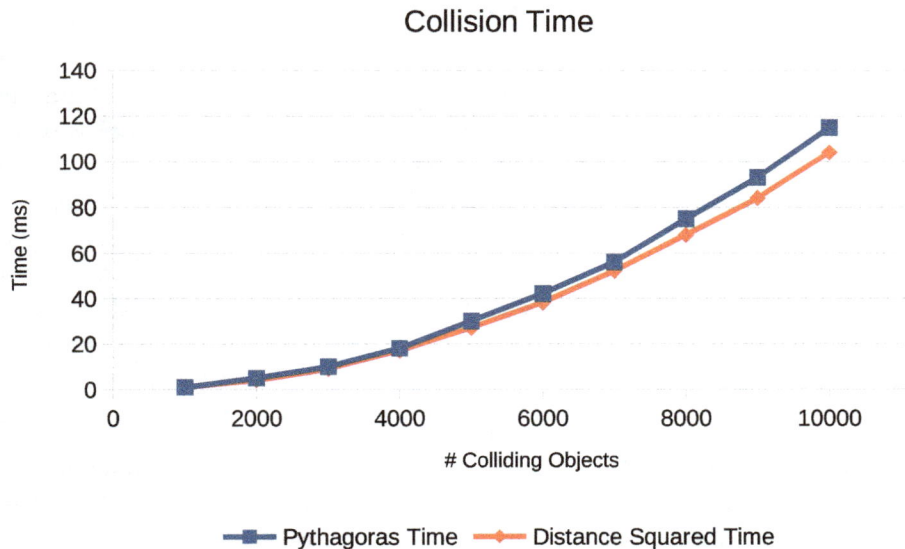

The algorithm remains firmly O(n²), but at least it scales *slightly* better now. Unfortunately, a simple circular collision isn't what you need, so let's operate on rectangles instead.

Improving Collision Detection with Bounding Boxes

There's a small problem with your collision detection: you're measuring distance between the center of each object, effectively drawing an imaginary circle around each one. The bouncing balls *are* circular, but the objects in

Flappy Dragon are rectangular in nature. Instead, you need to draw an imaginary rectangle around the objects and test if they overlap. The difference between bounding boxes and bounding circles (distances) looks like this:

**Bounding Circles
(Distance Checks)**   **Bounding Boxes**

The yellow behind each sprite displays an area that's included in the bounding type—rectangle or circle—but not occupied by a nontransparent pixel. For noncircular sprites, circular collision boundaries generally offer inferior collision detection with a higher chance of detecting a collision when no pixels in the colliding area are visible to the player.

Bounding boxes in games are typically aligned to the X/Y axes and are known as *axis-aligned bounding boxes* (*AABB*). Aligning with the axes allows for quick computation without taking into account rotation. Without rotation, you can reduce calculating overlap to a simple series of greater-than and less-than calculations, which are fast. If you include rotation in your bounding-box overlap calculation, the math becomes significantly more complicated: you need to rotate each point on the box around the bounding box's center point and then perform a "concave polygon collision detection" algorithm. Many such algorithms exist, but they are significantly more CPU-intensive than a single AABB check.

Concave Polygon Collisions

If you do want to perform full-scale concave polygon collisions, there are resources that can help you. The Rust Collision Detector crate contains working code with a permissive license.[2]

You can retain most of your high performance by first performing a coarse AABB check, and then following up with a more accurate collision detection algorithm. This lets you determine that a collision is possible, and you can then follow up with the accurate calculation. Using the coarse—but fast—algorithm first reduces the number of times you have to run the more expensive algorithm.

---

2.   https://github.com/JoelEager/Rust-Collision-Detector

Let's start by creating a bounding box type:

```
FlappyCollision/bouncy_bbox/src/main.rs
#[derive(Component)]
struct AxisAlignedBoundingBox {
  half_size: Vec2
}
```

Bounding boxes are going to have to move with their parent entity, but will never change size. So, rather than store the *position* of the box—and have to update it all the time—you can store the size of the attached sprite on the X and Y axis.

Let's define a *second* type to represent a two-dimensional rectangle:

```
FlappyCollision/bouncy_bbox/src/main.rs
#[derive(Debug, Clone, Copy)]
struct Rect2D {
  min: Vec2,
  max: Vec2,
}
```

The Rect2D type is straightforward; it contains two corners of the box (minimum and maximum). You can derive the rest of a rectangle's location from these values.

Next, you need to create a constructor for the AxisAlignedBoundingBox type and a function to convert a position into a Rect2D:

```
FlappyCollision/bouncy_bbox/src/main.rs
impl AxisAlignedBoundingBox {
  pub fn new(width: f32, height: f32) -> Self {
    Self {
      half_size: Vec2::new(width/2.0, height / 2.0)
    }
  }

  fn as_rect(&self, translate: Vec2) -> Rect2D {
    Rect2D::new(
      Vec2::new(translate.x - self.half_size.x,
        translate.y - self.half_size.y),
      Vec2::new(translate.x + self.half_size.x,
        translate.y + self.half_size.y),
    )
  }
}
```

The next step is to give Rect2D a constructor and an intersection test:

FlappyCollision/bouncy_bbox/src/main.rs
```
impl Rect2D {
  fn new(min: Vec2, max: Vec2) -> Self {
    Self { min, max }
  }

  fn intersect(&self, other: &Self) -> bool {
    self.min.x <= other.max.x
      && self.max.x >= other.min.x
      && self.min.y <= other.max.y
      && self.max.y >= other.min.y
  }
}
```

Let's attach an AABB to each ball in the simulation. Find the spawn_image! call in the spawn_bouncies function and add the following line:

FlappyCollision/bouncy_bbox/src/main.rs
```
spawn_image!(
  assets,
  commands,
  "green_ball",
  position.x,
  position.y,
  position.z,
  &loaded_assets,
  BouncyElement,
  Velocity::new(velocity.x, velocity.y, velocity.z),
➤ AxisAlignedBoundingBox::new(8.0, 8.0),
  Ball
);
```

Every ball now has a bounding box attached to it. Finally, you need to update the collision test to detect collisions between bounding boxes:

FlappyCollision/bouncy_bbox/src/main.rs
```
fn collisions(
  mut collision_time: ResMut<CollisionTime>,
➤ query: Query<(Entity, &Transform, &AxisAlignedBoundingBox)>,
  mut impulse: EventWriter<Impulse>
) {
  // Start the clock
  let now = std::time::Instant::now();

  // Bounding Box Naïve Collision
  let mut n = 0;
❶ for (entity_a, ball_a, box_a) in query.iter() {
❷   let box_a = box_a.as_rect(ball_a.translation.truncate());
❸   for (entity_b, ball_b, box_b) in query.iter() {
❹     if entity_a != entity_b {
```

```
❺          let box_b = box_b.as_rect(ball_b.translation.truncate());
           if box_a.intersect(&box_b) {
             bounce_on_collision(entity_a, ball_a.translation,
❻                ball_b.translation, &mut impulse);
           }
           n += 1;
         }
       }
     }
   }

   // Store the time result
   collision_time.time = now.elapsed().as_millis();
   collision_time.checks = n;
 }
```

❶ Iterate all entities that have a transformation and a bounding box.

❷ truncate() reduces a Vec3 to a Vec2 by dropping the z component. You don't want to include the render layer in your calculations. The truncated position is used to calculate entity_a's bounding box position.

❸ Iterate the same set of entities again, this time extracting entity_b—the other entity with whom entity_a may collide.

❹ Check that entity_a and entity_b aren't the same entity. Colliding with yourself is, at best, awkward.

❺ Calculate entity_b's bounding box.

❻ If the two bounding boxes intersect, a collision has occurred.

Now test the program with cargo run. If you look closely, the collisions are now inclusive of the faded-out pixels around the ball—the ball sprites are rectangular even if the ball is round. Unfortunately, the performance change is disastrous:

Collision Time

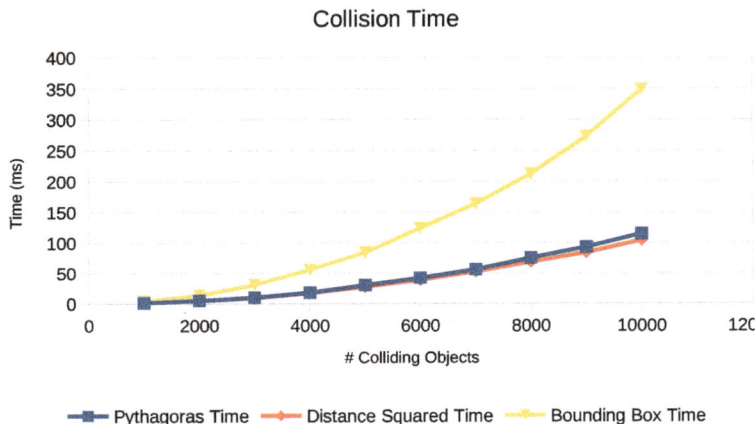

Legend: ■ Pythagoras Time ◆ Distance Squared Time ▼ Bounding Box Time

AABB checks are slightly slower than simple distance checks. You could probably optimize away much of the difference by first checking distance, and then testing bounding box overlap. But choosing between accurate collisions and fast collisions is a nasty decision. Let's avoid the decision altogether by examining ways to improve the underlying *algorithm*, rather than each collision, and check for fewer collisions per frame.

Reducing Collision Checks with Spatial Partitioning

You're still checking every ball against every other ball, so even with improvements in the "have we collided?" algorithm, the test bed still slows down badly as you increase the number of collidable entities.

What if instead of checking every ball against every other ball, you only check a ball for collision with nearby entities? That's the basic premise of a *Quad Tree*. Quad Trees are a *spatial partitioning* algorithm. The top level of a quad tree contains the entire screen. The second layer contains four sections, each containing one quarter of the parent layer. Additional layers can subdivide the layer above them.

An entity is added to a Quad Tree by starting at the base level (that's the entire screen). Its bounding box is compared to each of the quadrants making up the next level. If the entity only fits into one quadrant, you repeat the process for that layer, continuing until there are no choices in which an entity completely fits. This algorithm is inefficient at top-level quadrant boundaries—the entity remains on the top level rather than being inserted further down the tree. Unless you're aligning your entities in a perfect cross along the boundary, it shouldn't affect overall performance much.

That was quite a mouthful, so here's an illustration showing how entities are assigned to a one-layer quad tree (layer 0 being the whole screen and layer 1 being quarters of the tree):

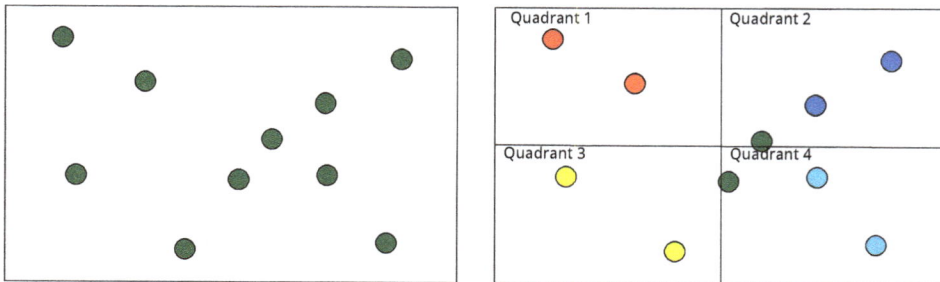

The dark green balls don't fit entirely inside any quadrant, so they remain at the top level. Balls that fit entirely within a quadrant are color-coded for that quadrant.

Let's start by implementing a static QuadTree, a tree with a fixed depth.

Implementing a Static QuadTree

You'll need a helper function added to Rect2D. Add the quadrants function to the impl Rect2D block:

```
FlappyCollision/bouncy_bbox_quadtree/src/main.rs
  fn quadrants(&self) -> Vec<Self> {
    let center = (self.min + self.max) / 2.0;
    vec![
      Self::new(self.min, center), // Top-left
      Self::new(
        Vec2::new(center.x, self.min.y),
        Vec2::new(self.max.x, center.y),
      ), // Top-Right
      Self::new(
        Vec2::new(self.min.x, center.y),
        Vec2::new(center.x, self.max.y),
      ), // Bottom-left
      Self::new(center, self.max), // Bottom-right
    ]
  }
}
```

The quadrants function returns an array of four more Rect2D variables, each representing one quarter of the parent rectangle. You'll use this function regularly throughout the QuadTree implementation.

Let's begin implementing a QuadTree by assigning a constant for the tree depth. Add the following line to main.rs:

```
const QUAD_TREE_DEPTH: usize = 1;
```

You'll start with a depth of 1, a single layer encompassing the entire screen, and a layer beneath it containing four quadrants.

Next, you need to implement a type to hold each "node" (element) of the QuadTree. Add the following to main.rs:

```
FlappyCollision/bouncy_bbox_quadtree/src/main.rs
#[derive(Debug)]
pub struct StaticQuadTreeNode {
  bounds: Rect2D,
  children: Option<[usize; 4]>,
}
```

Notice that the node contains an optional array of nodes named Children. Each child represents one of the four possible children of the node. You don't want to recursively divide the QuadTree forever, so the maximum depth of the tree will contain None rather than Some(children).

Next, you need to create a StaticQuadTree type into which you place the nodes. Add the following code to main.rs:

```
FlappyCollision/bouncy_bbox_quadtree/src/main.rs
#[derive(Debug, Resource)]
pub struct StaticQuadTree {
  nodes: Vec<StaticQuadTreeNode>,
}
```

The StaticQuadTree is a vector of nodes. Each node will be added to this vector, and its index in the vector used to reference it.

Now you need to implement a constructor for the StaticQuadTree type. Add the following code to main.rs:

```
FlappyCollision/bouncy_bbox_quadtree/src/main.rs
impl StaticQuadTree {
  fn new(screen_size: Vec2, max_depth: usize) -> Self {
    // Make the container
    let mut nodes = Vec::new();

    // Create the top-level, always the whole screen
    let half = screen_size / 2.0;
    let top = StaticQuadTreeNode {
      bounds: Rect2D::new(
        Vec2::new(0.0 - half.x, 0.0 - half.y),
        Vec2::new(half.x, half.y),
      ),
      children: None,
    };
    nodes.push(top);
    Self::subdivide(&mut nodes, 0, 1, max_depth);
    Self { nodes }
  }
```

❶ After creating a StaticQuadTreeNode encompassing the entire screen (remember that 0,0 is the middle)—add it as the first node in the tree.

❷ You'll write this function in a moment.

The constructor creates the top layer of the QuadTree, taking the coordinates of the visible display as a parameter. It then calls the subdivide function to create the rest of the tree.

Add the subdivide function to main.rs as part of the StaticQuadTree implementation:

FlappyCollision/bouncy_bbox_quadtree/src/main.rs

```
fn subdivide(
❶  nodes: &mut Vec<StaticQuadTreeNode>,
❷  index: usize,
❸  depth: usize,
   max_depth: usize,
) {
❹  let mut children = nodes[index].bounds.quadrants();
   let child_index = [
     nodes.len(),
     nodes.len() + 1,
     nodes.len() + 2,
     nodes.len() + 3,
   ];
❺  nodes[index].children = Some(child_index);
❻  children.drain(0..4).for_each(|quad| {
     nodes.push(StaticQuadTreeNode {
       bounds: quad,
       children: None,
     })
   });

❼  if depth < max_depth {
     for index in child_index {
       Self::subdivide(nodes, index, depth + 1, max_depth);
     }
   }
}
```

❶ Passing in a mutable reference to the nodes list is necessary because there's no &mut self—the tree hasn't been created yet.

❷ The index—in the nodes vector—of the node being subdivided.

❸ The current depth—in layers—of the node being divided. Tracking the depth through recursive calls prevents infinite recursion.

❹ Create a list of four quadrants, each covering one quarter of this node.

❺ You know that the node you're working on is located in the nodes vector at the position stored in the index. You aren't multithreading, so you can be certain that if you add four nodes, they'll have indices of (index+1), (index+2), and so on.

❻ drain() is a special iterator that removes items as it reads them—literally draining them out of the vector. Add each of the quadrants as a child node to the node list.

❼ If the recursion hasn't reached the maximum tree depth, repeat the process for each child node. If maximum depth has been reached, go no further. Execution will return to the previous function—eventually covering the entire QuadTree. Recursion is beautiful, but unconstrained recursion leads to stack overflow and crashes.

The subdivide function divides its bounding area into quadrants and creates a new node for each quarter of the bounded region. If the depth of the tree is less than the maximum depth, it recursively calls subdivide again on the new nodes. After it reaches the maximum depth, it stops subdividing. The constructor then returns the new tree.

Now that you have a static QuadTree, it's time to add entities to it. An entity occupies the smallest quadrant that completely contains it. Add the following function to main.rs:

FlappyCollision/bouncy_bbox_quadtree/src/main.rs
```
fn smallest_node(&self, target: &Rect2D) -> usize {
  let mut current_index = 0;
```
❶
❷
❸
```
  #[allow(clippy::while_let_loop)]
  loop {
    if let Some(children) = self.nodes[current_index].children {
      let matches: Vec<usize> = children
        .iter()
        .filter_map(|child| {
          if self.nodes[*child].bounds.intersect(target) {
            Some(*child)
          } else {
            None
          }
        })
```
❹
```
        .collect();
```
❺
```
      if matches.len() == 1 {
        current_index = matches[0];
      } else {
        break;
      }
    } else {
      break;
    }
  }

  current_index
}
```

❶ Clippy—Rust's linter—complains that this function is using an if let inside a loop construct. Clippy is correct, but this function is more readily explained as opposed to the shorthand while let syntax.

❷ Loop until a break statement is encountered.

❸ If the current node has children, examine them. Otherwise, break out of the loop.

❹ Check each child node to see if it intersects with the target bounding box. Collect the result into a vector of node indices.

❺ If exactly one child node matched, then begin evaluating that node—storing the current index. If more than one node intersects, then escape from the loop because the function has located the smallest node that completely contains the target bounding box.

The smallest_node function accepts a target rectangle—the bounding box of the entity you're adding. It then compares that bounding box with each child quadrant, counting how many quadrants intersect. If the entity only intersects with a single quadrant, it recursively calls itself against that quadrant. As soon as it finds a quadrant that intersects with more than one quadrant, it returns the current quadrant.

Now, let's pull this all together and implement the collision function—this time using a QuadTree.

You probably noticed earlier that the StaticQuadTree type is decorated as a Resource—a shared Bevy resource. One advantage of a *static* QuadTree—one that doesn't change—is that it can be used over and over again. The tree doesn't store entities; it provides node indices that you can store to indicate where an entity is. This means that you can use the same tree for every frame and only need to construct it once. To avoid repeated initialization, you want to create the QuadTree in the setup() function:

FlappyCollision/bouncy_bbox_quadtree/src/main.rs
```
fn setup(
  mut commands: Commands,
  mut rng: ResMut<RandomNumberGenerator>,
  assets: Res<AssetStore>,
  loaded_assets: Res<LoadedAssets>,
) {
  commands
    .spawn(Camera2d::default())
    .insert(BouncyElement);
  commands.insert_resource(CollisionTime::default());
  commands
    .insert_resource(StaticQuadTree::new(Vec2::new(1024.0, 768.0),
      QUAD_TREE_DEPTH));
  spawn_bouncies(1, &mut commands, &mut rng, &assets, &loaded_assets);
}
```

Now modify the collision() function to use the QuadTree. Modify the function signature to add a query to find every entity with a BBox component, and reference the QuadTree resource. Adjust the top of the collision() function:

FlappyCollision/bouncy_bbox_quadtree/src/main.rs
```
fn collisions(
  mut collision_time: ResMut<CollisionTime>,
❶  query: Query<(Entity, &Transform, &AxisAlignedBoundingBox)>,
  mut impulse: EventWriter<Impulse>,
❷  quad_tree: Res<StaticQuadTree>,
) {
```

❶ Find all entities with a bounding box and a transform.

❷ Request access to the QuadTree resource.

Now you need two helper functions. As part of the impl StaticQuadTree block, add the following functions:

FlappyCollision/bouncy_bbox_quadtree/src/main.rs
```
fn intersecting_nodes(&self, target: &Rect2D) -> HashSet<usize> {
  let mut result = HashSet::new();
  self.intersect(0, &mut result, target);
  result
}

fn intersect(
  &self,
  index: usize,
  result: &mut HashSet<usize>,
  target: &Rect2D,
) {
  if self.nodes[index].bounds.intersect(target) {
    result.insert(index);
    if let Some(children) = &self.nodes[index].children {
      for child in children {
        self.intersect(*child, result, target);
      }
    }
  }
}
```

This code iterates through child nodes, storing a HashMap of nodes that intersect with the target bounding box. intersect() recursively descends the QuadTree, collecting all entries that intersect with each QuadTree box.

Next, build a spatial index associating each entity with a QuadTree node index:

FlappyCollision/bouncy_bbox_quadtree/src/main.rs

```
// Start the clock
let now = std::time::Instant::now();

let mut spatial_index: HashMap<usize, Vec<(Entity, Rect2D)>> =
❶   HashMap::new();
❷ let tree_positions: Vec<(Entity, usize, Rect2D)> = query
    .iter()
    .map(|(entity, transform, bbox)| {
❸     let bbox = bbox.as_rect(transform.translation.truncate());
❹     let node = quad_tree.smallest_node(&bbox);
❺     for in_node in quad_tree.intersecting_nodes(&bbox) {
❻       if let Some(contents) = spatial_index.get_mut(&in_node) {
          contents.push((entity, bbox));
        } else {
          spatial_index.insert(in_node, vec![(entity, bbox)]);
        }
      }

      (entity, node, bbox)
    })
❼   .collect();
```

❶ Build a HashMap. The map is indexed by QuadTree node index and contains a vector of entities and bounding rectangles. This allows you to quickly look up the contents of a QuadTree node.

❷ Iterate through all entities that have a bounding box and a position.

❸ Translate the bounding box by the entity's position, and convert it into a Rect2D.

❹ Use the smallest_node() function to find the smallest possible QuadTree node in which the entity fits. This is the entity's position in the QuadTree.

❺ Now that you have the node in which the entity fits and its bounding box, you can list all nodes on the QuadTree that might contain the entity.

❻ Check the spatial tree. If the node id exists, add the entity's details to the spatial tree at the current position. If the node id doesn't exist, create the vector for that node id.

❼ Collect the entity, node index, and bounding box into a vector named tree_positions.

You've now built two indices:

- spatial_index is a map of QuadTree node indices to a vector of entities and their bounding boxes. The map is indexed by node index, allowing you to quickly retrieve a list of every entity in a node.

- tree_positions is a vector of entities, node indices, and bounding boxes. The tree_position index provides a list of every entity that might collide and of the bounding box and node index of each entity. You'll use it to determine which entities collided when you detect two bounding-box collisions.

FlappyCollision/bouncy_bbox_quadtree/src/main.rs

```rust
let mut n = 0;

for (entity, node, box_a) in tree_positions {
    if let Some(entities_here) = spatial_index.get(&node) {
        if let Some((entity_b, _)) = entities_here
            .iter()
            .filter(|(entity_b, _)| *entity_b != entity)
            .find(|(_, box_b)| {
                n += 1;
                box_a.intersect(box_b)
            })
        {
            // A Collision occurred
            let (_, ball_a, _) = query.get(entity).unwrap();
            let (_, ball_b, _) = query.get(*entity_b).unwrap();
            bounce_on_collision(entity, ball_a.translation,
                ball_b.translation, &mut impulse);
        }
    }
}

// Store the time result
collision_time.time = now.elapsed().as_millis();
collision_time.checks = n;
}
```

The collision code is similar to the code you used for bounding boxes: you iterate all possible colliding entities. Instead of iterating for a second time, you check what entities are in the spatial_index and only perform intersection tests on these. This massively reduces the number of intersection tests.

This Can Be a Lot Faster

You don't have to rebuild the positions every frame. You could share the spatial index as a mutable resource and adjust it when entities move. In the test bed, every entity moves on every frame, so the optimization doesn't help. If your game doesn't move everything all the time, you can save a lot of time by storing the QuadTree position in a component and lazily updating it if an entity moves.

Now run the game. The game runs as before, but it's a lot faster. You can add tens of thousands of balls before you start to slow down your computer.

Sometimes, you'll start to run out of graphics power before you run out of collision processing power. Here's a graph showing the relative performance of the algorithms you've tested so far:

Collision Time

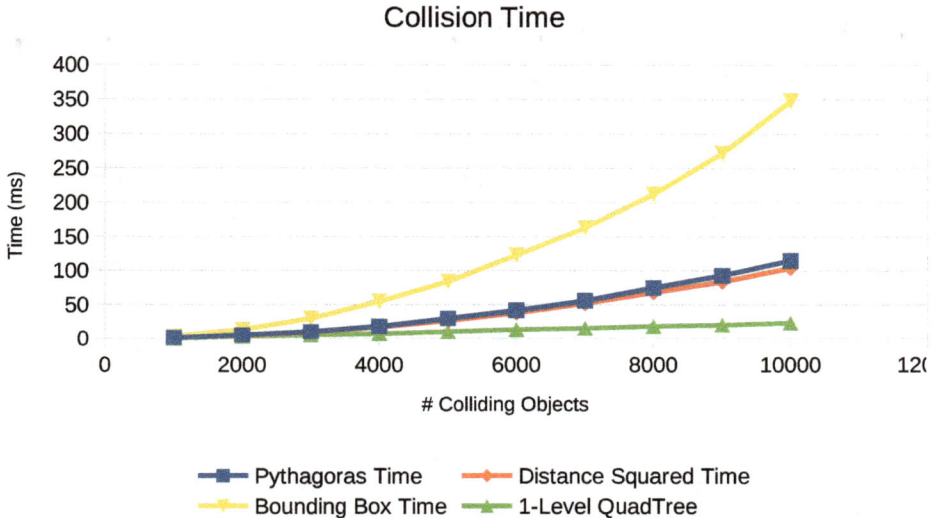

Legend: Pythagoras Time — Distance Squared Time — Bounding Box Time — 1-Level QuadTree

You can enhance performance further by changing the QUAD_TREE_DEPTH constant. Try a few different values. On a 12th-generation Intel Core i7 with 12 cores, the results were as follows:

Collision Time

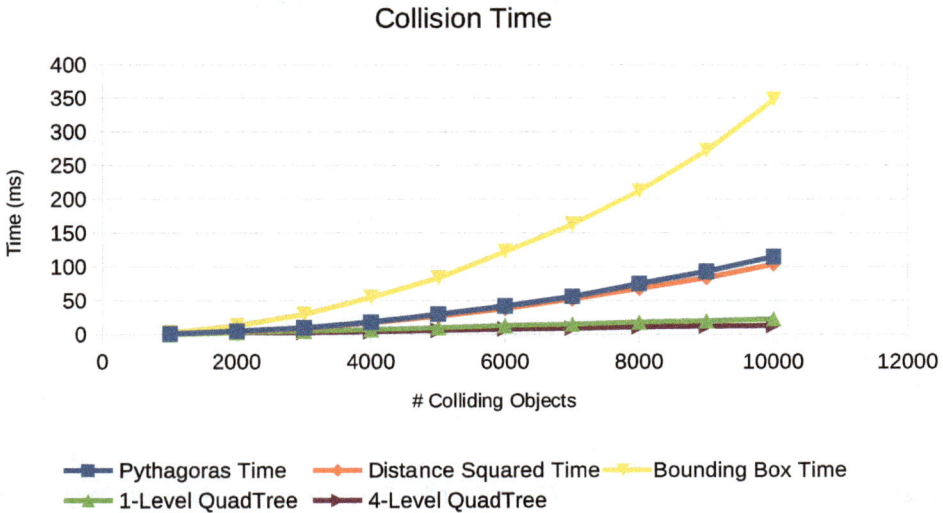

Legend: Pythagoras Time — Distance Squared Time — Bounding Box Time — 1-Level QuadTree — 4-Level QuadTree

Beyond a certain depth, you encounter diminishing returns and can even slow down processing. The optimal number varies by game, so be prepared to experiment.

Congratulations! You've mastered a complex spatial partitioning algorithm. Let's turn it into a library service to offer to users of my_library.

Upgrading Quad-Tree to a Library Service

You can reuse most of the code you've created in the billiards table test bed as library code, with minimal modification. Let's tidy things up a bit and separate the types into separate files.

Within my_library, create the following directory and file structure (with empty files for now):

```
my_library                      # Your library
  Cargo.toml                    # Configuration for your library
  src/                          # Source code for your library
    lib.rs                      # Library entry point
    bevy_framework/             # Bevy-specific code
      mod.rs                    # Module file
      bevy_collision/           # Collision detection
        mod.rs                  # Module file
        aabb.rs                 # Axis-aligned bounding box
        rect2d.rs               # Two-dimensional rectangle
        static_quadtree.rs      # Static QuadTree
```

Open my_library/src/bevy_framework/mod.rs and add the following code:

```
mod bevy_collision;
pub use bevy_collision::*;
```

Now, open my_library/src/bevy_framework/bevy_collision/mod.rs and add the following code:

FlappyCollision/my_library/src/bevy_framework/bevy_collision/mod.rs
```
mod aabb;
mod rect2d;
mod static_quadtree;
pub use aabb::AxisAlignedBoundingBox;
pub use rect2d::Rect2D;
pub use static_quadtree::*;
use bevy::{prelude::*, platform::collections::HashMap};
use std::marker::PhantomData;
```

Next, you'll port over the AxisAlignedBoundingBox. Open my_library/src/bevy_framework/bevy_collision/aabb.rs and copy and paste the AxisAlignedBoundingBox type. Change all of the `fn` to `pub fn` to ensure that the functions are accessible throughout your library:

FlappyCollision/my_library/src/bevy_framework/bevy_collision/aabb.rs
```
use bevy::prelude::*;
use super::rect2d::Rect2D;

#[derive(Component)]
pub struct AxisAlignedBoundingBox {
  half_size: Vec2,
}

impl AxisAlignedBoundingBox {
  pub fn new(width: f32, height: f32) -> Self {
    Self {
      half_size: Vec2::new(width / 2.0, height / 2.0),
    }
  }

  pub fn as_rect(&self, translate: Vec2) -> Rect2D {
    Rect2D::new(
      Vec2::new(translate.x - self.half_size.x,
        translate.y - self.half_size.y),
      Vec2::new(translate.x + self.half_size.x,
        translate.y + self.half_size.y),
    )
  }
}
```

Likewise, you can mostly copy and paste `Rect2D` into my_library/src/bevy_framework/bevy_collision/rect2d.rs. Again, make the functions public:

FlappyCollision/my_library/src/bevy_framework/bevy_collision/rect2d.rs
```
use bevy::prelude::*;

#[derive(Debug, Clone, Copy)]
pub struct Rect2D {
  min: Vec2,
  max: Vec2,
}

impl Rect2D {
  pub fn new(min: Vec2, max: Vec2) -> Self {
    Self { min, max }
  }

  pub fn intersect(&self, other: &Self) -> bool {
    self.min.x <= other.max.x
      && self.max.x >= other.min.x
      && self.min.y <= other.max.y
      && self.max.y >= other.min.y
  }

  pub fn quadrants(&self) -> Vec<Self> {
```

```rust
    let center = (self.min + self.max) / 2.0;
    vec![
      Self::new(self.min, center), // Top-left
      Self::new(
        Vec2::new(center.x, self.min.y),
        Vec2::new(self.max.x, center.y),
      ), // Top-Right
      Self::new(
        Vec2::new(self.min.x, center.y),
        Vec2::new(center.x, self.max.y),
      ), // Bottom-left
      Self::new(center, self.max), // Bottom-right
    ]
  }
}
```

Once more, copy and paste the StaticQuadTree into my_library/src/bevy_frame-work/bevy_collision/static_quadtree.rs with the functions changed to public. Start with the imports:

FlappyCollision/my_library/src/bevy_framework/bevy_collision/static_quadtree.rs
```rust
use bevy::{prelude::*, platform::collections::HashSet};
use super::rect2d::Rect2D;
```

Next, define the StaticQuadTree and StaticQuadTreeNode types:

FlappyCollision/my_library/src/bevy_framework/bevy_collision/static_quadtree.rs
```rust
#[derive(Debug, Resource)]
pub struct StaticQuadTree {
  nodes: Vec<StaticQuadTreeNode>,
}

#[derive(Debug)]
pub struct StaticQuadTreeNode {
  bounds: Rect2D,
  children: Option<[usize; 4]>,
}
```

Then add the constructor for StaticQuadTree:

FlappyCollision/my_library/src/bevy_framework/bevy_collision/static_quadtree.rs
```rust
impl StaticQuadTree {
  pub fn new(screen_size: Vec2, max_depth: usize) -> Self {
    // Make the container
    let mut nodes = Vec::new();

    // Create the top-level, always the whole screen
    let half = screen_size / 2.0;
    let top = StaticQuadTreeNode {
      bounds: Rect2D::new(
        Vec2::new(0.0 - half.x, 0.0 - half.y),
        Vec2::new(half.x, half.y),
```

```
            ),
            children: None,
        };
        nodes.push(top);

        Self::subdivide(&mut nodes, 0, 1, max_depth);

        Self { nodes }
    }
```

The smallest_node function is essentially unchanged and goes next:

FlappyCollision/my_library/src/bevy_framework/bevy_collision/static_quadtree.rs
```
pub fn smallest_node(&self, target: &Rect2D) -> usize {
    let mut current_index = 0;

    #[allow(clippy::while_let_loop)]
    loop {
        if let Some(children) = self.nodes[current_index].children {
            let matches: Vec<usize> = children
                .iter()
                .filter_map(|child| {
                    if self.nodes[*child].bounds.intersect(target) {
                        Some(*child)
                    } else {
                        None
                    }
                })
                .collect();

            if matches.len() == 1 {
                current_index = matches[0];
            } else {
                break;
            }
        } else {
            break;
        }
    }

    current_index
}
```

Add the subdivide function:

FlappyCollision/my_library/src/bevy_framework/bevy_collision/static_quadtree.rs
```
fn subdivide(
    nodes: &mut Vec<StaticQuadTreeNode>,
    index: usize,
    depth: usize,
    max_depth: usize,
) {
    let mut children = nodes[index].bounds.quadrants();
    let child_index = [
```

```
      nodes.len(),
      nodes.len() + 1,
      nodes.len() + 2,
      nodes.len() + 3,
    ];
    nodes[index].children = Some(child_index);
    children.drain(0..4).for_each(|quad| {
      nodes.push(StaticQuadTreeNode {
        bounds: quad,
        children: None,
      })
    });

    if depth < max_depth {
      for index in child_index {
        Self::subdivide(nodes, index, depth + 1, max_depth);
      }
    }
  }
}
```

And finally, add the intersecting_nodes function to the file:

FlappyCollision/my_library/src/bevy_framework/bevy_collision/static_quadtree.rs
```
  pub fn intersecting_nodes(&self, target: &Rect2D) -> HashSet<usize> {
    let mut result = HashSet::new();
    self.intersect(0, &mut result, target);
    result
  }

  fn intersect(
    &self,
    index: usize,
    result: &mut HashSet<usize>,
    target: &Rect2D,
  ) {
    if self.nodes[index].bounds.intersect(target) {
      result.insert(index);
      if let Some(children) = &self.nodes[index].children {
        for child in children {
          self.intersect(*child, result, target);
        }
      }
    }
  }
}
```

Now that you're done with the copying and pasting, it's time to think about
how to make collisions *generic*. You could run a single collision function that
checks every type with a bounding box for collisions against everything else
with a bounding box, but then you'd spend a lot of time figuring out what
type of object collided with what other type of object and ignoring any of the

collision types that you don't need in your game. Instead, let's make use of Rust generics to build a system that checks objects of type A with objects of type B and sends a message using the EventWriter system for the game to handle collisions.

We can name the message OnCollision and add the following code to my_library/bevy_framework/bevy_collision/mod.rs:

FlappyCollision/my_library/src/bevy_framework/bevy_collision/mod.rs

```
#[derive(Event)]
① pub struct OnCollision<A, B>
② where
     A: Component,
     B: Component,
{
③   pub entity_a: Entity,
     pub entity_b: Entity,
④   marker: PhantomData<(A, B)>,
}
```

❶ Specialize the message with two types, A and B. These should be tag components identifying the types of entities for whom you wish to check collisions, for example, Flappy and Obstacle.

❷ Require that both of these types be a Component.

❸ Store the Entity identifiers for each colliding object.

❹ PhantomData allows you to specialize a type, but not include the specializing types in the type you're creating.

Phantom Data

Rust structures can only be specialized to reference types that they contain or types that are used to further specialize other dependent types. A simple struct Foo<T> {} won't compile because it doesn't contain a T.

The PhantomData type exists to relax this requirement. You can include a PhantomData<T> in your structure to indicate that you require a T to be present, but you don't need to store it. The PhantomData type is a marker type that doesn't carry any data. It's compiled to zero bytes of code. The compiler uses PhantomData to provide compile-time type safety guarantees—without imposing runtime overhead.

Beware, phantom data frequently haunts data centers by night.

OnCollisioni is a double-specialized type; you specify A and B when you use it. Rust types are distinct when compiled with different specializations, so OnCollision<Flappy, Obstacle> is separate from OnCollision<Flappy, Gemstone>. This lets you use as many OnMessage types—and collision systems—as you need. Bevy will treat the message types and systems as being different types, and they can be run independently.

Now modify the collision function from the billiards example to emit the OnMessage type and be usable as a specialized service so that you can specify multiple collision types. Add the following to my_library/src/bevy_framework/bevy_collision/mod.rs:

FlappyCollision/my_library/src/bevy_framework/bevy_collision/mod.rs

```
❶ pub fn check_collisions<A, B>(
❷   quad_tree: Res<StaticQuadTree>,
❸   query_a: Query<(Entity, &Transform, &AxisAlignedBoundingBox), With<A>>,
    query_b: Query<(Entity, &Transform, &AxisAlignedBoundingBox), With<B>>,
❹   mut sender: EventWriter<OnCollision<A, B>>,
  ) where
    A: Component,
    B: Component,
  {
❺   let mut spatial_index: HashMap<usize, Vec<(Entity, Rect2D)>> =
      HashMap::new();

    query_b.iter().for_each(|(entity, transform, bbox)| {
      let bbox = bbox.as_rect(transform.translation.truncate());
      let in_node = quad_tree.smallest_node(&bbox);
      if let Some(contents) = spatial_index.get_mut(&in_node) {
        contents.push((entity, bbox));
      } else {
        spatial_index.insert(in_node, vec![(entity, bbox)]);
      }
    });

    query_a.iter().for_each(|(entity_a, transform_a, bbox_a)| {
      let bbox_a = bbox_a.as_rect(transform_a.translation.truncate());
      for node in quad_tree.intersecting_nodes(&bbox_a) {
        if let Some(contents) = spatial_index.get(&node) {
          for (entity_b, bbox_b) in contents {
            if entity_a != *entity_b && bbox_a.intersect(bbox_b) {
❻             sender.write(OnCollision {
                entity_a,
                entity_b: *entity_b,
❼               marker: PhantomData,
              });
            }
          }
        }
      }
    });
  }
```

❶ Make the check_collisions system generic, using the same specialization as OnMessage.

❷ Request the QuadTree as a read-only resource. Multiple collision detection checks can run concurrently.

❸ You can use generic types in queries, too. The specialized queries retrieve entity, transformation, and bounding box information for entities that also have the tag class A.

❹ Specializing the EventWriter to use A and B links it to the correct OnCollision message.

❺ The basic collision logic is the same as before.

❻ Submit an OnCollision message.

❼ When you use PhantomData, you have to initialize it, even though it won't do anything. You can just enter PhantomData as the value.

The library code for collision detection is now complete. Let's adjust Flappy Dragon to use the new system.

Update Flappy Dragon

Open flappy_dragon/src/main.rs. Find the macro that lists the systems to run, and add a collision detection request to the systems:

FlappyCollision/flappy_dragon_base/src/main.rs
```
run => [ flap, clamp, move_walls, hit_wall, cycle_animations,
    continual_parallax, physics_clock, sum_impulses, apply_gravity,
➤   apply_velocity, check_collisions::<Flappy, Obstacle> ],
```

You've specialized the collisions to refer to collisions between Flappy and Obstacle. This is the only type of collision present in Flappy Dragon: the dragon hitting a wall.

At the end of the Bevy initialization—after you add the animation resources—add the following code:

FlappyCollision/flappy_dragon_base/src/main.rs
```
.add_event::<OnCollision<Flappy, Obstacle>>()
```

Each OnCollision type is distinct. If you were using more collision types, you'd add them all here.

Next, in the setup() function, you need to create a QuadTree and give Flappy the Dragon a bounding box:

FlappyCollision/flappy_dragon_base/src/main.rs
```rust
fn setup(
  mut commands: Commands,
  mut rng: ResMut<RandomNumberGenerator>,
  assets: Res<AssetStore>,
  loaded_assets: Res<LoadedAssets>,
) {
  commands
    .spawn(Camera2d::default())
    .insert(FlappyElement);
  spawn_animated_sprite!(
    assets, commands, "flappy", -490.0, 0.0, 10.0, "Straight and Level",
    Flappy, FlappyElement,  Velocity::default(), ApplyGravity,
➤    AxisAlignedBoundingBox::new(62.0, 65.0)
  );
➤  commands.insert_resource(StaticQuadTree::new(Vec2::new(1024.0, 768.0), 4));
  build_wall(&mut commands, &assets, rng.range(-5..5), &loaded_assets);
```

Then, add a bounding box to walls spawned with the build_wall() function:

FlappyCollision/flappy_dragon_base/src/main.rs
```rust
fn build_wall(commands: &mut Commands, assets: &AssetStore, gap_y: i32,
  loaded_assets: &LoadedAssets)
{
  for y in -12..=12 {
    if y < gap_y - 4 || y > gap_y + 4 {
      spawn_image!(
        assets,
        commands,
        "wall",
        512.0,
        y as f32 * 32.0,
        10.0,
        loaded_assets,
        Obstacle,
        FlappyElement,
        Velocity::new(-4.0, 0.0, 0.0),
➤        AxisAlignedBoundingBox::new(32.0, 32.0)
      );
    }
  }
}
```

Finally, you can replace the inefficient hit_wall() function with a new function that receives messages from the collision detection system:

FlappyCollision/flappy_dragon_base/src/main.rs
```rust
fn hit_wall(
  mut collisions: EventReader<OnCollision<Flappy, Obstacle>>,
  mut state: ResMut<NextState<GamePhase>>,
  assets: Res<AssetStore>,
```

```
    loaded_assets: Res<LoadedAssets>,
    mut commands: Commands,
) {
    for _collision in collisions.read() {
        assets.play("crash", &mut commands, &loaded_assets);
        let _ = state.set(GamePhase::GameOver);
    }
}
```

And that's it. Run the game, and it's noticeably smoother. Collisions remain accurate, and the frame rate has improved. You've also extended my_library to provide a high-performance collision detection system.

Wrapping Up

In this chapter, you worked through a common library developer task. You identified a performance problem, built a focused test bed to examine different solutions, and ported the resulting solution into generic library code. You also learned about PhantomData, multitype generic specialization, and function type signatures. Flappy Dragon is now running fast, and your collision detection system is ready for prime time.

In the next chapter, you'll fine-tune your physics system to provide smooth rendering—even on the highest-end computer systems. You'll also learn how to use physics to predict the future. Finally, you'll apply a little polish to my_library and be ready to move on to another game that uses your library.

CHAPTER 9

Smooth Physics with Tweening

Flappy Dragon is looking pretty good. You've built a reusable assets system with integrated audio, an animation state machine, a parallax scrolling backgrounds, a reusable physics system, and a high-performance collision detection system. You could ship Flappy as is, but a few minor improvements can take Flappy from being a good game to being a great game.

Until now, the physics system has been running a fixed time step. That's perfect for physics calculations, and you've avoided the gradual accumulation of floating-point errors over time that accompany performing each physics calculation based on frame time. Unfortunately, fixed time steps also lead to some jerkiness in the game's rendering. If you slow down the physics time step, Flappy will visibly jump from position to position rather than rendering smoothly.

You're going to fix the jerkiness by adding a deterministic physics integration. You already know the starting position for each frame and the ending position for each frame—the positions are determined by the sum of velocities for an entity. This allows you to *tween* (smoothly interpolate) between the start and end positions, giving you smooth rendering, while also retaining the benefits of a fixed time step. Knowing the end position of a time step—effectively peering into the near future—also gives you the ability to predict pending collisions. It also helps with the common "falling through an object" problem found in some physics engines. "Fall through" occurs when a colliding object is moving so fast that it finishes a frame so deeply embedded in an object that a collision vector based on the ending position will be incorrect. If you watch the test bed closely, you occasionally see two balls "merge" and shoot off in inappropriate directions once they achieve sufficient velocity.

Smoothly Integrating Physics Steps

You already have the information you need for a smooth time step; you just haven't gathered it into one place yet. Let's start by collating the start and end frame positions for the physics entity into a new component:

```
FlappyWrap/my_library/src/bevy_framework/bevy_physics.rs
#[derive(Component)]
pub struct PhysicsPosition {
  pub start_frame: Vec2,
  pub end_frame: Vec2,
}

impl PhysicsPosition {
  pub fn new(start: Vec2) -> Self {
    Self {
      start_frame: start,
      end_frame: start,
    }
  }
}
```

This component stores the starting and ending positions for each frame. You'll use this to smoothly interpolate between the two positions. The constructor sets both the starting and ending positions to the initial position—no forces have been applied yet. You'll need to add this component to Flappy:

```
FlappyWrap/flappy_dragon_base/src/main.rs
spawn_animated_sprite!(
  assets, commands, "flappy", -490.0, 0.0, 10.0, "Straight and Level",
  Flappy, FlappyElement,  Velocity::default(), ApplyGravity,
  AxisAlignedBoundingBox::new(62.0, 65.0),
➤  PhysicsPosition::new(Vec2::new(-490.0, 0.0))
);
```

You've set the initial physics position to the same location as Flappy's rendering coordinates. Do the same for the walls:

```
FlappyWrap/flappy_dragon_base/src/main.rs
spawn_image!(
  assets,
  commands,
  "wall",
  512.0,
  y as f32 * 32.0,
  10.0,
  loaded_assets,
  Obstacle,
  FlappyElement,
  Velocity::new(-8.0, 0.0, 0.0),
```

```
    AxisAlignedBoundingBox::new(32.0, 32.0),
➤   PhysicsPosition::new(Vec2::new(512.0, y as f32 * 32.0))
);
```

Now that you have starting and ending positions attached to each physics entity, you need to update the apply_velocity() function to update the ending position instead of the actual screen/transformation position:

FlappyWrap/my_library/src/bevy_framework/bevy_physics.rs
```
pub fn apply_velocity(
  mut tick: EventReader<PhysicsTick>,
  mut movement: Query<(&Velocity, &mut PhysicsPosition)>,
) {
  for _tick in tick.read() {
    movement.iter_mut().for_each(|(velocity, mut position)| {
      position.end_frame += velocity.0.truncate();
    });
  }
}
```

Instead of editing the Transform component, you're now updating the PhysicsPosition component. The update logic remains the same; you add the sum of velocities to the position. Instead of directly moving the sprite, you're updating its future position.

The last step is to update the physics_clock() function to interpolate between the start and end positions. The first step is to add a new query to the function:

FlappyWrap/my_library/src/bevy_framework/bevy_physics.rs
```
pub fn physics_clock(
  mut clock: Local<PhysicsTimer>,
  time: Res<Time>,
  mut on_tick: EventWriter<PhysicsTick>,
➤ mut physics_position: Query<(&mut PhysicsPosition, &mut Transform)>,
) {
```

The physics_position query gives mutable access to the PhysicsPosition component and the Transform component.

Next, you need to update the logic for what happens when a physics tick is firing:

FlappyWrap/my_library/src/bevy_framework/bevy_physics.rs
```
let ms_since_last_call = time.delta().as_millis();
clock.0 += ms_since_last_call;
if clock.0 >= PHYSICS_TICK_TIME {
  clock.0 = 0;
➤ physics_position.iter_mut().for_each(|(mut pos, mut transform)| {
➤   transform.translation.x = pos.end_frame.x;
➤   transform.translation.y = pos.end_frame.y;
```

```
    pos.start_frame = pos.end_frame
  });
  on_tick.write(PhysicsTick);
}
```

Whenever a frame ends and the physics clock fires, you set each entity's transformation position to the end_frame from their PhysicsPosition component. Moving to the pre-determined ending position ensures that you know *exactly* where the entity is at the end of the frame, reducing error accumulation. You then set the PhysicsPosition's start_frame to equal the position at the end of the previous frame. You can run the game now, and it will behave similarly to before, but you've now laid the groundwork for smooth interpolated movement.

Finally, you need to add an else clause and perform interpolation when a frame is rendering and the physics clock hasn't fired:

FlappyWrap/my_library/src/bevy_framework/bevy_physics.rs
```
else {
  let frame_progress = clock.0 as f32 / PHYSICS_TICK_TIME as f32;
  physics_position.iter_mut().for_each(|(pos, mut transform)| {
    transform.translation.x = pos.start_frame.x
      + (pos.end_frame.x - pos.start_frame.x) * frame_progress;
    transform.translation.y = pos.start_frame.y
      + (pos.end_frame.y - pos.start_frame.y) * frame_progress;
  });
}
```

You start by calculating the portion (from 0 to 1) of the frame that has elapsed. You then use this fraction to interpolate between the start_frame and end_frame positions. This calculation is a simple linear interpolation; you can use fancier interpolation functions to get different effects. You then set the Transform component to the interpolated position.

Run the game now, and you'll see that it's moving smoothly, even if you have a 120Hz monitor. You've successfully added a deterministic integration to the physics system and smoothed out the rendering.

Now that you can reliably foresee the future, let's use your knowledge of the upcoming frame to make Flappy look towards its destination.

Rotating Your Dragon

Armed with the knowledge of the starting and ending positions for each frame, you can now predict collisions. You can also use this information to rotate Flappy to face its destination. This doesn't affect gameplay, but it makes the game look more alive, providing near instant feedback on the player's actions and the extent to which gravity is getting Flappy down.

Dead Reckoning

Simple linear interpolations are useful in networked gameplay. Because of lag, dogs chewing network cables, and random solar flares, you can't always be sure that every position update sent over the network will arrive. Networked games often send the current position and future position in updates and continue using the previously sent velocity to assume that movement continues in the event of packet loss. Dead reckoning can greatly improve the appearance of a networked game, and it can also be responsible for characters suddenly warping across the map when the player's Internet connection starts working again.

Add a new function to flappy_dragon_base/src/main.rs:

```
FlappyWrap/flappy_dragon_base/src/main.rs
fn rotate(
  mut physics_position: Query<(&PhysicsPosition, &mut Transform),
    With<Flappy>>,
) {
    physics_position.iter_mut().for_each(|(position, mut transform)| {
      if position.start_frame != position.end_frame {
        let start = position.start_frame;
        let end = position.end_frame;
        let angle = end.angle_to(start) * 10.0;
        transform.rotation = Quat::from_rotation_z(angle);
      }
    });
}
```

❶ Don't apply rotation if the starting and ending positions are the same. The positions will be the same at the very start of a physics tick, and resetting Flappy's rotation to horizontal looks bad.

❷ Flappy's position at the beginning of the physics cycle.

❸ Flappy's position at the end of the cycle.

❹ Make use of Bevy's Vec2 type's included angle_between() to calculate the angle between the start and end frame position vectors. The angles are rather small, so multiply by 10 to exaggerate Flappy's rotation.

❺ You can set the Transform's rotation variable to apply rotation to a sprite. Rotations are calculated as quaternions—a math construct similar to vectors, but good at calculating rotations. In 3D math, quaternions avoid the problem of *gimball lock*—when rotations can't be applied, leaving you stuck facing a particular direction.

You also need to add rotate to the list of systems Bevy will call:

FlappyWrap/flappy_dragon_base/src/main.rs

```
add_phase!(app, GamePhase, GamePhase::Flapping,
    start => [ setup ],
    run => [ flap, clamp, move_walls, hit_wall, cycle_animations,
➤      continual_parallax, physics_clock, sum_impulses, apply_gravity,
        apply_velocity, check_collisions::<Flappy, Obstacle>, rotate ],
    exit => [ cleanup::<FlappyElement> ]
);
```

Run the game. When you press the spacebar to flap the dragon's wings, Flappy rotates upwards. As gravity pulls Flappy toward their inevitable doom, Flappy rotates downward. With a simple system, you've taken advantage of the interpolating physics system and given the player great feedback about their actions.

Visualizing the near-future position of Flappy is a great way to give the player feedback about their actions. You can use this technique to do more than rotate Flappy. You can also use it to predict collision moments before they occur. Let's adjust the collision system to take advantage of your knowledge of both current and future positions.

Predicting Imminent Collisions

Now that you're predicting the future, you can use that information to predict collisions. The collision is inevitable because the position at the end of the physics frame is fixed. Predicting a collision before it occurs is useful when you want to play a sound effect prior to the collision or when you want to calculate the angle of the collision. If you calculate angles *after* a collision has occurred, the objects are already overlapping, and it becomes difficult to calculate the angle of collision without "backtracking" to previous positions.

Fortunately, notifying of future—but unavoidable—collisions is straightforward now that you're storing the beginning and ending positions for each physics frame.

Open src/my_library/bevy_framework/bevy_collision/mod.rs and add a use clause importing your PhysicsPosition component:

```
FlappyWrap/my_library/src/bevy_framework/bevy_collision/mod.rs
mod aabb;
mod rect2d;
mod static_quadtree;
pub use aabb::AxisAlignedBoundingBox;
pub use rect2d::Rect2D;
pub use static_quadtree::*;
use bevy::{prelude::*, platform::collections::HashMap};
use std::marker::PhantomData;
➤ use crate::PhysicsPosition;
```

Next, you need to update the check_collisions function to use the PhysicsPosition component instead of Bevy's built-in Transform component. Start by updating the queries in the function signature:

```
FlappyWrap/my_library/src/bevy_framework/bevy_collision/mod.rs
pub fn check_collisions<A, B>(
  quad_tree: Res<StaticQuadTree>,
➤   query_a: Query<
➤     (Entity, &PhysicsPosition, &AxisAlignedBoundingBox),
➤     With<A>
➤   >,
➤   query_b: Query<
➤     (Entity, &PhysicsPosition, &AxisAlignedBoundingBox),
➤     With<B>
➤   >,
  mut sender: EventWriter<OnCollision<A, B>>,
) where
  A: Component,
  B: Component,
```

You've replaced Transform with PhysicsPosition, giving you the end-of-frame positions. The remaining task is to replace all instances of transform.translate.truncate() with transform.end_frame:

FlappyWrap/my_library/src/bevy_framework/bevy_collision/mod.rs

```
query_b.iter().for_each(|(entity, transform, bbox)| {
    let bbox = bbox.as_rect(transform.end_frame);
    let in_node = quad_tree.smallest_node(&bbox);
    if let Some(contents) = spatial_index.get_mut(&in_node) {
        contents.push((entity, bbox));
    } else {
        spatial_index.insert(in_node, vec![(entity, bbox)]);
    }
});

query_a.iter().for_each(|(entity_a, transform_a, bbox_a)| {
    let bbox_a = bbox_a.as_rect(transform_a.end_frame);
    for node in quad_tree.intersecting_nodes(&bbox_a) {
        if let Some(contents) = spatial_index.get(&node) {
            for (entity_b, bbox_b) in contents {
                if entity_a != *entity_b && bbox_a.intersect(bbox_b) {
                    sender.write(OnCollision {
                        entity_a,
                        entity_b: *entity_b,
                        marker: PhantomData,
                    });
                }
            }
        }
    }
});
```

And that's all you need to use the interpolating physics system for collisions. Run the game now. You'll notice there's little visible change, but now your collision detection is future-proof. You'll make use of this feature in Chapter 11, Build a Mining Outpost on Mars, on page 219.

Wrapping Up

Congratulations! Flappy Dragon is in great shape. Despite only being 277 lines of code, you've implemented the following:

- A generic game state manager
- A reusable game assets system, including both graphics and audio
- Frame-based animation
- An animation state machine with scripting and transitions
- Parallax scrolling background layers
- QuadTree-based rapid collision detection

- Smooth physics via time-based integration
- Prediction of future positions and collisions

Best of all, the majority of these features are implemented in my_library, and you have a solid base on which to build future games.

As you worked through this chapter, you learned a lot about Bevy's features. You also mastered Rust declarative macros, generics, and traits, and you're well on your way to becoming a Rust expert.

In the next part of this book, you'll build a more advanced game: Mars Base One. You'll use all of the library features you've created so far and build a completely different game. You'll learn how to combine rendered entities into a mesh to improve rendering performance, and you'll use serialization and networking to build an online high-score table. You'll also discover a bunch of fun tricks to make your game look better.

Part IV

Mars Base One

CHAPTER 10

Welcome to Mars Base One

The first half of this book focused on library creation, and then using that library to help develop *Flappy Dragon* and *Pig*. As you built those games, you added assets, animation, physics, collision detection, and game state management. You also learned how to work with the Bevy engine.

With that work behind you, you're now ready to use your library to help create your next game: *Mars Base One*. As you build this game, you'll learn about multithreading, asynchronous network calls, and how to handle external data. You'll also learn about optimization, as well as a few visual tricks to draw your players into this game. But before you get started, let's work on an outline.

Building a Mars Base One Outline

It's always a good idea to have a plan before you start coding. Rather than build a full game design document, you'll outline only the high-level concepts. Let's consider the following ideas:

- Mars Base One is a game in which a rescue ship visits a tragedy-stricken mining base in orbit around Mars.
- The player must navigate the ship through a series of obstacles to reach the base.
- The player gains points for picking up stranded miners.
- The player loses health for hitting obstacles.
- The player has a finite amount of fuel and must hover near fuel pickups to acquire more.
- The game is physics-based, requiring careful navigation in a world that simulates exoatmospheric maneuvering and a weak gravitational pull.

You'll add these features to the game, building each one up as you go. You'll start with the game's skeleton, and then you'll add the rest of the content.

Let's start by building the game's skeleton.

Creating a Starting Point

First of all: some good news. You've already done most of the hard work by building my_library. You can start with a simple skeleton that initializes the library and gets the game running.

Start by choosing the parent directory into which you want to build the game. Then, create a new project like this:

```
cargo new mars_base_one
```

Next, edit the Cargo.toml file to include your library:

```
[package]
name = "mars_base_one"
version = "0.1.0"
edition = "2021"

[dependencies]
bevy = "0.16"
my_library = { path = "../my_library" }
```

Replace ../my_library with the path to the library you built in the previous chapters of this book.

Now you need to fill in src/main.rs. Start by importing Bevy's prelude and your library:

```
MarsBaseOneSkeleton/mars_base_zero/src/main.rs
use bevy::prelude::*;
use my_library::*;
```

Then—just as you did with Flappy Dragon—add a GamePhase and some elements to identify the player and game elements:

```
MarsBaseOneSkeleton/mars_base_zero/src/main.rs
#[derive(Clone, Copy, PartialEq, Eq, Debug, Hash, Default, States)]
enum GamePhase {
  #[default]
  Loading,
  MainMenu,
  Playing,
  GameOver,
}

#[derive(Component)]
struct GameElement;
```

```
#[derive(Component)]
struct Player;
```

Next, set up your main function to initialize the game and your library systems:

MarsBaseOneSkeleton/mars_base_zero/src/main.rs
```
fn main() -> anyhow::Result<()> {
  let mut app = App::new();
  add_phase!(app, GamePhase, GamePhase::Playing,
    start => [ setup ],
    run => [ end_game, physics_clock, sum_impulses, apply_gravity,
      apply_velocity ],
    exit => [ cleanup::<GameElement> ]
  );

  app.add_event::<Impulse>();
  app.add_event::<PhysicsTick>();
  app
    .add_plugins(DefaultPlugins.set(WindowPlugin {
      primary_window: Some(Window {
        title: "Mars Base One".to_string(),
        resolution: bevy::window::WindowResolution::new(1024.0, 768.0),
        ..default()
      }),
      ..default()
    }))
    .add_plugins(RandomPlugin)
    .add_plugins(GameStatePlugin::new(
      GamePhase::MainMenu,
      GamePhase::Playing,
      GamePhase::GameOver,
    ))
    .add_plugins(AssetManager::new())
    .insert_resource(Animations::new())
    .run();

  Ok(())
}
```

Finally, create a setup and game_over function to handle the game's setup and end:

MarsBaseOneSkeleton/mars_base_zero/src/main.rs
```
fn setup(
  mut commands: Commands,
  assets: Res<AssetStore>,
  loaded_assets: Res<LoadedAssets>,
) {
  commands
    .spawn(Camera2d::default())
    .insert(GameElement);
}
```

```
fn end_game(
  mut state: ResMut<NextState<GamePhase>>,
  assets: Res<AssetStore>,
) {
  //let _ = state.set(GamePhase::GameOver);//
}
```

❶ Uncomment this line to have the game immediately end when it starts, so you can see the game over screen.

The game will fail to run until you give it some menu graphics. You can copy game_over.png and main_menu.png from the code accompanying this book. Copy these files into your assets directory. The menu graphics look like this:

Run the game with cargo run, and you'll be greeted with a main menu. Press P to play, and the game will start—a blank window.

Congratulations! You created a short stub of a game in very little time. Even with the brevity, thanks to your library, you already support many features, including:

- A main menu
- A game over menu
- Game state tracking
- A physics system
- An animation system
- Asset handling

This is the power of creating a library: you can save yourself a ton of work and have a workable game skeleton in very little time.

All right, let's start adding the content.

Adding a Ship

Let's add a spaceship to the game. The ship is the
player's character that navigates Mars Base One.
Copy ship.png into the assets directory.

Now, let's add the ship to the game. First, you
need to add the ship to the game's assets. In the
main function, update the asset loader to include
the ship:

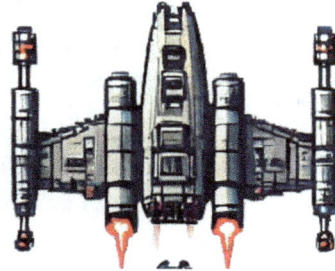

MarsBaseOneSkeleton/mars_base_one/src/main.rs
```
.add_plugins(GameStatePlugin::new(
  GamePhase::MainMenu,
  GamePhase::Playing,
  GamePhase::GameOver,
))
.add_plugins(AssetManager::new().add_image("ship", "ship.png")?)
.insert_resource(Animations::new())
```

Let's also spawn the ship into the game. In the setup function, add the following
code to spawn the ship:

MarsBaseOneSkeleton/mars_base_one/src/main.rs
```
commands
    .spawn(Camera2d::default())
    .insert(GameElement);

spawn_image!(
  assets,
  commands,
  "ship",
  0.0,
  0.0,
  1.0,
  &loaded_assets,
  GameElement,
  Player,
  Velocity::default(),
  PhysicsPosition::new(Vec2::new(0.0, 0.0)),
  ApplyGravity
);
```

Run the game now, and your ship is sitting in the middle of the screen.
Gravity pulls it down off the screen, and nothing happens.

Time to get the ship moving.

What Do the Components Do?

All of the components you're adding to the ship are part of the library you built in the previous section. You're applying Velocity and PhysicsPosition and using ApplyGravity to enable the physics engine's gravity support.

This is a good example of why it's useful to fill out the documentation tabs in your library code. Providing a quick description of what each component does makes it easier to remember how to use it later.

Moving the Ship

A game about a ship sitting alone in space and wondering why gravity still works might make for a good artistic statement, but it's not much of a game. Let's make the ship move.

Your library contains most of the code you need for this to work. The same physics system you used in Flappy Dragon can also work for ships, but you'll need to add a few more elements.

First, you need to know which way the ship is facing. Space vehicles typically work by facing a direction and firing their engines. Reaction mass is expelled from the engines, and the ship moves in the opposite direction—Newtonian physics in action. Bevy's rotation system—the same one you used to rotate Flappy—provides a way to track the ship's rotation. You can access a function on the Transform entity named rotation_y() to access the ship's rotation. Then you can combine this with the physics impulse system you built to move the ship.

Build the following system to move the ship:

MarsBaseOneSkeleton/mars_base_one/src/main.rs
```
fn movement(
  keyboard: Res<ButtonInput<KeyCode>>,
  mut player_query: Query<(Entity, &mut Transform), With<Player>>,
  mut impulses: EventWriter<Impulse>,
) {
  let Ok((entity, mut transform)) = player_query.single_mut() else {
    return;
  };
  if keyboard.pressed(KeyCode::ArrowLeft) {
❶   transform.rotate(Quat::from_rotation_z(f32::to_radians(2.0)));
  }
  if keyboard.pressed(KeyCode::ArrowRight) {
❷   transform.rotate(Quat::from_rotation_z(f32::to_radians(-2.0)));
  }
  if keyboard.pressed(KeyCode::ArrowUp) {
```

```
❸      impulses.write(Impulse {
         target: entity,
❹        amount: transform.local_y().as_vec3(),
         absolute: false,
         source: 1,
       });
   }
}
```

❶ When the left arrow is pressed, modify the ship's Transform to rotate counter-clockwise with a negative angle (in radians).

❷ When the right arrow is pressed, do the opposite and rotate the spaceship clockwise.

❸ Firing the ship's thruster applies an impulse. Just like flapping the dragon's wings provided an upward impulse, this impulse will provide a push forward.

❹ Using the local_y() function provides a vector indicating the local—already transformed—direction of the sprite. Bevy provides local_*() vectors for all three axes: X, Y, and Z.

You also need to enable the system in the main function:

```
add_phase!(app, GamePhase, GamePhase::Playing,
  start => [ setup ],
  run => [ movement, end_game, physics_clock,
    sum_impulses, apply_gravity, apply_velocity,
    terminal_velocity.after(apply_velocity) ],
  exit => [ cleanup::<GameElement> ]
);
```

If you run the game now, you'll notice the ship behaves as if it's on an ice rink. Press the "up" arrow to add velocity and the "left" and "right" arrows to rotate your ship. You'll see that you can slide around the screen, but you can't stop, and nothing happens when you hit the edges—but hey, at least you're moving.

Did you happen to notice something else?

If you press the "up" arrow for too long, you'll see that the ship moves *really* fast. That happens because the movement impulses are being added every frame—the longer you hold the key, the faster you go. This can be fun, but it makes it far too easy to exceed a reasonable velocity, which ultimately will cause the ship to zoom uncontrollably off the screen. Let's clamp the ship's maximum velocity with a terminal_velocity system:

MarsBaseOneSkeleton/mars_base_one/src/main.rs

```
fn terminal_velocity(mut player_query: Query<&mut Velocity, With<Player>>) {
  let Ok(mut velocity) = player_query.single_mut() else {
    return;
  };
  let v2 = velocity.0.truncate();
  if v2.length() > 5.0 {
    let v2 = v2.normalize() * 5.0;
    velocity.0.x = v2.x;
    velocity.0.y = v2.y;
  }
}
```

Enable this system in main as well:

```
add_phase!(app, GamePhase, GamePhase::Playing,
  start => [ setup ],
  run => [ movement, end_game, physics_clock,
    sum_impulses,
    apply_gravity,
    apply_velocity,
    terminal_velocity.after(apply_velocity) ],
  exit => [ cleanup::<GameElement> ]
);
```

Notice that we have something new! terminal_velocity.after(apply_velocity) means that the terminal_velocity system will run after the apply_velocity system. This is important because you want to clamp the velocity after it has been applied, so that the ship's speed is limited to a maximum value.

Normalizing Vectors

"Normalizing" a vector is a math term, meaning that you scale the vector so that its total length equals 1. The relative lengths of the vector's components remain the same. This allows you to retain the direction of travel for the ship, even while limiting maximum velocity.

Excellent, now you can't move too fast. You can still slide around the screen, but your speed is constrained. You can have some fun zooming around, fighting gravity.

With the movement system in place, it's time to add the game over conditions.

Adding Game Over Conditions

Let's set up a temporary game over condition so that the game will end when the ship leaves the screen. You'll add the actual end-game conditions as you flesh out the game, but this is a good start. Update the end_game function to end the game if the ship leaves the screen:

MarsBaseOneSkeleton/mars_base_one/src/main.rs
```
fn end_game(
  mut state: ResMut<NextState<GamePhase>>,
  player_query: Query<&Transform, With<Player>>,
) {
  let Ok(transform) = player_query.single() else {
    return;
  };
  if transform.translation.y < -384.0 || transform.translation.y > 384.0 ||
    transform.translation.x < -512.0 || transform.translation.x > 512.0
  {
    state.set(GamePhase::GameOver);
  }
}
```

You now have the basis of a working game. Run the game (cargo run), and you'll see a menu screen. Press P to play and move your ship around the screen. To test the new game over condition, move the ship to the edge of the screen and attempt to keep going. If all goes well, the game should end.

You can't do much else, but you have a working game skeleton.

Wrapping Up

In this chapter, you built a game skeleton, demonstrating the power of the library you created. With the help of the library code, you added a ship, gravity, physics-based movement, and a menu system—using very little code. You also learned to retrieve direction vectors from Bevy's rotation system and apply them for simple movement. You also learned to clamp the ship's velocity to prevent it from moving too fast. In other words, your hard work so far has paid off, and you can get started on the fun bits of a game in very little code.

In the next chapter, you'll add some more content to the game. You'll build a world and learn how to hide world-building in a system thread. You'll discover the "secrets" to passing data between threads, which allows you to keep the player entertained during world-building. You'll also find out how to optimize the rendering of many entities at once.

CHAPTER 11

Build a Mining Outpost on Mars

In the previous chapter, you built the beginnings of a game. The player—a spaceship—can rotate, thrust, move around the screen, and is affected by gravity. A title screen welcomes the new player, and a game over screen—albeit a temporary placeholder—heralds the end of the game. And, thanks to your fancy new library, you built all of this with relatively little code.

In this chapter, you're going to turn the empty "space" into a Mars mining colony. Girders will fence off the playable area, and players won't be able to fly through them. You'll use procedural generation to generate maps, so they'll be different with each new game. You'll adjust the game camera for a more immersive experience, and you'll enable collision detection—letting you explore the depths of the mine. After you get all that done, you'll move this world-building process into a separate thread and learn about inter-thread communication.

Let's get started with the camera actions.

Zooming In

Bevy's camera system is pretty comprehensive—and so far, you've used the bare minimum. It can do a lot more than provide a fixed view of the world. Let's adjust the camera to be closer to the player. This gives both a better sense of speed and direction, but it also makes the game more immersive—you can't see the whole map, only what's in front of you. You're also going to add a component to label your camera as MyCamera. Adding the component makes it easy to find the camera later when you want to adjust it.

Start by defining the MyCamera component in src/main.rs:

MarsBaseOneWorldBuilder/mars_base_one/src/main.rs
```
#[derive(Component)]
struct MyCamera;
```

MyCamera is a tag component, which doesn't contain any data. The next step is to adjust the camera itself. You aren't going to move the world around the camera; instead, you're going to move Bevy's camera and let it take care of the transformation for you.

Edit src/main.rs and adjust the setup() function:

MarsBaseOneWorldBuilder/mars_base_one/src/main.rs
```
fn setup(
  mut commands: Commands,
  assets: Res<AssetStore>,
  loaded_assets: Res<LoadedAssets>,
  mut rng: ResMut<RandomNumberGenerator>,
) {
❶  let cb = Camera2d::default();
❷  let projection = Projection::Orthographic(OrthographicProjection {
    scaling_mode: ScalingMode::WindowSize,
    scale: 0.5,
    ..OrthographicProjection::default_2d()
  });

  commands
    .spawn(cb).insert(projection)
    .insert(GameElement)
❸    .insert(MyCamera);
```

❶ Create the Camera2d like you did before, but this time as a mutable variable so that you can edit it prior to spawning the camera into the world.

❷ Divide the default scale by 2.0. This halves the size of the visible region, effectively zooming in. Bevy will take care of the transformation for you.

❸ Spawn the camera and label it as a GameElement and MyCamera. The first label ensures that the camera is included in the cleanup phase, and the second label makes it easy to find the camera later.

Run the game now, and you'll see a double-sized spaceship. You'll also notice that the camera is closer to the player:

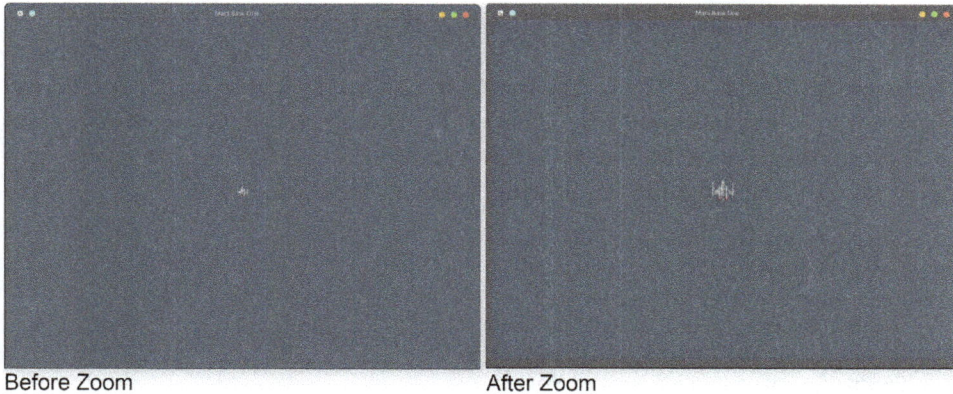

Before Zoom · After Zoom

How Do Game Cameras Work?

All your entities and components' locations are specified in *world space*. World space is a fixed coordinate system that doesn't change; everything in your scene is located relative to world space. The camera is a special entity that transforms world space into *screen space*. Screen space is a coordinate system based on pixels inside your game window. Screen space can change if the window is resized, while world space remains constant.

When you specify a camera's position, rotation, scale, and scaling mode, you're telling Bevy how to transform world space into screen space. Bevy then manages the transformation for you: items that are off-screen won't be rendered, and everything is scaled to fit the current window viewport.

Under the hood, the transformation from world space to screen space is done with a *projection matrix*. The projection matrix is a mathematical construct that takes into account the camera's position, rotation, and scale and transforms its world space into screen space. As each frame is prepared, every entity's position is multiplied by the projection matrix to determine where it should be rendered on the screen.

Video cards are optimized for matrix multiplication, and they can often perform millions of them per second. This is why modern games can render thousands of entities at once and still maintain a high frame rate.

If you move the spaceship around, it's possible for it to move out of the camera's view. Let's make a few changes so that the camera follows the player.

Making the Camera Follow the Player

There are pre-existing Bevy plugins that can make the camera follow the player. It's a simple enough task, so you're going to write your own system to do it. Adding a dependency for a tiny function is overkill, and this way, you know how to write it. Start by adding a new function to src/main.rs:

MarsBaseOneWorldBuilder/mars_base_one/src/main.rs
```
fn camera_follow(
  player_query: Query<&Transform,
❶    (With<Player>, Without<MyCamera>)>,
  mut camera_query: Query<&mut Transform,
❷    (With<MyCamera>, Without<Player>)>,
) {
❸  let Ok(player) = player_query.single() else {
    return;
  };
❹  let Ok(mut camera) = camera_query.single_mut() else {
    return;
  };
  camera.translation = Vec3::new(player.translation.x, player.translation.y,
❺    10.0);
}
```

❶ Query for the player's position. This is a read-only query, which means it isn't mutable. You're using two Bevy query helpers here: With, which lets you require that a component exist without having to actually read it, and Without, which lets you require that a component doesn't exist.

❷ Query for the camera's position. This is a mutable query, which you're going to use to update the camera's position.

❸ The single function retrieves only one entity from a query. Since there shouldn't ever be more than one player, this makes sense. This function returns a reference to the player's Transform component, which contains the player's position in the translation field.

❹ single_mut retrieves a single entity, giving a mutable reference to the entity's Transform component.

❺ Update the camera's position to match the player's position. You're hard-coding the z position to 10.0. This process ensures that the player remains rendered on top of any other entities in the game.

This is a relatively simple system that reads the player's position and updates the camera's position to match it.

Now that the camera_follow system is written, you need to add it to the game loop. Edit src/main.rs, and in the main function, adjust the add_phase macro to include the camera_follow systems. Notice that we're making sure we apply camera movement after the terminal_velocity system—so we know exactly where the spaceship is:

```
add_phase!(app, GamePhase, GamePhase::Playing,
    start => [ setup ],
    run => [ movement, end_game, physics_clock, sum_impulses, apply_gravity,
        apply_velocity,
        terminal_velocity.after(apply_velocity),
        camera_follow.after(terminal_velocity) ],
    exit => [ cleanup::<GameElement> ]
);
```

Run the game now, and you'll see the camera is closer to the player. You'll also notice that the camera follows the player around.

Now that you have a ship and camera system in place, it's time to build a world for the player to explore.

Building a Martian Mining Outpost

Designing great levels is an art form. You could spend hours creating the perfect level, sharing it with friends, and tweaking it until it's "just right." I'd encourage you to experiment with that process.

However, for this book, you're going to use procedural level generation. The map will never be the same twice, and you can tweak the algorithm to make it more or less challenging. Some maps will be better than others, but the game will be much more replayable because it's different every time.

Let's set some map-generation goals:

- The whole map should be walkable. There should be no "islands" that the player can't reach.

- There should be a central column entry into the world that represents the initial borehole that started the mining operation.

- The map should include rooms that are connected by corridors. The corridors need to be wide enough to fly through.

- No boring, rectangular rooms. Each room should have a heavily eroded look with lots of nooks and crannies.

To accomplish these goals, you're going to combine some procedural generation algorithms. These algorithms are derived from the Rust Roguelike Tutorial.[1] Combining algorithms is often the best way to "fine-tune" a generation to ensure you get what you want, but it isn't the same each time.

1. Create a solid map.
2. Clear the center.
3. Blast some holes in the map to represent rooms.
4. Carve a linear corridor between rooms.
5. Carve a vertical borehole.
6. Apply "outwards diffusion" to the map to give it a more eroded look.

You're going to need the MarsBaseOneWorldBuilder/assets/ground.png image for this section. Download the file and place it in the assets directory of your project.

Center the Player

While we're building the world, we want the player to start at 0,0—right next to the world. Edit the setup() function as follows:

```
spawn_image!(
  assets,
  commands,
  "ship",
  0.0,
➤ 0.0,
  1.0,
  &loaded_assets,
  GameElement,
  Player,
  Velocity::default(),
➤ PhysicsPosition::new(Vec2::new(0.0, 0.0))//,
  //ApplyGravity(0.2),
  //AxisAlignedBoundingBox::new(24.0, 24.0)
);
```

You'll want to change this back at the end of the chapter.

Create a Solid Map

Start by adding a structure to src/main.rs to represent the world:

MarsBaseOneWorldBuilder/mars_base_one/src/main.rs
```
struct World {
  solid: Vec<bool>,
  width: usize,
  height: usize,
```

---

1. http://bfnightly.bracketproductions.com/chapter23-prefix.html

```
}
```

The solid field is an array of booleans. If a cell is true, it's a solid wall. Otherwise, it's an open space. The width and height fields are the dimensions of the world.

It'll be helpful to have a function to convert a 2D coordinate into a 1D index. Add this function to src/main.rs:

MarsBaseOneWorldBuilder/mars_base_one/src/main.rs
```
impl World {
  fn mapidx(&self, x: usize, y: usize) -> usize {
    y * self.width + x
  }
```

Next, let's add the beginnings of a constructor to the World structure. This constructor will create a solid map. Add the following code to src/main.rs:

```
// inside impl World
fn new(width: usize, height: usize, rng: &mut RandomNumberGenerator) -> Self {
  let mut result = Self {
    width,
    height,
    solid: vec![true; width * height],
  };
  // ... more to come
}
```

This is a pretty normal constructor. You're creating a new World structure with width and height passed in as parameters. The solid vector sets every entry to true—representing a solid tile—for a width x height grid. The grid represents rows of tiles, indexed as (y * width)+1. You'll be clearing some of these tiles later.

It helps to be able to see your progress, so let's add a function to spawn the world into the game. Add this code to src/main.rs:

MarsBaseOneWorldBuilder/mars_base_one/src/main.rs
```
fn spawn(&self, assets: &AssetStore, commands: &mut Commands,
  loaded_assets: &LoadedAssets)
{
  for y in 0 .. self.height {
    for x in 0 .. self.width {
      if self.solid[y * self.width + x] {
        let position = Vec2::new(
          (x as f32 * 24.0) - ((self.width as f32 / 2.0) * 24.0),
          (y as f32 * 24.0) - ((self.height as f32) * 24.0),
        );

        // spawn a solid block
        spawn_image!(
          assets,
          commands,
```

```
        "ground",
        position.x,
        position.y,
        -1.0,
        &loaded_assets,
        GameElement,
        Ground,
        PhysicsPosition::new(Vec2::new(
          position.x,
          position.y,
        )),
        AxisAlignedBoundingBox::new(24.0, 24.0)
      );
    }
  }
 }
}
```

There's no new functionality here. You iterate over the map tiles, and if a tile is solid, you spawn it into the world using the spawn_image! macro from Chapter 6, Manage Your Game Assets, on page 111.

You also need to load the image. In your Bevy setup, add the following:

```
.add_plugins(
  AssetManager::new().add_image("ship", "ship.png")?
  .add_image("ground", "ground.png")?
)
```

You're going to be using the collision detection system from Chapter 8, Build Obstacles and Collision Detection, on page 163, to handle collisions, so you need to include a PhysicsPosition and AxisAlignedBoundingBox component on each solid tile. You've also referenced a Ground type, identifying a ground tile. Add that to src/main.rs:

MarsBaseOneWorldBuilder/mars_base_one/src/main.rs
```
#[derive(Component)]
struct Ground;
```

Finally, add the following code to the end of the setup() function:

```
let world = World::new(200, 200, &mut rng);
world.spawn(&assets, &mut commands, &loaded_assets);
commands.insert_resource(StaticQuadTree::new(Vec2::new(10240.0, 7680.0), 6));
```

Run the game now, and you'll see a solid world:

Yes, you *can* fly through solid walls but only because you haven't implemented collision detection yet. Before you get to that, let's make the map more interesting.

Clear the Center of the Map

At the center of the map, the miners have dug out a core chamber. The central chamber is used as the basis of a lot of the rest of the procedural generation—it's not all that amazing. You're going to need to clear tiles on the map to create rooms and corridors. Implement another function as part of World:

MarsBaseOneWorldBuilder/mars_base_one/src/main.rs
```
fn clear_tiles(&mut self, x: usize, y: usize) {
  for offset_x in -1 ..= 1 {
    for offset_y in -1 ..= 1 {
      let x = x as isize + offset_x;
      let y = y as isize + offset_y;
      if x > 0 && x < self.width as isize -1 &&
        y > 0 && y < self.height as isize
      {
        let idx = self.mapidx(x as usize, y as usize);
        self.solid[idx] = false;
      }
    }
  }
}
```

Rather than clearing one tile, you're clearing a block of tiles around the specified tile. By doing so, you make the game less "fiddly" by not requiring the player's reflexes to be *quite* as perfect to avoid continually bouncing off walls. You've added bounds-checking to ensure that you don't try to clear tiles outside the map.

Let's start by clearing the exact center of the map. Add the following code to the end of the new function in World:

```
// Set the center tile and surrounding tiles to be empty
result.clear_tiles(width / 2, height / 2);
```

Run the game now, and your ship will fall into a gap at the center of the map:

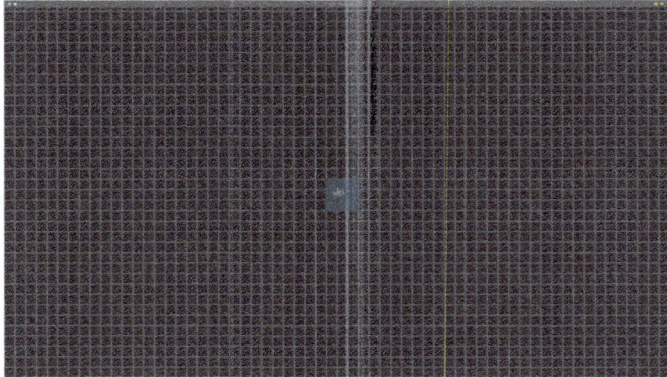

That's a useful starting point because now you know that clearing tiles works. Let's make some more holes in the world.

Blast Some Holes in the Map

The generation strategy assumes that miners have carved chambers into the solid rock they're mining, which means you need to randomly blast these chambers. You also need to ensure these holes are connected. It makes logical sense—the miners had to dig from one position to another. It also makes the game playable, since the ship can't fly through solid tiles. The player is guaranteed to be able to reach the whole map.

Let's start by making a vector to store the locations of the holes. Add the following code to the new() function immediately after clearing the center of the map:

```
// Blast some holes in the center
let mut holes = vec![(width / 2, height / 2)];
```

The initial center hole is pre-added, ensuring that when you come to carve corridors, you have a starting point. Next, let's carve some big holes:

MarsBaseOneWorldBuilder/mars_base_one/src/main.rs
```
for _ in 0 .. 10 {
  let x = rng.range(5 .. width-5);
  let y = rng.range(5 .. height-5);
  holes.push((x, y));
  result.clear_tiles(x, y);
```

```
    result.clear_tiles(x+2, y);
    result.clear_tiles(x-2, y);
    result.clear_tiles(x, y+2);
    result.clear_tiles(x, y-2);
}
```

Run the game now, and you'll see a map with a few holes in it. Note that the camera shot was adjusted to zoom out for this image so that you could see the entire map:

You can fly around, but there's no connection between the holes. Let's add some corridors.

Carving a Linear Corridor Between Rooms

You're going to add corridors by carving a line between points on the map. Add the following function to your World implementation:

```
MarsBaseOneWorldBuilder/mars_base_one/src/main.rs
fn clear_line(&mut self, start: (usize, usize), end: (usize, usize)) {
  let (mut x, mut y) = (start.0 as f32, start.1 as f32);
  let (slope_x, slope_y) = (
    (end.0 as f32 - x) / self.width as f32,
    (end.1 as f32 - y) / self.height as f32,
  );
  loop {
    let (tx, ty) = (x as usize, y as usize);
    if tx < 1 || tx > self.width-1 || ty < 1 || ty > self.height-1 {
      break;
    }
    if tx == end.0 && ty == end.1 {
      break;
    }
    self.clear_tiles(x as usize, y as usize);
    x += slope_x;
    y += slope_y;
  }
}
```

❶ Calculate the slope between the start and the end points. This is the difference between each x and y coordinate divided by the distance. This value serves as the amount by which to increment the cursor's position as you iterate along the line.

❷ Repeat until break; is called.

❸ Exit the loop if the line has left the map.

❹ Exit the loop if the cursor has reached the destination.

❺ Clear the tiles at the current cursor position, and move the cursor by adding the slope.

The clear_line() function implements a basic line-drawing algorithm by calculating the slope between the start and the end, and clearing tiles along the way.

Line Drawing in Games

There are many ways to plot a line. In 2D games, Bresenham's line algorithm is often used. It's fast and takes into account the fact that pixels have integer coordinates.[an]

When working with an engine that works with floating-point coordinates, it's more common to use floating-point numbers and let the video card handle the transformation from world space to screen space. This is what you're doing here. This can result in lines that aren't perfectly straight, but it's good enough for what you need here.

Let's use the clear_line() to connect the rooms. Add the following to the end of the new function in World:

```
MarsBaseOneWorldBuilder/mars_base_one/src/main.rs
// Cut a line between each hole
for i in 0 .. holes.len() {
  let start = holes[i];
  let end = holes[(i + 1) % holes.len()];
  result.clear_line(start, end);
}
```

If you run the game and zoom around a bit, you'll find that all of the rooms are now connected, giving you the beginnings of a mine-like structure:

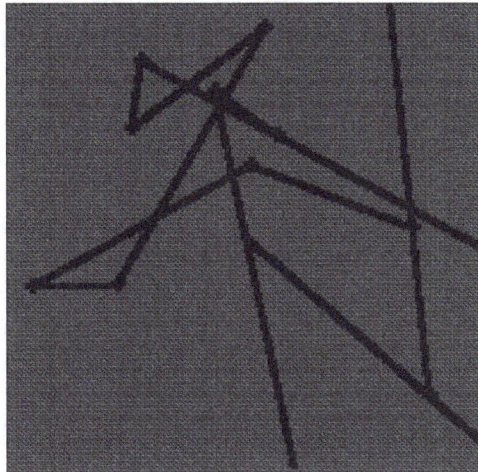

There's no obvious way into the mine from above, so let's add a vertical borehole.

Carve a Vertical Borehole

You're going to add a vertical borehole to the map. This hole will be the entrance to the mine. Add the following code to the end of the new function in World:

```
// Carve a borehole
for y in height/2 .. height {
  result.clear_tiles(width / 2, y);
}
```

There's now a vertical entrance carved into the map:

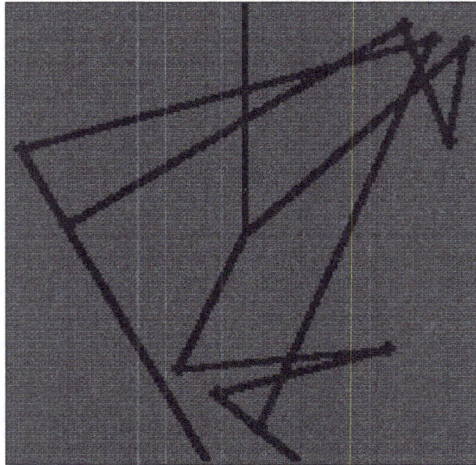

That's better. Now you can fly into the mine. But the map is a bit boring. Let's add some erosion.

Apply Outwards Diffusion to Erode the Map

Outward diffusion is a popular procedural generation technique for making a boring structure look more natural. It works by picking a "starting point" from a known open location and randomly selecting a "target" point. A ray is then traced from the starting point to the ending point, checking for collisions with a solid tile at each step. If a collision is detected, the tile is marked as open. This is repeated many times, giving the map a more eroded look.

You'll need a support function to find a target—a solid tile, selected randomly from the map. Add the following function to your World implementation's new() function:

MarsBaseOneWorldBuilder/mars_base_one/src/main.rs

```rust
fn find_random_closed_tile(&self, rng: &mut RandomNumberGenerator)
  -> (usize, usize)
{
  loop {
    let x = rng.range(0 .. self.width);
    let y = rng.range(0 .. self.height);
    let idx = self.mapidx(x, y);
    if self.solid[idx] {
      return (x, y);
    }
  }
}
```

Next, add the following function to your World implementation:

MarsBaseOneWorldBuilder/mars_base_one/src/main.rs

```rust
    // Outward diffusion
    let mut done = false;
    while !done {
      let start_tile = holes[rng.range(0..10)];
      let target = result.find_random_closed_tile(rng);
      let (mut x, mut y) = (start_tile.0 as f32, start_tile.1 as f32);
      let (slope_x, slope_y) = (
        (target.0 as f32 - x) / width as f32,
        (target.1 as f32 - y) / height as f32,
      );

      loop {
        if x < 1.0 || x > width as f32 || y < 1.0 || y > height as f32 {
          break;
        }
        let tile_id = result.mapidx(x as usize, y as usize);
        if result.solid[tile_id] {
          result.clear_tiles(x as usize, y as usize);
          break;
        }
        x += slope_x;
        y += slope_y;
      }

      let solid_count = result.solid.iter().filter(|s| **s).count();
      let solid_percent = solid_count as f32 / (width * height) as f32;
      if solid_percent < 0.6 { done = true; }
    }

    result
}
```

Run the game now, and you'll see the ship is flying around a much more interesting map:

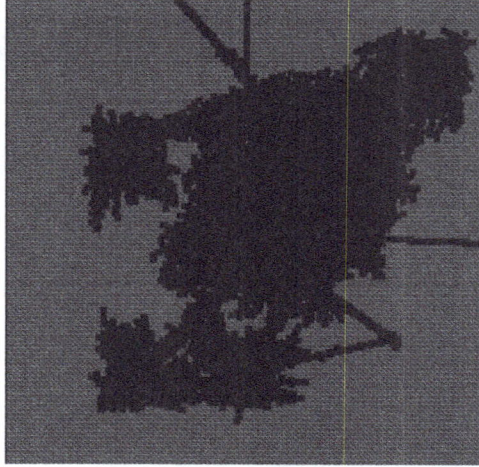

There's a borehole, defined rooms and corridors, and a relatively natural, eroded look.

You'll also see a few "floating" pieces of ground. That's ok, you're going to use those later.

You can radically change the look and feel of the map with a few simple changes:

- Changing the number of holes and corridors you carve will change the complexity of the map.
- Changing the if solid_percent < 0.6 { done = true; } line lets you decide how much of the world should be eroded away. Higher numbers will give you more rock.

Your ship still isn't interacting with the map, so you need to add collision detection.

Bouncing Off Walls

You created an efficient, QuadTree-based collision-detection system in Chapter 8, Build Obstacles and Collision Detection, on page 163. In your world spawning function, you already added tag components to walls and added a Ground type to identify them. All that remains is to wire up the collision system and handle bouncing off walls.

Your library's extended collision detection becomes very important here. You know the position of the player and the walls *at the beginning* of the frame, and you also know that at the *end* of the frame, a collision will occur. So you have the player's location as a valid position, not clipped inside the wall. This is important because you're going to be bouncing the player off the wall. If you clipped the player's position inside the wall, the player would be stuck inside the wall, and the collision system would keep bouncing the player back and forth.

Let's start by enabling collisions between the player and the walls. In the setup() function, enable Player versus Ground collision events:

```
.add_event::<OnCollision<Player, Ground>>()
```

Next, add the following system to GamePhase:

```
add_phase!(app, GamePhase, GamePhase::Playing,
    start => [ setup ],
    run => [ movement, end_game, physics_clock, sum_impulses,
      apply_gravity, apply_velocity,
      terminal_velocity.after(apply_velocity),
      check_collisions::<Player, Ground>, bounce,
      camera_follow.after(terminal_velocity)
    ],
    exit => [ cleanup::<GameElement> ]
);
```

You've enabled collision detection, but you still need to write the bounce() system. The plan is to take the player's position and the wall position and apply an impulse that prevents the collision from actually occurring. Add the following code to src/main.rs:

MarsBaseOneWorldBuilder/mars_base_one/src/main.rs
```
fn bounce(
❶   mut collisions: EventReader<OnCollision<Player, Ground>>,
❷   mut player_query: Query<&PhysicsPosition, With<Player>>,
❸   ground_query: Query<&PhysicsPosition, With<Ground>>,
❹   mut impulses: EventWriter<Impulse>,
) {
    let mut bounce = Vec2::default();
    let mut entity = None;
    let mut bounces = 0;
❺   for collision in collisions.read() {
        if let Ok(player) = player_query.single_mut() {
            if let Ok(ground) = ground_query.get(collision.entity_b) {
                entity = Some(collision.entity_a);
❻               let difference = player.start_frame - ground.start_frame;
                bounces += 1;
❼               bounce = difference;
            }
        }
    }
❽   if bounce != Vec2::default() {
❾       bounce = bounce.normalize();
```

```
      impulses.write(Impulse {
        target: entity.unwrap(),
        amount: Vec3::new(
          bounce.x / bounces as f32,
          bounce.y / bounces as f32,
          0.0
        ),
        absolute: true,
        source: 2,
      });
  }
}
```

❶ Read any collision events.

❷ Query the player's position to allow you to update the player.

❸ Query ground positions.

❹ An EventWriter to let you send impulses to the physics system.

❺ Iterate through detected collisions.

❻ If a collision occurred and both the player and the wall they're going to hit are valid, then calculate a vector describing the difference in position between the player and the wall at the start of the frame.

❼ It's possible that the player will be about to hit more than one wall. Add the player-to-wall vectors together and note how many collisions were encountered.

❽ Only apply an impulse if the sum of bounces isn't zero. This prevents any division by zero errors from occurring.

❾ Normalize the bounce vector: preserve the direction, but scale it to a total length of 1.0.

❿ Apply the average of the bounces to the player as an absolute impulse. It's absolute, so it replaces any other impulses that may be occurring. This simplifies the overall math as gravity is no longer part of the equation.

You also need to give the player and the walls a bounding box. In the setup() function, uncomment the AxisAlignedBoundingBox component for the player:

```
spawn_image!(
  assets,
  commands,
  "ship",
  0.0,
  200.0,
  1.0,
```

```
    &loaded_assets,
    GameElement,
    Player,
    Velocity::default(),
    PhysicsPosition::new(Vec2::new(0.0, 200.0))//,
    //ApplyGravity(0.2),
➤   AxisAlignedBoundingBox::new(24.0, 24.0)
  );
```

In the spawn() function of World, uncomment the AxisAlignedBoundingBox component for the walls:

```
spawn_image!(
  assets,
  commands,
  "ground",
  position.x,
  position.y,
  -1.0,
  &loaded_assets,
  GameElement,
  Ground,
  PhysicsPosition::new(Vec2::new(
    position.x,
    position.y,
  )),
➤   AxisAlignedBoundingBox::new(24.0, 24.0)
  );
```

Run the game now, and your ship will bounce off walls. You can explore the map, and it feels like the game is coming together. But there's a problem: a noticeable pause while the world generates. Let's fix that next.

Adding a Background Thread for World Building

Generating the world is a slow process, which gets even slower as you add more functionality to the game. That's ok; it's a normal price to pay for using procedural generation. What isn't ok is that the game pauses while the world is being generated.

On some platforms, if the main loop pauses for too long, the operating system will kill the game. You need to move the world building into a separate thread.

World generation is a great candidate for a separate thread: world creation doesn't rely on any volatile game state, runs independently of the game loop, and has well-defined starting and ending points. You just need a way to indicate when the world is ready and add it to the game.

Let's make use of the game state system to add a new state for world building:

You Already Have Threads

Your game is already multithreaded. Bevy divides your systems between threads and handles the concurrency for you. Bevy even provides a built-in mechanism for background tasks, but this book is going to rely on Rust primitives, giving you an opportunity to learn more about threading.

MarsBaseOneWorldBuilder/mars_base_one_threaded/src/main.rs
```
#[derive(Clone, Copy, PartialEq, Eq, Debug, Hash, Default, States)]
enum GamePhase {
  #[default]
  Loading,
  MainMenu,
  WorldBuilding,
  Playing,
  GameOver,
}
```

In the setup() function, add a new phase for it immediately after the GamePhase::Playing setup:

MarsBaseOneWorldBuilder/mars_base_one_threaded/src/main.rs
```
add_phase!(app, GamePhase, GamePhase::WorldBuilding,
  start => [ spawn_builder ],
  run => [ show_builder ],
  exit => [ ]
);
```

When the world-building phase starts, you're going to call its own spawn_builder function. On each tick, your show_builder function will keep the player apprised of progress and check to see if the world is ready yet. If it is, the game will spawn the world and transition into the Playing state.

In Chapter 3, Optimize and Benchmark Your Library, on page 49, you learned to use a Mutex to provide runtime locking for access to a variable between threads. Rust's fearless concurrency guarantees won't let you avoid using a locking primitive, which is a good thing—race conditions are a *bear* to debug. The benchmarking in that chapter showed a downside to using a Mutex. Mutex access is quite slow compared to "normal" code. You need a way to indicate that the world is ready (or not), and it'll be checked on every rendered frame, so it would be nice to not have to lock a Mutex every frame.

Rust provides *atomic* types for faster—but still safe—access to shared data. Atomics are only available for "primitive" types like integers, booleans, and other types that are directly supported by your CPU. You're going to use an

AtomicBool to indicate when the world is ready. Add the following code to the WorldBuilder structure:

MarsBaseOneWorldBuilder/mars_base_one_threaded/src/main.rs
```
static WORLD_READY: AtomicBool = AtomicBool::new(false);
```

Atomics

An *atomic* operation is an operation that's guaranteed to execute in a single CPU cycle, without being interrupted. It also provides a guarantee that if you have multiple CPU cores executing at once, the operation will be completed in order and without the potential for multiple cores to interfere with one another. Atomics are a great way to provide thread-safe access to shared data without the overhead of a Mutex.

Setting a variable is normally a three-stage process: you read the variable, update the variable, and write the result. If there's no locking, another thread could change the variable between the read and write stages. This results in a "race condition" and corrupted data. Atomics let you avoid this problem.

You'll also need a way to transmit the world from the builder thread to the game setup. This *is* a good candidate for a Mutex as you'll only need to lock it when setting the world and when reading it—once in each case—so there's minimal performance overhead. Since your world isn't a primitive type, it can't be an atomic. Add the following code to src/main.rs:

MarsBaseOneWorldBuilder/mars_base_one_threaded/src/main.rs
```
use std::sync::Mutex;
use bevy::render::camera::ScalingMode;

static NEW_WORLD: Mutex<Option<World>> = Mutex::new(None);
```

Add the new system:

MarsBaseOneWorldBuilder/mars_base_one_threaded/src/main.rs
```
fn spawn_builder() {
❶  use std::sync::atomic::Ordering;
    // Clear the build state
❷  WORLD_READY.store(false, Ordering::Relaxed);

    // Spawn a "building world" message

    //Start a world building thread
    std::thread::spawn(|| {
      // Make our own random number generator
❸    let mut rng = my_library::RandomNumberGenerator::new();

      // Spawn the world
❹    let world = World::new(200, 200, &mut rng);
```

```
    // Store the world
⑤   let mut lock = NEW_WORLD.lock().unwrap();
    *lock = Some(world);

    // Notify of success
⑥   WORLD_READY.store(true, Ordering::Relaxed);
  });
}
```

❶ Atomic operations rely on a system called *Ordering*. There are different levels of guarantee for how isolated operations are from one another.[3]

❷ You can set the value of an atomic with the store() function. You're using *relaxed* ordering here—the fastest, but also the lowest level of ordering guarantee. It doesn't matter in this case because no other processes will be reading the value yet. If you'd like to know more about ordering, Mara Bos's excellent *Rust Atomics and Locks* gives a comprehensive guide.[4]

❸ Your thread will be running outside of Bevy's normal systems, so it won't have access to Bevy's dependency injection. Keeping a reference across frames is dangerous and usually won't compile, so you'll make your own RandomNumberGenerator here and use it to seed the world builder.

❹ Call the world builder as you did before.

❺ The world is now ready to use. You acquire a lock on the shared NEW_WORLD Mutex and store the world inside.

❻ The world is now ready to use. You indicate to the rest of the program that the world is ready by setting the WORLD_READY atomic to true.

The world builder will now run in the background and flag that it has completed its task by setting the WORLD_READY atomic to true. You need to check this atomic in your game loop and spawn the world when it's ready.

While the world-building thread is running in the background, Bevy continues to run the normal game loop. The game is in the WorldBuilding state, so it's running the show_builder function for every frame. Add the show_builder function to your src/main.rs file:

MarsBaseOneWorldBuilder/mars_base_one_threaded/src/main.rs
```
fn show_builder(
  mut state: ResMut<NextState<GamePhase>>,
  mut egui_context: egui::EguiContexts,
) {
```

---

3. https://doc.rust-lang.org/std/sync/atomic/enum.Ordering.html
4. https://marabos.nl/atomics/atomics.html

```
egui::egui::Window::new("Performance").show(
  egui_context.ctx_mut(),
  |ui| {
    ui.label("Building World");
  });
  if WORLD_READY.load(std::sync::atomic::Ordering::Relaxed) {
    state.set(GamePhase::Playing);
  }
}
```

The show_builder function displays an egui window indicating that the world is being constructed using the same egui commands you used in previous chapters. It then checks the atomic. Once again, it uses Relaxed ordering because the order of operations isn't important; you just need to know if the world is ready or not. If the world is ready, the game transitions to the Playing state.

Run the game now, and you'll see a "Building World" message while the world is being generated. The game will then fluidly start as soon as the world is ready, giving the player a much better experience. You can now fly around, enjoy your world, and be safe from having your process killed for blocking the main thread's message loop for too long.

Wrapping Up

In this chapter, you started with an almost blank slate: a spaceship flying around in an open area. Gravity worked, but that's about it. You added a camera, zoomed in, and made it follow the player. You then built a procedurally generated world, complete with rooms, corridors, and a borehole. You added collision detection, which prevents the player from flying through walls. You moved the world building into a separate thread so that the game doesn't pause while the world is being generated. You also learned about one mechanism for communicating between threads: Atomic variables and shared state protected by a Mutex. You'll learn about other inter-thread communication mechanisms in Chapter 14, Build a High Score Server, on page 279.

In the next chapter, you're going to tackle one of the thorniest issues of game development—and development in general—optimization. Even though Bevy is a great renderer, and your collision detection code is highly optimized already, as Mars Base One grows, there are a few sticking points that will slow down your game.

CHAPTER 12

Optimize Mars Base One

At this point, you've got the start of a fun game. Your ship can fly around a procedurally generated mining colony, bounce off walls, and move with realistic physics. You've solved one performance problem by moving world generation into another thread. On lower-end systems, and especially when compiling in Debug mode—omitting --release from your build commands—rendering performance can stutter a little. In this chapter, you'll improve the performance of two parts of your program: rendering and collision detection.

Game Optimization

When you build bigger games, you'll get a "feel" for where performance problems appear. It's almost always render batching, collision detection, doing too much work, or map navigation!

Warning: Optimization can be addictive. It's easy to spend hours and hours making your algorithms better and forget to write the game!

Last, the old adage "premature optimization is the root of all evil" remains true. Start by making your game work. Then, identify the bottlenecks and optimize them. Don't spend days adding every little optimization you can think of at the expense of finishing your game and having readable code.

Let's start by ensuring that you can measure your progress.

Displaying the Frame Rate

When you were optimizing collision detection in Chapter 8, Build Obstacles and Collision Detection, on page 163, you built a frame-rate display. A similar display for Mars Base One will give you immediate feedback on optimizations, so let's add one now.

In the main() function, add the following to your application builder:

```
.add_plugins(FrameTimeDiagnosticsPlugin{
  ..default()
})
```

Now, you can make a simple system to display frames per second:

MarsBaseOneOptimize/mars_base_one/src/main.rs
```
fn show_performance(
  diagnostics: Res<DiagnosticsStore>,
  mut egui_context: egui::EguiContexts,
) {
  let fps = diagnostics
      .get(&FrameTimeDiagnosticsPlugin::FPS)
      .and_then(|fps| fps.average())
      .unwrap_or(0.0);
  egui::egui::Window::new("Performance").show(
    egui_context.ctx_mut(),
    |ui| {
      let fps_text = format!("FPS: {fps:.1}");
      let color = match fps as u32 {
        0..=29 => Color32::RED,
        30..=50 => Color32::GOLD,
        _ => Color32::GREEN,
      };
      ui.colored_label(color, &fps_text);
    });
}
```

Finally, add it to the list of systems executed in the GamePhase:

```
add_phase!(app, GamePhase, GamePhase::Playing,
  start => [ setup ],
  run => [ movement, end_game, physics_clock, sum_impulses,
    apply_gravity, apply_velocity,
    terminal_velocity.after(apply_velocity),
    check_collisions::<Player, Ground>, bounce,
    camera_follow.after(terminal_velocity),
    show_performance
  ],
  exit => [ cleanup::<GameElement> ]
);
```

Run the game, and you'll see a performance indicator:

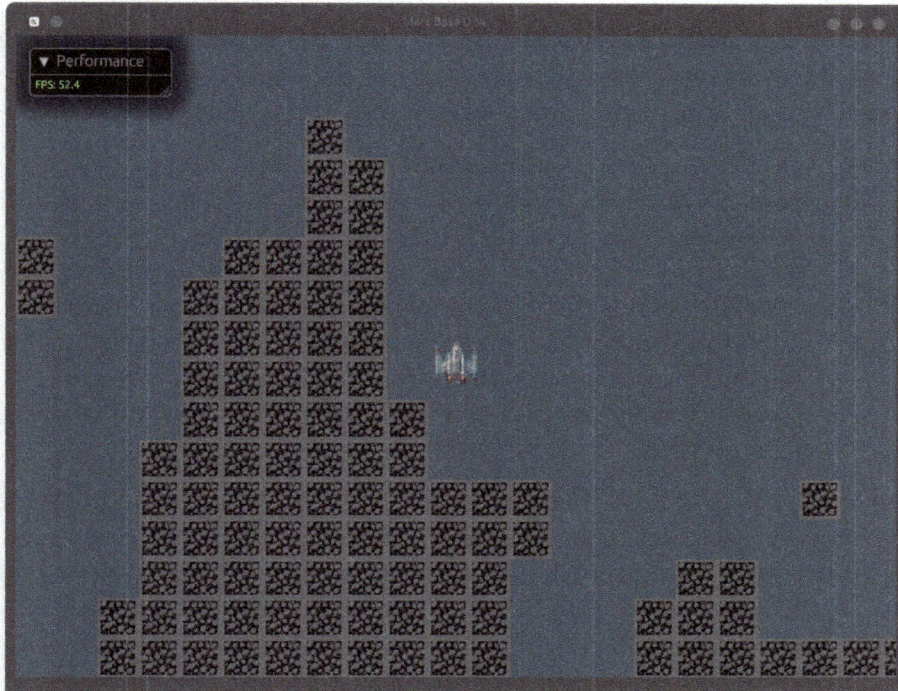

Now that you can measure your progress, let's tackle two bigger optimization targets.

Making a Mesh

Play the current game for a bit. Maximize your window and watch your frame rate. On my high-end Intel i7 (20 core) with a pretty great AMD video card, I see a frame rate of about 45 frames per second (FPS). That's not amazing. It's a little worse on some older computers and a little better on others. Running in release mode (with cargo run-release), my frame rate is a solid 60 FPS, so the performance problems aren't awful but could be improved. (As an aside, older versions of Bevy struggled a lot more.)

Your map is 200 x 200 tiles, for a maximum of 40,000 tiles. The Bevy engine is smart enough to batch sprites together that share a common texture (texture switches can be slow), but it's still checking whether a wall is visible up to 40,000 times per frame before building the rendered batch and submitting it. That's a lot of work, so Bevy's performance is impressive.

Fortunately, you know some things that Bevy doesn't: the walls are static, and some will always be visible. You can use this knowledge to massively reduce the amount of work that Bevy has to do. You'll build a single *mesh* representing the entire map and submit it as a single draw call.

GPUs and Draw Calls

Your computer's *Graphics Processing Unit (GPU)* is a special type of computer in and of itself. It specializes in running the same operation over and over again, really fast and in parallel. GPUs typically perform better with large workloads—lots of operations to perform. Otherwise, they spend most of their time waiting for the next instruction. Batching as many draw calls together as possible is a popular and effective method of speeding up rendering performance.

Meshes are a way of describing tasks to your GPU and are close to how the GPU actually processes data. Meshes are made up of buffers of vector data. The buffers are then uploaded, and the GPU processes them in parallel. The more data you can send to the GPU at once, the faster it can process that data.

The mesh you need to build consists of "vertex data." A vertex is a point in 3D space—a Vec3. Bevy provides a Mesh type to help you build vertex buffers and submit them to the video card. Vertex buffers can hold many kinds of data, including points, triangle strips, triangle lists, lines, and raw data to be processed by shader programs. You're going to build a "triangle list" describing the world-space location of each tile.

Modern GPUs are designed to work with triangles. Triangles are an excellent choice because you can compose almost anything from triangles if you put your mind to it. In this game, each tile is made up of two triangles to form a square.

You're also going to provide *two* pieces of data for each point: the vertex's world-space coordinates and the vertex's *texture space* ("UV") coordinates. Texture space ranges from 0 to 1 in the X and Y directions and determines which part of the texture to draw at that point. Bevy likes to receive the coordinates in counter-clockwise order. When rendering 3D, the order of the vertices that make up a face determines if a triangle is facing toward the player (and should be rendered) or away from the player (and should be culled).

Vertex 2 (Top-Left)   Vertex 3 (Top-Right)   Vertex 1 (Top-Right)

Vertex 1 (Bottom-Left)   Vertex 2 (Bottom-Left)   Vertex 3 Bottom-Rightt)

Triangle 1   Triangle 2

Each triangle must specify the UV texture coordinates in "texture space." Textures are treated as rectangles with x and y axes ranging from 0.0 to 1.0 (floating point). The top-left corner of the texture is 0.0, 0.0, and the bottom-right corner is 1.0, 1.0. Since you're only rendering whole tiles, you can align 0 with the left or bottom, and 1 with the top or right.

You already have the most challenging part done: knowing where the triangles should go. You just need to decompose them into individual vertices (also known as points on the triangle) and add them to a *TriangleList*—a list of triangle vertices in a GPU-friendly format. You also need to add UVs—texture coordinates—describing where on the sprite each point lies relative to the texture. You'll also provide a list of tile locations for the physics engine.

You'll need somewhere to store the generated mesh. Let's add a pair of new fields to the World struct:

MarsBaseOneOptimize/mars_base_one/src/main.rs
```rust
struct World {
  solid: Vec<bool>,
  width: usize,
  height: usize,
➤ mesh: Option<Mesh>,
➤ tile_positions: Vec<(f32, f32)>,
}
```

The mesh field is an option—it might not have been created yet. Rust doesn't have null—not in safe code—so an Option is the preferred way to indicate that something may not exist yet. The tile_positions field stores the world-space positions of each tile so that they can be used for collision detection.

You also need to update the World::new function to initialize the new fields:

MarsBaseOneOptimize/mars_base_one/src/main.rs
```rust
fn new(
  width: usize, height: usize,
  rng: &mut RandomNumberGenerator
) -> Self {
  let mut result = Self {
    width,
    height,
    solid: vec![true; width * height],
    mesh: None,
    tile_positions: Vec::new(),
  };
```

Now that you have a structure in which to store it, let's build the mesh:

MarsBaseOneOptimize/mars_base_one/src/main.rs
```rust
fn build_mesh(&self) -> (Mesh, Vec<(f32, f32)>) {
  let mut position = Vec::new();
  let mut uv = Vec::new();
  let mut tile_positions = Vec::new();
  let x_offset = (self.width as f32 / 2.0) * 24.0;
  let y_offset =(self.height as f32) * 24.0;
  for y in 0 .. self.height {
    for x in 0 .. self.width {
      if self.solid[self.mapidx(x, y)] {

        let left = (x as f32 * 24.0) - x_offset;
        let right = ((x as f32 + 1.0) * 24.0) - x_offset;
        let top = (y as f32 * 24.0) - y_offset;
        let bottom = ((y as f32 + 1.0) * 24.0) - y_offset;

        position.push([left, bottom, 1.0]);
        position.push([right, bottom, 1.0]);
        position.push([right, top, 1.0]);
        position.push([right, top, 1.0]);
        position.push([left, bottom, 1.0]);
        position.push([left, top, 1.0]);

        uv.push([0.0, 1.0]);
        uv.push([1.0, 1.0]);
        uv.push([1.0, 0.0]);
        uv.push([1.0, 0.0]);
        uv.push([0.0, 1.0]);
        uv.push([0.0, 0.0]);

        tile_positions.push((left + 12.0, top + 12.0));
      }
    }
  }
  (
    Mesh::new(PrimitiveTopology::TriangleList, RenderAssetUsages::default())
      .with_inserted_attribute(Mesh::ATTRIBUTE_POSITION, position)
```

```
        .with_inserted_attribute(Mesh::ATTRIBUTE_UV_0, uv),
    tile_positions
  )
}
```

❶ Create vectors for the vertices (position), texture position (UVs), and tile position (world space).

❷ Rather than repeatedly calculate the shift required to align with Bevy's coordinate system, precalculate it once.

❸ Calculate the position of each of the four corners of the tile. This is the same calculation you used when spawning all the sprites individually.

❹ Add each position as a vertex for a total of six vertices or two triangles. This follows the counter-clockwise order described earlier.

❺ Add the texture positions for each vertex. These are derived from the texture position graphic in the first step.

❻ Push the tile positions into their vector, ready for use in collision detection.

You can now simplify the spawn function quite a bit:

MarsBaseOneOptimize/mars_base_one/src/main.rs
```rust
fn spawn(
  &self,
  assets: &AssetStore,
  commands: &mut Commands,
  loaded_assets: &LoadedAssets,
  meshes: &mut Assets<Mesh>,
  materials: &mut Assets<ColorMaterial>,
) {
  let mesh = self.mesh.as_ref().unwrap().clone();
  let mesh_handle = meshes.add(mesh);
  let material_handle = materials.add(ColorMaterial {
    texture: Some(assets.get_handle("ground", loaded_assets).unwrap()),
    ..Default::default()
  });
  commands.spawn(Mesh2d(mesh_handle ))
      .insert(MeshMaterial2d(material_handle ))
      .insert(Transform::from_xyz(0.0, 0.0, 0.0));

  for (x, y) in self.tile_positions.iter() {
    commands.spawn_empty()
      .insert(GameElement)
      .insert(Ground)
      .insert(PhysicsPosition::new(Vec2::new(*x, *y)))
      .insert(AxisAlignedBoundingBox::new(24.0, 24.0));
  }
}
```

Rather than repeatedly calling spawn_image!, you're just spawning the mesh. You're still spawning physics positions for each tile, but there's no render data attached. The physics tiles are now detached from the rendering system.

Run the game, and you'll notice it's a lot faster. On my machine, it's a silky smooth 58 frames per second, a decent improvement. You could stop now, but there's one more obvious area for improvement.

Indexed Meshes

If the texture positions remain the same for each point, you don't have to list six vertices for a four-vertex shape. Instead, you can build your vertex buffer to represent only the unique points and then add an *index buffer* to refer to the points when describing the triangles. This saves some video card memory and bandwidth and can result in faster rendering.

This book won't cover indexed meshes, but you can learn more from Bevy's documentation.[1] Experimentation while writing this book showed a negligible benefit.

You've made a significant improvement in rendering performance, which was the big bottleneck standing in your way. But there's one more obvious area for improvement: collision detection.

Optimizing Collision Detection

You've already made collision detection fast with QuadTrees. You're not checking up to 40,000 tiles for collision; you're checking a tiny subset. But once again, you can use your knowledge of the game to reduce the work that must be done.

Many wall tiles are inaccessible to the player. Unless your physics engine has gone horribly wrong, the player will never be able to reach tiles surrounded by other tiles. You can use this knowledge and not include those tiles as collidable objects. The fastest collision detection is the one that doesn't have to be done.

Instead of generating physics bounds for every solid tile, let's create bounds only for tiles players can reach. In the build_mesh() function, let's make adding tiles to the tile list optional:

---

1.   https://docs.rs/bevy/latest/bevy/prelude/struct.Mesh.html

```
MarsBaseOneOptimize/mars_base_one_collision/src/main.rs
// Delete this
//tile_positions.push((left + 12.0, top + 12.0));

// Only push the physics position if the tile is on the edge,
// and the tile isn't completely surrounded by solid tiles.
let mut needs_physics = false;
```
❶
```
if x==0 || x > self.width-3 || y==0 || y > self.height-3 {
  // On the edge
  needs_physics = true;
} else {
  // Are we surrounded by solid tiles?
```
❷
```
  let solid_count =
      self.solid[self.mapidx(x-1, y)] as u8
    + self.solid[self.mapidx(x+1, y)] as u8
    + self.solid[self.mapidx(x, y-1)] as u8
    + self.solid[self.mapidx(x, y+1)] as u8;
```
❸
```
  if solid_count < 4 {
    needs_physics = true;
  }
}
```
❹
```
if  needs_physics {
  tile_positions.push((left + 12.0, top + 12.0));
}
```

❶ Perform a boundary check. You don't want to try to read outside of the map array. If a tile is on the edge of the map, it's always collidable.

❷ Count the number of adjacent tiles.

❸ If there are fewer than four adjacent tiles, the tile is collidable; it has an exposed edge that the player could run into.

❹ If the tile is collidable, push it into the physics collision tile list.

Run the game now. My system runs at a perfect 60.0 frames per second, even in Debug mode. Despite having a complicated world to model, performance is very, very good.

Let's add a few embellishments before calling world generation done.

Adding Visual Embellishments

There are a few ways to help make Mars Base One *pop*—adding visual effects that make the game more engaging. You'll add a background graphic, a mothership, and some particle effects to the game. Let's start with a background graphic.

Add a Background Graphic

The map has large open spaces, and players may find themselves in a predominantly black/unrendered area. Modern game design typically avoids this "dead space," as there should always be *something* players can look at. So, let's add a huge background image stretched across the mine.

You'll use the following image, which was generated with ChatGPT v40, edited with the GIMP, and provided royalty-free:[2,3]

Let's make use of the image. In the setup() function, add the following after you spawn the player:

MarsBaseOneOptimize/mars_base_one_collision/src/main.rs
```
// Backdrop
let x = 100.0;
let y = 100.0;
let x_scale = (200.0 * 24.0) / 1720.0;
let y_scale = (300.0 * 24.0) / 1024.0;
let center_x = (x as f32 * 24.0) - ((200.0 / 2.0) * 24.0);
let center_y = ((y as f32 + 1.0) * 24.0) - (200.0 * 24.0);
let mut transform = Transform::from_xyz(center_x, center_y, -10.0);
transform.scale = Vec3::new(x_scale, y_scale, 1.0);
commands
  .spawn(Sprite::from_image(
    assets.get_handle("backdrop", &loaded_assets).unwrap())
  )
  .insert(transform)
  .insert(GameElement);
```

---

2. https://chat.openai.com/
3. https://www.gimp.org/

❶ Calculate the scale for the x-axis required to stretch the image across the entire map.

❷ The y-axis scale is similar but uses a larger value to stretch the image vertically. The player starts above the generated world, and the extra space avoids having an ugly band at the top of the map.

❸ Create a transform for the image, placing it over the center of the generated map.

❹ Apply the scaling you calculated to the sprite.

❺ Add the sprite into the world. You aren't using the spawn_image!() macro because you need to apply a transform to the sprite. This is a downside of macros: you can either keep adding options to them—resulting in large macros—or, occasionally, write the underlying code yourself.

Run the game now, and instead of dull "dead space," you have a lovely backdrop as you zoom around the map:

The look and feel are coming together. Inquiring minds may wonder why your ship starts floating above the world with no context. It's such a small ship that interplanetary travel seems like a lot to ask. Let's add a mothership to provide some context.

Add a Mothership

It's disconcerting that the player starts above the world with no sense of context. Gravity will generally ensure they reach the outpost, but providing a visual cue that you were dropped from a mothership and are exploring the mining outpost is a good idea.

This is the image of the Mothership, which is in the code/MarsBaseOneOptimize/mars_base_one_collision/assets directory.

Once again, the image was generated with ChatGPT—many iterations until it produced something useful—and then hand-edited with the GIMP. It's provided royalty-free.

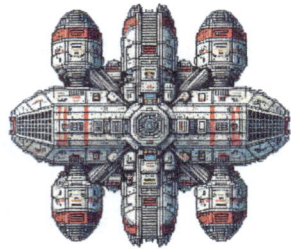

AI-Generated Content

Generative AI is a powerful tool. You can quickly create a lot of game content. But it's far from being a magic bullet, as you'll have to hand-tune everything you make with it. It's a great way to create graphics to get you started and give you a playground with which to rapidly iterate your designs. When you're ready to ship your game, finding a professional—human—artist to help you with your design is absolutely worth it. Human artists understand context, storytelling, and the emotional impact of art in a way that AI doesn't.

Let's add a mothership graphic to the top. First, in the main() function, add the mothership graphic to the list of assets being loaded:

```
AssetManager::new().add_image("ship", "ship.png")?
  .add_image("ground", "ground.png")?
  .add_image("backdrop", "backing.png")?
  .add_image("particle", "particle.png")?
  .add_image("mothership", "mothership.png")?
)
```

Then, in the setup() function, add the following after you spawn the player:

```
MarsBaseOneOptimize/mars_base_one_collision/src/main.rs
spawn_image!(
  assets,
  commands,
  "mothership",
  0.0,
  400.0,
  10.0,
  &loaded_assets,
  GameElement
);
```

Run the game, and your ship slides out of the mothership and into the world:

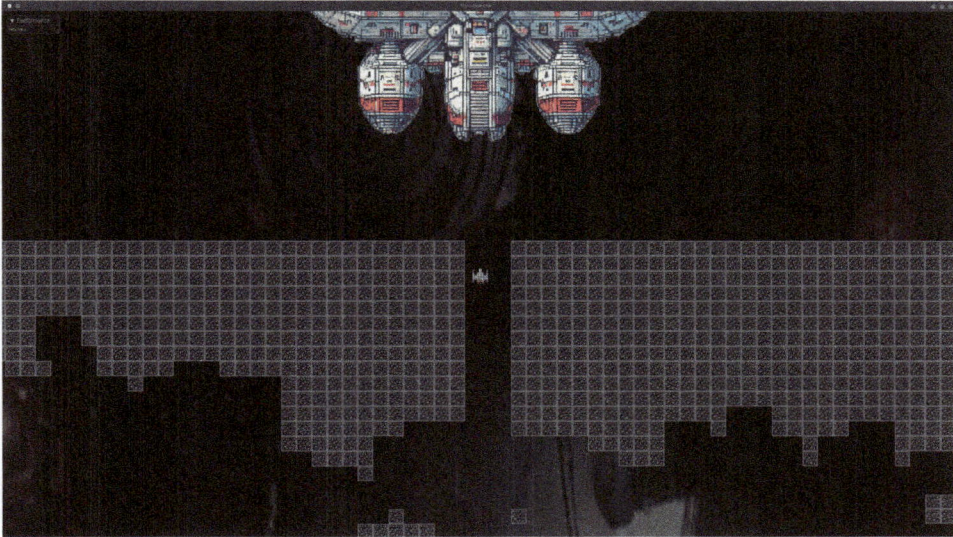

The game looks pretty good, but let's add one more source of "juice": particle effects.

Particle Effects

Particle effects are a great way to add some flair to your game. They can be used for explosions, fire, smoke, rocket trails, and more. They're "cheap" to render—not using too much CPU or GPU time—and can add a lot of visual interest to your game. Let's use particle effects to add some feedback to firing your ship's maneuvering thrusters.

Particle Effects

Particle effects are common in lots of games. As a result, there are many great implementations available premade for Bevy. If you're writing a big game, you may want to use one of them. The particle system in this book is deliberately lightweight to show you how to build one from scratch. Many freely available systems are more impressive and offer a much wider range of effects.

You should start by deciding what to render as a particle. The file code/Mars-BaseOneOptimize/assets/particle.png is provided for your use. It's a single, white pixel—not rendered in the book because that would be silly. Because of its simplicity, it's an ideal base for a particle system. So let's start by adding it to the asset loading list in the main() function:

```
.add_image("particle", "particle.png")?
```

You're going to want spawning particles to be fast and easy. Events are perfect for this; you already use them throughout the physics system, so you don't need to learn anything new. Add a new event to your setup list in main():

```
MarsBaseOneOptimize/mars_base_one_collision/src/main.rs
.add_event::<OnCollision<Player, Ground>>()
.add_event::<SpawnParticle>()
```

Now that you've told Bevy to use SpawnParticle events, it's a great time to define them:

```
MarsBaseOneOptimize/mars_base_one_collision/src/main.rs
#[derive(Event)]
pub struct SpawnParticle{
  position: Vec2,
  color: LinearRgba,
  velocity: Vec3,
}
```

Spawning a particle requires some basic information: The position at which the particle should spawn. The color of the particle. The velocity of the particle.

Spawning particles requires a Component—an indicator that an entity is a particle—and also a storage area for any data you need to retain about that particle:

```
MarsBaseOneOptimize/mars_base_one_collision/src/main.rs
#[derive(Component)]
pub struct Particle {
  pub lifetime: f32,
}
```

For now, you're just storing the "lifetime" of the particle. In other words, how long until it fades away and leaves the game.

Next, let's create a system to spawn the particles when a SpawnParticle message is received:

```
MarsBaseOneOptimize/mars_base_one_collision/src/main.rs
// Receive messages to spawn particles
fn spawn_particle_system(
  mut commands: Commands,
  mut reader: EventReader<SpawnParticle>,
  assets: Res<AssetStore>,
  loaded_assets: Res<LoadedAssets>,
) {
  for particle in reader.read() {
    let mut sprite = Sprite::from_image(
      assets.get_handle("particle", &loaded_assets).unwrap());
    sprite.color = particle.color.into();
```

```
  commands
    .spawn(sprite)
    .insert(Transform::from_xyz(
      particle.position.x, particle.position.y, 5.0))
    .insert(GameElement)
    .insert(Particle { lifetime: 2.0 })
    .insert(Velocity(particle.velocity))
    .insert(PhysicsPosition::new(particle.position));
  }
}
```

There's nothing in this function that you haven't already learned. You iterate through received SpawnParticle messages; for each message, you create a new particle entity with the provided data.

Great news! The physics system is already handling the movement of your particles—you gave the particles a Velocity component, and the physics system does the rest. You don't have a mechanism for tracking the age of a particle and making it fade away. Part of the "cheapness" of particles is that they're transient and don't accumulate vast lists of render data. Add the following system to your game:

MarsBaseOneOptimize/mars_base_one_collision/src/main.rs
```
fn particle_age_system(
  time: Res<Time>,
  mut commands: Commands,
  mut query: Query<(Entity, &mut Particle, &mut Sprite)>,
) {
  for (entity, mut particle, mut sprite) in
    query.iter_mut()
  {
    particle.lifetime -= time.delta_secs();
    if particle.lifetime <= 0.0 {
      commands.entity(entity).despawn();
    }

    // Adjust the color
    sprite.color.set_alpha(particle.lifetime / 2.0);
  }
}
```

The new particle_age_system is simple. It iterates through all of your particles and reduces their lifetime. If the lifetime is zero, the particle is removed from the game. Otherwise, the particle has its "alpha" channel (transparency) reduced, making it fade away.

Next, add the systems you created to your game phase handler in the main() function. (The code is on the next page.)

```
add_phase!(app, GamePhase, GamePhase::Playing,
  start => [ setup ],
  run => [ movement, end_game, physics_clock, sum_impulses,
    apply_gravity, apply_velocity,
    terminal_velocity.after(apply_velocity),
    check_collisions::<Player, Ground>, bounce,
    camera_follow.after(terminal_velocity),
    show_performance,
➤   spawn_particle_system, particle_age_system
    ],
  exit => [ cleanup::<GameElement> ]
);
```

Finally, you need to spawn some particles. Let's add a particle effect to the player's thrusters. In the movement() function, add the following highlighted sections:

MarsBaseOneOptimize/mars_base_one_collision/src/main.rs
```
fn movement(
  keyboard: Res<ButtonInput<KeyCode>>,
  mut player_query: Query<(Entity, &mut Transform), With<Player>>,
  mut impulses: EventWriter<Impulse>,
  mut particles: EventWriter<SpawnParticle>,
) {
  let Ok((entity, mut transform)) = player_query.single_mut()
  else { return; };
  if keyboard.pressed(KeyCode::ArrowLeft) {
    transform.rotate(Quat::from_rotation_z(f32::to_radians(2.0)));
➤   particles.write(SpawnParticle{
➤     position: -transform.local_x().truncate() + Vec2::new(
➤       transform.translation.x, transform.translation.y),
➤     color: LinearRgba::new(0.0, 1.0, 1.0, 1.0),
➤     velocity: transform.local_x().as_vec3(),
➤   });
  }
  if keyboard.pressed(KeyCode::ArrowRight) {
    transform.rotate(Quat::from_rotation_z(f32::to_radians(-2.0)));
➤   particles.write(SpawnParticle{
➤     position: transform.local_x().truncate() + Vec2::new(
➤       transform.translation.x, transform.translation.y),
➤     color: LinearRgba::new(0.0, 1.0, 1.0, 1.0),
➤     velocity: -transform.local_x().as_vec3(),
➤   });
  }
  if keyboard.pressed(KeyCode::ArrowUp) {
    impulses.write(Impulse {
      target: entity,
      amount: transform.local_y().as_vec3(),
      absolute: false,
```

```
      source: 1,
    });
➤   particles.write(SpawnParticle{
➤     position: transform.local_y().truncate() + Vec2::new(
➤       transform.translation.x, transform.translation.y),
➤     color: LinearRgba::new(0.0, 1.0, 1.0, 1.0),
➤     velocity: -transform.local_y().as_vec3(),
➤   });
  }
}
```

You also submit a SpawnParticle event whenever you generate a physics impulse. You set the particle's initial position to that of the player and apply a velocity derived from the helper function local_x or local_y (you used these functions to rotate Flappy the Dragon). The particles are cyan, representing the use of compressed gas for maneuvering. The particles gradually fade away over one second.

When the player fires their maneuvering thrusters, particles are added to the world. This gives a much nicer overall effect to your game:

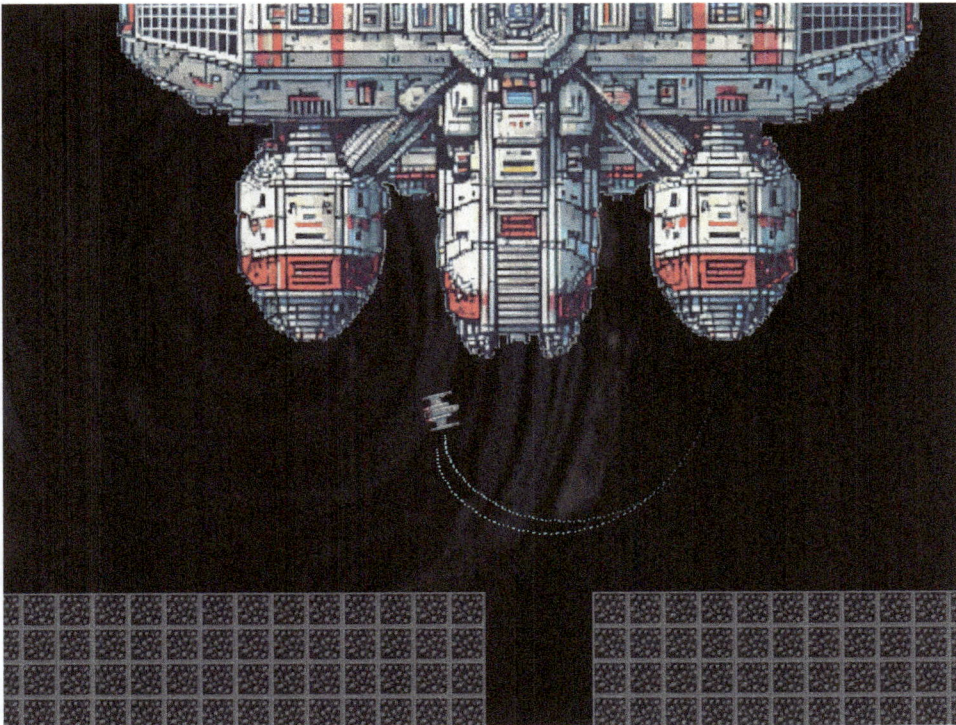

The particle system provides instant feedback for your player's actions and will also be helpful as you add other elements to the game.

Wrapping Up

You've made some serious performance improvements. You reduced world rendering from thousands of draw calls to only one, taking advantage of the static nature of the walls. You used greedy meshing to divide your collision detection workload so you don't have to worry about checking *thousands* of walls that the player can't reach. And you "juiced" the basic game by adding a backdrop, a mothership, and particle effects. The game is looking and feeling great!

In the next chapter, you'll add some fun elements to the game: astronauts to collect and shields so you don't die instantly. This will make navigating the world feel more like an arcade game than an exploration simulation.

CHAPTER 13

Add Miners and Energy Shields

Now that you've got a ship the player can fly around, working gravity, procedurally generated terrain, and particle effects, it's time to add an objective to the game: to save the miners! It's also time to make it possible to lose the game by either running out of fuel or hitting the walls too many times and depleting your shields. As you work through this chapter, you'll learn how traits and generics can greatly reduce the repetitive nature of writing systems like this. Let's get started.

Adding Some Graphics

To begin, you'll first need the spaceman.png, fuel.png, and battery.png files from the book's code archive. Put these files in the assets directory.

For reference, the graphics look like this:

Once you have those files where they need to be, add them to your game's asset loader, just as you did before. Edit main.rs:

```
MarsElements/mars_base_one/src/main.rs
AssetManager::new().add_image("ship", "ship.png")?
    .add_image("ground", "ground.png")?
    .add_image("backdrop", "backing.png")?
    .add_image("particle", "particle.png")?
    .add_image("mothership", "mothership.png")?
➤    .add_image("spaceman", "spaceman.png")?
➤    .add_image("fuel", "fuel.png")?
➤    .add_image("battery", "battery.png")?
```

You'll also need to define components to tag each of these asset types:

MarsElements/mars_base_one/src/main.rs
```
#[derive(Component)]
struct Miner;

#[derive(Component)]
struct Battery;

#[derive(Component)]
struct Fuel;
```

The game engine now knows how to render these asset types and uniquely identify them in game. The engine work you did before has simplified the process, making it easier to add assets to the game.

Next, you need to spawn the entities into the game world.

Placing Miners, Batteries, and Fuel Tanks

Before you distribute miners, batteries, and fuel tanks around the game world, you need to make sure their placement makes sense. For example, you don't want miners floating in the air, batteries buried in the ground, or entities in a location that's impossible to reach. You can achieve this by building a set of valid, usable spawn locations while you build the world.

Add a spawn_positions field to the World structure in main.rs. This will list locations that could contain a valid spawn point.

MarsElements/mars_base_one/src/main.rs
```
struct World {
  solid: Vec<bool>,
  width: usize,
  height: usize,
  mesh: Option<Mesh>,
  tile_positions: Vec<(f32, f32)>,
➤ spawn_positions: Vec<(f32, f32)>,
}
```

You also need to update the World constructor to initialize the new field:

MarsElements/mars_base_one/src/main.rs
```
fn new(width: usize, height: usize, rng: &mut RandomNumberGenerator) -> Self {
  let mut result = Self {
    width,
    height,
    solid: vec![true; width * height],
    mesh: None,
    tile_positions: Vec::new(),
➤   spawn_positions: Vec::new(),
  };
```

You're using the same data format as you did for world tiles: an x and y location. Now, update your build_mesh() function signature to return more data:

```
fn build_mesh(&self) -> (Mesh, Vec<(f32, f32)>, Vec<(f32, f32)>) {
```

Tuples, Tuples Everywhere, and Not a Name to Use

Tuples are wonderful. You can keep adding data to them and use them to easily return ever-increasing amounts of data from functions. They're a great way to extend functions quickly. Be warned: tuples are also addictive, and because you don't name individual fields, it can be difficult to remember what each field represents. As you add complexity to your return types, it's often clearer to replace your tuple with a structure. Structures have named fields, and there's little risk of ambiguity.

(Mesh, Vec<(f32, f32)>, Vec<(f32, f32)>) sits right on the border between an excessively complicated tuple and a structure. Replacing it with struct WorldInfo { mesh: Mesh, tiles: Vec<(f32, f32)>, spawn_positions: Vec<(f32, f32)> } would be a good idea if you were planning to add more fields or use the data in multiple places.

In the previous version of the world builder, you've already checked to see if a tile is solid while you build the list of tile positions. If a tile *is not* solid, it may be a possible spawn location for a game element. You also want to check that the tile isn't too close to the edge of the map, and that the tile above is *also* open, ensuring that the tile is reachable. Add an else clause to your if self.solid condition to add the tile to the list of possible spawn locations:

MarsElements/mars_base_one/src/main.rs

```
        }
➤       else {
➤         if x > 1 && x < self.width-3 && y > 1 && y < self.height-3 &&
➤         self.solid[self.mapidx(x, y-1)] {
➤           possible_miner_positions.push((left + 12.0, top + 12.0));
➤         }
➤       }
      }
    }
    (
      Mesh::new(PrimitiveTopology::TriangleList, RenderAssetUsages::default())
        .with_inserted_attribute(Mesh::ATTRIBUTE_POSITION, position)
        .with_inserted_attribute(Mesh::ATTRIBUTE_UV_0, uv),
      tile_positions,
➤     possible_miner_positions
    )
}
```

When your call to build_mesh returns, you'll have a list of possible spawn locations. The locations are built in-line while your world-building thread runs, so the additional time taken is nicely hidden from the user. There's still one problem with the locations list: it's sorted by the order in which the world builder traversed the tile grid. You want to randomize the list. Fortunately, the rand crate includes a shuffle function that can do this for you. Adjust your spawn_builder function as follows:

MarsElements/mars_base_one/src/main.rs
```rust
//Start a world building thread
std::thread::spawn(|| {
  // Make our own random number generator
  let mut rng = my_library::RandomNumberGenerator::new();
  // Spawn the world
  let mut world = World::new(200, 200, &mut rng);

  // Shuffle possible miner positions and limit the size to 20
➤ use my_library::rand::seq::SliceRandom;
➤ world.spawn_positions.shuffle(&mut rng.rng);
```

Now that you have a shuffled list of possible locations, you can simply take them in turn and add an element to the world at that location.

You've already spawned the tiles that make up the world in the spawn function. This is an ideal place to add the other game elements as well. Let's consider the logic you can use:

1. Take the first 20 elements from the shuffled list of spawn locations.
2. At each location, spawn a miner.
3. Take the *next* 20 elements (from index 20 to 40) from the shuffled list of spawn locations.
4. At each location, spawn a battery.
5. Take the *next* 20 elements (from index 40 to 60) from the shuffled list of spawn locations.
6. At each location, spawn a fuel tank.

Each of these elements will be an entity, comprised of a sprite, position, a tag, velocity, and a bounding box. Making the bounding box artificially large will make it easier to collect the elements, which will reduce the player's frustration. So let's add the code to spawn miners to the spawn function:

MarsElements/mars_base_one/src/main.rs
```rust
// Spawn miners
❶ for (x, y) in self.spawn_positions.iter().take(20) {
❷   spawn_image!(
      assets,
      commands,
      "spaceman",
```

```
❸     *x,
      *y,
      10.0,
      loaded_assets,
      GameElement,
      Miner,
      Velocity::default(),
      PhysicsPosition::new(Vec2::new(*x, *y)),
      // Extra Large Hitbox
      AxisAlignedBoundingBox::new(48.0, 48.0)
   );
}
```

❶ Using iter gives you an iterator over elements of the collection. You receive a reference to each element—the original isn't destroyed. Calling take(20) gives you the first 20 elements of the iterator.

❷ Use the spawn_image macro you created to take care of the boilerplate code for spawning an entity with a sprite, and make use of your assets system.

❸ The iterator is giving you a reference to each element. You need to dereference it to get the actual value.

Thanks to the work you did in the previous chapters, you don't need to write as much boilerplate code to get these elements added to the world. You can simply repeat this process for fuel tanks:

MarsElements/mars_base_one/src/main.rs
```
// Spawn fuel
❶ for (x, y) in self.spawn_positions.iter().skip(20).take(20) {
   spawn_image!(
      assets,
      commands,
      "fuel",
      *x,
      *y,
      10.0,
      loaded_assets,
      GameElement,
      Fuel,
      Velocity::default(),
      PhysicsPosition::new(Vec2::new(*x, *y)),
      // Extra Large Hitbox
      AxisAlignedBoundingBox::new(48.0, 48.0)
   );
}
```

❶ Obtain the iterator and take 20 elements, but this time use skip(20) to skip the positions you've already used.

Finally, you can do the same again for batteries:

MarsElements/mars_base_one/src/main.rs

```
// Spawn batteries
for (x, y) in self.spawn_positions.iter().skip(40).take(10) {
  spawn_image!(
    assets,
    commands,
    "battery",
    *x,
    *y,
    10.0,
    loaded_assets,
    GameElement,
    Battery,
    Velocity::default(),
    PhysicsPosition::new(Vec2::new(*x, *y)),
    // Extra Large Hitbox
    AxisAlignedBoundingBox::new(48.0, 48.0)
  );
```

Run the game now, and you'll find miners, batteries, and fuel tanks littering your Mars base in all the right places:

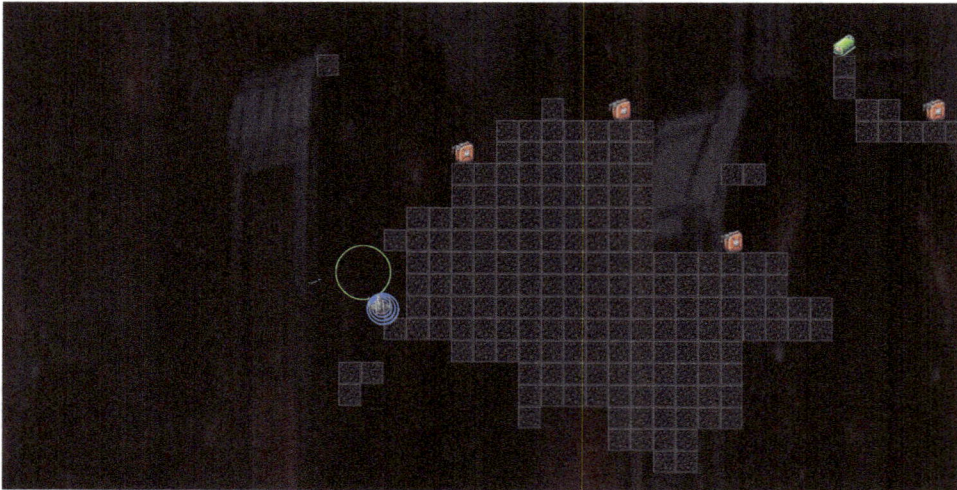

Having fuel and shields in the game implies that they *do something*. Fuel—predictably—represents your ship's reaction mass. You burn fuel to maneuver. Shields protect you from collisions. Let's add these features to the game.

Adding Shields and Fuel

Now that the game features miners to rescue, fuel to burn, and batteries to recharge your shields, let's model those in the game. You'll need to add three fields to the Player component structure:

MarsElements/mars_base_one/src/main.rs
```
#[derive(Component)]
struct Player {
  miners_saved: u32,
  shields: i32,
  fuel: i32,
}
```

These should be pretty self-explanatory: the number of miners you've saved, your shield level, and how much fuel is left in your tanks.

Your Player is instantiated in the setup() function. Let's update it to include the new fields with default starting values:

```
Player { miners_saved: 0, shields: 500, fuel: 100_000 },
```

Now that you have the fields in place, let's make them visible to the player. You'll use egui once again to provide a heads-up display (HUD) for the player. Create a new function/system to display the score:

MarsElements/mars_base_one/src/main.rs
```
fn score_display(
  player: Query<&Player>,
  mut egui_context: egui::EguiContexts,
) {
  let Ok(player) = player.single() else {
    return;
  };
  egui::egui::Window::new("Score").show(
    egui_context.ctx_mut(),
    |ui| {
      ui.label(format!("Miners Saved: {}", player.miners_saved));
      ui.label(format!("Shields: {}", player.shields));
      ui.label(format!("Fuel: {}", player.fuel));
    });
}
```

Don't forget to add show_performance to the add_phase! macro for the playing phase.

Run the game now, and you have a display of your game's statistics:

Default Values

When you first add a new game element, the correct way to determine starting values for things like shields and fuel is to make an educated guess, play the game a bit, and adjust your guesswork. If you decide to add difficulty levels to your game, you can adjust these values as part of the difficulty selection. For now, pick a value that seems reasonable and adjust it as you playtest.

You'll often find yourself changing these for a single test. Want to test that your "oh no, I'm out of shields" system is working? Start with a lower number of shields. Games are as much an art as a science—there isn't a "right" answer to these questions. Gradually changing parameters and seeing what happens is often the path to building a genuinely fun game.

Let's add a little more "juice" to the game. The map is large, so let's make it easier to find the miners.

Adding Particle Bursts

Your particle system is pretty nifty. So far, you've only been spawning linear particles—particles that come out of your ship when you maneuver. There are *lots* of other ways to spawn particles. Let's add a radial burst of particles moving outwards. You can use this to indicate the position of miners and make it easier for the player to find them. It also provides a great basis for explosions, markers when you pick up a collectible, and more. Add a new function named particle_burst:

MarsElements/mars_base_one/src/main.rs
```rust
fn particle_burst(
  center: Vec2,
  color: LinearRgba,
  spawn: &mut EventWriter<SpawnParticle>,
  velocity: f32,
) {
  for angle in 0 .. 360 {
    let angle = (angle as f32).to_radians();
    let velocity = Vec3::new(angle.cos() * velocity,
      angle.sin() * velocity, 0.0);
    spawn.write(SpawnParticle {
      position: center,
      color,
      velocity,
    });
  }
}
```

This function iterates through a circle, spawning a particle for each degree.
It accepts a color, a position, and a velocity for the particles, which will burst
outward from the center point before fading away. Now that you can spawn
particle bursts, let's add some more visual flair to the game.

Finding the Miners

With miners appearing in random locations on a large map, it's easy to end-
lessly, never finding miners. Let's give the player a hint: a periodic burst of
particles from miners, indicating their position. This is easy to explain in the
game's fiction. The miners are sending out a distress signal, and you can see
it as a burst of particles. You'll add a new system to the game that spawns
these bursts, and you'll use the particle burst function you just wrote:

MarsElements/mars_base_one/src/main.rs
```rust
fn miner_beacon(
  mut rng: ResMut<RandomNumberGenerator>,
  miners: Query<&Transform, With<Miner>>,
  mut spawn: EventWriter<SpawnParticle>,
) {
  for miner in miners.iter() {
    if rng.range(1 ..= 100) == 100 {
      particle_burst(
        miner.translation.truncate(),
        LinearRgba::new(1.0, 1.0, 0.0, 1.0),
        &mut spawn,
        10.0)
    }
  }
}
```

Now that your player has a chance of finding some miners, let's make it possible to save them.

A Generic System for Collecting Things

You could easily set up separate functions for miners, fuel, and batteries, but you'd be duplicating a lot of code. The steps are the same: check for collisions, if a collision occurred, despawn the item, and adjust the player's statistics. You then spawn a particle burst to indicate that the consumable was collected. Instead of writing the same code three times, you can write it once and use generics to make it work for all three types of consumables.

Looking back at what you've learned about generics, the Rust generic and trait system can help you here. You can define a trait that all collectable items implement, specifying a function to call when an item is collected. You can then write a generic system that performs all of the identical steps—and delegates collection for the specific item type to the trait function.

Let's start by defining an OnCollect trait:

MarsElements/mars_base_one/src/main.rs
```rust
trait OnCollect {
  fn effect(player: &mut Player);
}
```

Remember that traits are an *interface*, not a concrete implementation. Which means your trait doesn't do anything at all yet. You need to implement it for each of the collectable types:

MarsElements/mars_base_one/src/main.rs
```rust
impl OnCollect for Miner {
  fn effect(player: &mut Player) {
    player.miners_saved += 1;
  }
}

impl OnCollect for Fuel {
  fn effect(player: &mut Player) {
    player.fuel += 1000;
  }
}

impl OnCollect for Battery {
  fn effect(player: &mut Player) {
    player.shields += 100;
  }
}
```

Spawning the same particle burst for each collectable type is a bit repetitive and not too much fun. So let's add a bit of color and take advantage of another one of Rust's generic features: constants. Let's start by defining some possible colors for particle bursts:

MarsElements/mars_base_one/src/main.rs
```rust
#[repr(u8)]
enum BurstColor {
  Green,
  Orange,
  Magenta,
}
```

This is a simple enough enumeration. The #[repr(u8)] is new. You're telling Rust to represent the enumeration as a single unsigned byte. You'll see why in a moment. Note that this only works for enumerations that don't contain additional data.

Now, let's write a function that converts a u8—the enumeration's type—into a BurstColor value:

MarsElements/mars_base_one/src/main.rs
```rust
impl From<u8> for BurstColor {
  fn from(value: u8) -> Self {
    match value {
      0 => BurstColor::Green,
      1 => BurstColor::Orange,
      2 => BurstColor::Magenta,
      _ => panic!("Invalid BurstColor value"),
    }
  }
}
```

Here, you're working around a limitation of Rust's constant parameter system. You can only use primitive types in constants at this time. Adding the converter up-front gives us a much nicer interface to work with later on.

The particle system is storing color as a Vec3, so you should also implement a conversion from the BurstColor enumeration to a Vec3:

MarsElements/mars_base_one/src/main.rs
```rust
impl Into<LinearRgba> for BurstColor {
  fn into(self) -> LinearRgba {
    match self {
      BurstColor::Green => LinearRgba::new(0.0, 1.0, 0.0, 1.0),
      BurstColor::Orange => LinearRgba::new(1.0, 0.5, 0.0, 1.0),
      BurstColor::Magenta => LinearRgba::new(1.0, 0.0, 1.0, 1.0),
    }
  }
}
```

You now have all the building blocks to create a generic system for collecting items: you can implement the OnCollect trait for each collectable item and store a color for each item type that should spawn as a particle burst when the item is collected. Let's pull that together and create a generic system to handle all collectable items:

MarsElements/mars_base_one/src/main.rs

```rust
fn collect_game_element_and_despawn<T:Component + OnCollect, const COLOR: u8>
(
❶  mut collisions: EventReader<OnCollision<Player, T>>,
   mut commands: Commands,
   mut player: Query<(&mut Player, &Transform)>,
❷  mut spawn: EventWriter<SpawnParticle>,
)
 {
❸  let mut collected = Vec::new();
   for collision in collisions.read() {
     collected.push(collision.entity_b);
   }

   let Ok((mut player, player_pos)) = player.single_mut() else {
     return;
   };

❹  for miner in collected.iter() {
     if commands.get_entity(*miner).is_ok() {
       commands.entity(*miner).despawn();
     }
❺    T::effect(&mut player);
   }

   if !collected.is_empty() {
     // Spawn burst of particles
     particle_burst(
       player_pos.translation.truncate(),
       BurstColor::from(COLOR).into(),
       &mut spawn,
       2.0,
     );
   }
}
```

❶ Specify the collision type. Notice how the second collision is generic—of type T. You can specialize the system multiple times to handle every collision type without having to rewrite it.

❷ Event sender to let you send messages to the particle system, requesting particle spawning.

❸ Build a vector to collect a list of entities with whom you've collided. You read all collisions and add the non-player entity (of type T) into here.

❹ For each entity the player has collided with, call Bevy's despawn function to remove them from the game. You have to check that the entity exists —if it doesn't, Bevy will crash.

❺ The T::effect() functions you created are provided by your trait as associated functions. You can call T::effect to call the trait, which will be associated with the correct function at compile time. Since you're specializing the function's generics at compile time, this provides a zero-overhead way of determining what to do with the collision.

The collision function can now handle all of the items in the game, and you've only had to write it once. The compiler will create a new copy of the function, specialized to the specified T type for each invocation. Now you need to call the systems to enable functionality:

```
add_phase!(app, GamePhase, GamePhase::Playing,
  start => [ setup ],
  run => [ movement, end_game, physics_clock, sum_impulses,
      apply_gravity, apply_velocity,
    terminal_velocity, check_collisions::<Player, Ground>, bounce,
      camera_follow,
    show_performance, spawn_particle_system, particle_age_system,
    miner_beacon,
    score_display, check_collisions::<Player, Miner>,
    check_collisions::<Player, Fuel>, check_collisions::<Player, Battery>,
    collect_game_element_and_despawn::<Miner, { BurstColor::Green as u8 }>,
    collect_game_element_and_despawn::<Fuel,  { BurstColor::Orange as u8 }>,
    collect_game_element_and_despawn::<Battery,{ BurstColor::Magenta as u8 }>
    ],
  exit => [ cleanup::<GameElement> ]
);
```

Notice how you're handling all of the collectable items with a single system, creating specializations for each in your game phase enumeration. That's nice and easy to read; you aren't duplicating code, and you can easily add new collectable items in the future.

You also need to register the collisions. At the end of your initialization code, add the following:

```
    .insert_resource(Animations::new())
➤   .add_event::<OnCollision<Player, Ground>>()
➤   .add_event::<OnCollision<Player, Miner>>()
➤   .add_event::<OnCollision<Player, Fuel>>()
➤   .add_event::<OnCollision<Player, Battery>>()
➤   .add_event::<SpawnParticle>()
    .run();
```

Code Bloat and Compile Time

Generic specialization is free at runtime, but there's no such thing as a free lunch. The compiler is generating a new copy of your function for each generic type with which it's called. Your binary is getting bigger, and your compile time is getting longer every time you do this. Like everything else in engineering, it's a trade-off, and you're the only one who can decide on the correct balance between compile-time overhead and runtime overhead.

Now that you can handle collisions and their effects on game score, you need to add a few effects that *result* from collisions.

Depleting Shields

You've added shields to the game, but they don't do anything yet. You need to deplete them when the player collides with the ground. You'll do this in the bounce function:

MarsElements/mars_base_one/src/main.rs
```
fn bounce(
  mut collisions: EventReader<OnCollision<Player, Ground>>,
  mut player_query: Query<(&PhysicsPosition, &mut Player)>,
  ground_query: Query<&PhysicsPosition, With<Ground>>,
  mut impulses: EventWriter<Impulse>,
  mut particles: EventWriter<SpawnParticle>,
  mut state: ResMut<NextState<GamePhase>>,
) {
  let mut bounce = Vec2::default();
  let mut entity = None;
  let mut bounces = 0;
  // Re-using the bounce techniques from the collisions chapter.
  for collision in collisions.read() {
    if let Ok((player, _)) = player_query.single_mut() {
      if let Ok(ground) = ground_query.get(collision.entity_b) {
        entity = Some(collision.entity_a);
        let difference = player.start_frame - ground.start_frame;
        bounces += 1;
        bounce = difference;
      }
    }
  }
  if bounce != Vec2::default() {
    bounce = bounce.normalize();
    impulses.write(Impulse {
      target: entity.unwrap(),
      amount: Vec3::new(bounce.x / bounces as f32,
        bounce.y / bounces as f32, 0.0),
      absolute: true,
```

```
      source: 2,
    });

    // Spawn a burst of particles
    let Ok((player_pos, mut player)) = player_query.single_mut()
      else {
        return;
      };
    particle_burst(
      player_pos.end_frame,
      LinearRgba::new(0.0, 0.0, 1.0, 1.0),
      &mut particles,
      3.0,
    );
    // Reduce the player's shield level
    player.shields -= 1;
    if player.shields <= 0 {
      state.set(GamePhase::GameOver);
    }
  }
}
```

There's nothing new to you here (it's all been covered before). You used the "bounce" system from Chapter 8, Build Obstacles and Collision Detection, on page 163, to make the player bounce off walls and combined it with the particle burst system from this chapter. The player now loses shields when they collide with the ground, and a burst of particles is spawned to indicate the collision.

Running Out of Fuel

The game features fuel, but it doesn't do anything yet either. You need to deplete fuel when the player fires their thruster and also refuse to fire the thruster when there's no fuel. You'll do this in the movement function:

MarsElements/mars_base_one/src/main.rs
```
fn movement(
  keyboard: Res<ButtonInput<KeyCode>>,
  mut player_query: Query<(Entity, &mut Transform, &mut Player)>,
  mut impulses: EventWriter<Impulse>,
  mut particles: EventWriter<SpawnParticle>,
) {
  let Ok((entity, mut transform, mut player)) = player_query.single_mut()
    else {
      return;
    };
  if keyboard.pressed(KeyCode::ArrowLeft) {
    transform.rotate(Quat::from_rotation_z(f32::to_radians(2.0)));

    particles.write(SpawnParticle{
```

```
        position: -transform.local_x().truncate() + Vec2::new(
          transform.translation.x, transform.translation.y),
        color: LinearRgba::new(0.0, 1.0, 1.0, 1.0),
        velocity: transform.local_x().as_vec3(),
      });
    }
    if keyboard.pressed(KeyCode::ArrowRight) {
      transform.rotate(Quat::from_rotation_z(f32::to_radians(-2.0)));

      particles.write(SpawnParticle{
        position: transform.local_x().truncate() + Vec2::new(
          transform.translation.x, transform.translation.y),
        color: LinearRgba::new(0.0, 1.0, 1.0, 1.0),
        velocity: -transform.local_x().as_vec3(),
      });
    }
    if keyboard.pressed(KeyCode::ArrowUp) {
➤     if player.fuel > 0 {
➤       impulses.write(Impulse {
➤         target: entity,
➤         amount: transform.local_y().as_vec3(),
➤         absolute: false,
➤         source: 1,
➤       });
➤       particles.write(SpawnParticle{
➤         position: transform.local_y().truncate() + Vec2::new(
➤           transform.translation.x, transform.translation.y),
➤         color: LinearRgba::new(0.0, 1.0, 1.0, 1.0),
➤         velocity: -transform.local_y().as_vec3(),
➤       });
➤       player.fuel -= 1;
➤     }
    }
  }
}
```

Running out of fuel is handled by not allowing the thruster to fire anymore, causing the ship to drop like a paperweight. It will bounce off the ground repeatedly, and you'll lose shields each time. You can't die from running out of fuel, but you can lose all of your shields.

Winning the Game

The last thing you need to do is add a "win" condition. If the player has collected all of the miners, they've won the game. This is a relatively simple system:

MarsElements/mars_base_one/src/main.rs
```rust
fn end_game(
  mut state: ResMut<NextState<GamePhase>>,
  player_query: Query<&Player>,
) {
  let Ok(player) = player_query.single() else {
    return;
  };
  if player.miners_saved == 20 {
    // You won!
    state.set(GamePhase::GameOver);
  }
}
```

Finalizing the Systems

Finally, you need to ensure that all of the systems you've created are being executed. Your GamePhase setup should look like this:

MarsElements/mars_base_one/src/main.rs
```rust
add_phase!(app, GamePhase, GamePhase::Playing,
  start => [ setup ],
  run => [ movement, end_game, physics_clock, sum_impulses, apply_gravity,
      apply_velocity,terminal_velocity.after(apply_velocity),
      check_collisions::<Player, Ground>, bounce,
      camera_follow.after(terminal_velocity),
    show_performance, spawn_particle_system, particle_age_system,
    miner_beacon,
    score_display, check_collisions::<Player, Miner>,
    check_collisions::<Player, Fuel>, check_collisions::<Player, Battery>,
    collect_game_element_and_despawn::<Miner, { BurstColor::Green as u8 }>,
    collect_game_element_and_despawn::<Fuel, { BurstColor::Orange as u8 }>,
    collect_game_element_and_despawn::<Battery, { BurstColor::Magenta
      as u8 }>
    ],
  exit => [ cleanup::<GameElement> ]
);
```

Wrapping Up

Congratulations! You've officially built a complete game. In the process, you used the library you created to quickly add elements to the game. You can now save stranded space miners, refuel your ship, recharge your shields, and die horribly when you hit the ground too often.

At this point, you learned how to use traits and generics to reduce code duplication and how to add visual flair to your game with particle effects. You also learned how to display text on a heads-up display (HUD) using egui.

In the next chapter, you'll turn the statistics into a game score and build a high-score server. You'll also learn a bit about using Rust for networking, network services, and creating asynchronous code.

Extending the Game

It would be fun to keep adding features to Mars Base One. It's a powerful base for a game. You could add more collectible items, like VIP miners who need priority rescue. You could track playtime and reward fast wins. You could add more levels and increase difficulty. You could add turrets that fire missiles at the player—a remnant of the base's defense systems. You could add a story and a reason for the player to be saving miners.

Due to size constraints and the desire to keep the book focused on teaching new concepts, this book won't include all of these features. But you can implement them. You have the tools and the knowledge to extend Mars Base One into a full game.

Some additional game features will appear as bonus content on this book's website.[1]

CHAPTER 14

Build a High Score Server

In the previous chapter, you finished Mars Base One and now have a complete game that players can enjoy. While this might be a good place to stop, there's one more feature you can add: high scores.

High scores are popular because they encourage people to keep playing your game long after their first win. But, before you can add this new feature, you need to add a way to keep score. Let's get started.

Calculating Scores

Scores are conceptually simple. When players do something good, they score points. When they do something bad, they might lose points—depending on your game's rules. In Mars Base One, players will earn points for saving stranded miners and for maintaining a high level of resources such as fuel and shields.

The first step is to decide where to keep track of the score. Attaching the scorekeeper to the player tends to make the most sense, so you'll add it there. In the Player struct, add a score field:

```
MarsScore/mars_base_one/src/main.rs
#[derive(Component)]
struct Player {
  miners_saved: u32,
  shields: i32,
  fuel: i32,
➤  score: u32,
}
```

Now that the Player structure has a score field, you need to update the structure's initialization to set the score to zero. In the setup() function, add a zero initialization to the score field:

MarsScore/mars_base_one/src/main.rs

```
spawn_image!(
  assets,
  commands,
  "ship",
  0.0,
  200.0,
  10.0,
  &loaded_assets,
  GameElement,
➤ Player { miners_saved: 0, shields: 500, fuel: 100_000, score: 0 },
  Velocity::default(),
  PhysicsPosition::new(Vec2::new(0.0, 200.0)),
  ApplyGravity,
  AxisAlignedBoundingBox::new(24.0, 24.0)
);
```

With initialization out of the way, it's time to award some points.

The most obvious place to start is when the player collides with miners, saving them from certain doom. Collisions between the player and miners are handled in the OnCollect implementation for the Miner type. Currently, the code increments the player.miners_saved field. Let's add some points to the player's score as well:

MarsScore/mars_base_one/src/main.rs

```
impl OnCollect for Miner {
  fn effect(player: &mut Player) {
    player.miners_saved += 1;
❶  player.score += 1000;
❷  if player.shields > 0 {
      player.score += player.shields as u32;
    }
❸  if player.fuel > 1000 {
      player.score += player.fuel as u32;
    }
  }
}
```

❶ Award 1,000 points for saving the miner.

❷ If the player still has shields remaining, award a bonus.

❸ Likewise, if the player still has fuel above the starting level, award a bonus.

You could add more scoring opportunities or keep it simple and reward saving miners. Adding more dimensions to score calculations can make the game more interesting but also more complex. It's a balancing act, and only your game design and playtesting can guide you to what's right.

The last change to the actual game code is to display the score.

Offering continuous feedback to players helps drive engagement; it also keeps them from feeling like they're playing in a vacuum. More importantly, feedback lets them know what they're doing well and what rewards they're earning for their efforts. You're already displaying shields, fuel, and miners saved—you just need to add the score to the score_display() system:

MarsScore/mars_base_one/src/main.rs
```
fn score_display(
  player: Query<&Player>,
  mut egui_context: egui::EguiContexts,
) {
  let Ok(player) = player.single() else {
    return;
  };
  egui::egui::Window::new("Score").show(
    egui_context.ctx_mut(),
    |ui| {
➤      ui.label(format!("Score: {}", player.score));
      ui.label(format!("Miners Saved: {}", player.miners_saved));
      ui.label(format!("Shields: {}", player.shields));
      ui.label(format!("Fuel: {}", player.fuel));
    });
}
```

Perfect. Now, as players zoom around the base, they'll have continual feedback on how well they're doing:

Adding a score to the game was relatively straightforward mostly because you had all the elements in place to make it happen—it just needed some glue. Next up, you'll need to consider how to connect the score to the other game phases.

Passing the Score to the Game Over Phase

In previous chapters, game phases were self-contained. Sure, you transitioned between them—starting the game, ending the game, and so on—but they didn't (and still don't) share data between them.

Self-contained code is generally a good design practice and is much easier to understand, manage, and debug. But there are times when you need to pass data between phases. In this case, when the player's game ends, you need to pass the score to the "game over" phase. Passing the score will allow you to display the final score and give players the opportunity to submit their score to a high-score server.

There are a few approaches to passing data between phases:

- You can use a shared resource, keeping it around at the end of the phase. You already use this approach for game assets. But for data that isn't global data—data that's shared between phases, but not all phases—you run the risk of creating a "code smell." It's easy to create an overabundance of shared resources, but then you run into structural questions like who owns this data, where was this data updated, and did I remember to clean it up? As you can imagine, questions like these can get out of hand quickly.

- You can work some magic with threads and channels, building an "actor system." This is a great idea for some persistent systems because you isolate ownership and access to the data. But it's a bit heavyweight for passing a single score.

- You can use Bevy's event system. You already use it for passing messages between systems. It's less obvious that you can post a message in one game phase and receive it in the next, but it works. This solution offers a nice balance between simplicity and isolation: you *move* the score out of the game phase and into the event system. The next phase can then read the score from the event system. Ownership, access, and cleanup are clear, and there's little room for confusion. The best part: your architecture remains easy to understand.

Since you've created a few message types already for the physics system, you can use the same approach to pass the score to the game over phase. First, create a message type:

MarsScore/mars_base_one/src/main.rs
```
#[derive(Event)]
struct FinalScore(u32);
```

FinalScore is a simple tuple type that holds the score. In the engine creation step, you need to register the message type. This is a simple call to add_event():

MarsScore/mars_base_one/src/main.rs
```
app.add_event::<FinalScore>();
```

Next, create a game system that emits an event with the player's score when the game ends:

MarsScore/mars_base_one/src/main.rs
```
fn submit_score(
  player: Query<&Player>,
  mut final_score: EventWriter<FinalScore>,
) {
  for player in player.iter() {
    final_score.write(FinalScore(player.score));
  }
}
```

The system needs to run when the game ends, but before the game phase's cleanup. Fortunately, your game phase macro supports this type of process. Adjust the add_phase! call to execute the new system:

MarsScore/mars_base_one/src/main.rs
```
add_phase!(app, GamePhase, GamePhase::Playing,
  start => [ setup ],
  run => [ movement, end_game, physics_clock, sum_impulses, apply_gravity,
    apply_velocity, terminal_velocity.after(apply_velocity),
    check_collisions::<Player, Ground>, bounce,
    camera_follow.after(terminal_velocity),
    show_performance, spawn_particle_system, particle_age_system,
    miner_beacon,
    score_display, check_collisions::<Player, Miner>,
    check_collisions::<Player, Fuel>, check_collisions::<Player, Battery>,
    collect_game_element_and_despawn::<Miner,{ BurstColor::Green as u8 }>,
    collect_game_element_and_despawn::<Fuel, { BurstColor::Orange as u8 }>,
    collect_game_element_and_despawn::<Battery,
      { BurstColor::Magenta as u8 }>
    ],
➤   exit => [ submit_score, cleanup::<GameElement>.after(submit_score) ]
);
```

When the game ends—for any reason—the submit_score() system will emit a FinalScore event. The next phase can then read the score from the event system. That leads you to the next phase: displaying the final score on the game over screen.

You need to create a system that displays the final score. The system will read the FinalScore event and use egui to display a score window. Eventually, submission to the high-score table will go here—but for now, let's display the score.

Let's start by creating a structure to hold the score and the player's name:

```
❶ #[derive(Default)]
   struct ScoreState {
❷   score: Option<u32>,
     player_name: String,
     submitted: bool,
   }
```

This is a simple Rust structure, but notice the following:

❶ Deriving default allows for easy construction of an empty structure with default values. It will set options to None and strings to be empty.

❷ score is optional. You may not have one immediately. You could use a "sentinel" value (for example, 0), but explicitly noting that a score isn't present yet makes your intent much clearer.

Let's create a system that receives the FinalScore event and displays the score, with placeholders for letting players enter their names and submit their scores:

```
   fn final_score(
❶   mut final_score: EventReader<FinalScore>,
❷   mut state: Local<ScoreState>,
     mut egui_context: egui::EguiContexts,
   ) {
     // Receive any score messages
❸   for score in final_score.read() {
       state.score = Some(score.0);
     }

     // Display the score input
❹   if let Some(score) = state.score {
       egui::egui::Window::new("Final Score").show(
         egui_context.ctx_mut(),
         |ui| {
           ui.label(format!("Final Score: {}", score));
           ui.label("Please enter your name:");
❺         ui.text_edit_singleline(&mut state.player_name);
❻         if ui.button("Submit Score").clicked() {
             // TODO: Submit the score here
           }
         });
     }
   }
```

❶ Request an EventReader for the FinalScore event. This allows you to read the event queue.

❷ Bevy supports LocalState as a way to persist between calls to a single system. This is great for storing the state that only applies to a single system— and shouldn't be shared with other systems. LocalState must implement Default, which is why you derive it on the ScoreState structure. An empty— defaulted—value will be created the first time that the system runs.

❸ Poll the message queue. If any FinalScore events have arrived, update the local state's score to match the value. This will almost always run on the first system execution—and never again.

❹ If a score has been recorded, then extract the score option into a local variable for easy access and build the egui window.

❺ Egui offers the text_edit_singleline() function as an easy way to display a text box and have changes to the text value be reflected in the bound string.

❻ If the Submit Score button is clicked, this code will be executed. You're not ready for that yet, so for now, stub it as a placeholder.

In your events initialization, don't forget to register the FinalScore event type:

MarsScore/mars_base_one/src/main.rs
```
app.add_event::<FinalScore>();
```

Finally, in your application setup, you need to add the final_score() system to the game over phase:

MarsScore/mars_base_one/src/main.rs
```
app.add_systems(Update, final_score.run_if(in_state(GamePhase::GameOver)));
```

If you run the game now, you can build up a score, and when you get to the game over screen, you'll see your score submission, as shown at the top of the next page.

You have a working local score system. The next step is to submit the score to a server.

Serializing Scores

You can send pretty much anything over the Internet. When it first came online, it was common to write a full socket-based program in C that would open a TCP or UDP socket, submit data in a bespoke, custom format, and write another program to receive your custom format. That's fast and effi- cient—and still worth doing for high-performance systems—but it imposes a heavy learning curve in Enterprise systems. Every new employee has to learn

the intricacies of your own personal protocol, and bugs tend to proliferate. As the Internet has evolved, so has the way we send data. The most common way to send data over the Internet is *JSON* over HTTP.

What Is JSON?

JSON—or JavaScript Object Notation—is a simple, human-readable data format. It's based on JavaScript and uses the JavaScript object syntax to represent data. It's more compact than XML and easier to read. JSON is a great way to send data over the Internet and is supported by almost every programming language.

For something as simple as a high score, you could simply write:

```
let score = format!("{{\"name\":\"{}\",\"score\":{}}}", name, score);
```

That would work well until someone entered a name with a double quote in it. Then your JSON would be invalid, and your server would reject it. You could escape the double quotes, but then you'd have to escape the escape character, and so on. So you modify your code to escape that pattern—and inevitably miss something. It's a rabbit hole of complexity that you want to avoid. Instead, let's make use of a library that can serialize your data into JSON for you. Rust has a great library for this, known as *Serde*.

Serde

Serde does a lot more than just JSON. Serde is language agnostic and can serialize and deserialize data into many formats. It's a great library to learn from and is used in many Rust projects. It's a bit complex, but it's worth learning.

When I was first learning Rust and encountered Serde for the first time, I was amazed. It made serialization easy, elegant, and fast. It was one of the reasons I stuck with Rust.

Let's add Serde to your project:

```
cargo add serde -F derive
```

The "-F derive" is a feature flag. Serde optionally provides "derive" macros to make serialization easy. Not using them is quite painful, so be sure to include them! cargo add should have added Serde to your Cargo.toml file. You can check by opening the file and looking for the serde dependency:

```
[dependencies]
...
serde = { version = "1.0.210", features = ["derive"] }
```

Now, let's build a structure to hold the high-score entry for submission to a server:

```
MarsScore/mars_base_one/src/main.rs
#[derive(serde::Serialize, serde::Deserialize)]
struct HighScoreEntry {
  name: String,
  score: u32,
}
```

That's all you need to support serialization: add a #[derive(Serialize)]. Deserialization is supported with #[derive(Deserialize)]. Serde runs a procedural macro at compile time that builds the serialization and deserialization code for you. And best of all: escaping is handled for you, compliance with formats is handled for you, and it's fast.

Now that you can serialize to JSON, you need to submit the score to a server.

Submitting Scores with Ureq

There are several Rust crates that can submit data to a server. The most popular is reqwest, but it's pretty heavy for what you need. Instead, you're

Put Shared Structures in a Crate

When you have data structures shared between clients and a server, it's a good idea to put them into their own crate and have both use the shared crate. This ensures that you don't accidentally change the structure in one place and forget to change it in the other.

going to use ureq. ureq is a simple, lightweight HTTP client that doesn't require asynchronous code, a lot of setup, or a lot of resources. It's perfect for submitting high scores.

Add ureq to your project (version 2):

```
cargo add ureq@2 -F json
```

Double-check your Cargo.toml file to ensure that ureq has been added:

```
[dependencies]
...
serde = { version = "1.0.210", features = ["derive"] }
ureq = { version = "2.10.1", features = ["json"] }
```

You now have a serializable type to submit—the HighScoreEntry—and an HTTP client with which to submit it. It's time to write some client code to submit the score to a server. Let's go back to the final_score system and flesh it out.

Before the if let Some(score) = state.score { block, add a check to see if the score has already been submitted. If it has, return early:

```
// Don't show the window if the score has been submitted
➤ if state.submitted {
➤     return;
➤ }
  if let Some(score) = state.score {
      egui::egui::Window::new("Final Score").show(
      //etc...
```

Next, you modify the "Submit Score" button to submit the score to the server. You'll spawn a thread and call ureq inside the thread. This ensures that the submission is detached from the rest of the program. If the program changes state, the submission thread will continue on its own. If the submission fails, it won't affect the rest of the program. Let's work through the code:

```
MarsScore/mars_base_one/src/main.rs
if let Some(score) = state.score {
    egui::egui::Window::new("Final Score").show(
        egui_context.ctx_mut(),
        |ui| {
```

```
        ui.label(format!("Final Score: {}", score));
        ui.label("Please enter your name:");
      ui.text_edit_singleline(&mut state.player_name);
❶    if ui.button("Submit Score").clicked() {
❷      state.submitted = true;
❸      let entry = HighScoreEntry {
          name: state.player_name.clone(),
          score,
        };
❹      std::thread::spawn(move || {
❺        ureq::post("http://localhost:3030/scoreSubmit")
❻        .timeout(std::time::Duration::from_secs(5))
❼        .send_json(entry)
❽        .expect("Failed to submit score");
        });
      }
    }
  );
}
```

❶ The player clicks the Submit Score button.

❷ Set submitted to true, so the player can't repeatedly submit a score.

❸ Create an instance of HighScoreEntry containing the name and high score.

❹ Create a new thread to run in the background so that you don't lock up the UI while the network request runs, and so the execution is detached from the rest of the program.

❺ Initialize ureq with the "post" constructor. You want to use the HTTP POST method since it's designed for submitting form data to a server.

❻ If you don't set a timeout, a server that isn't responding will keep this thread sitting around for a long time.

❼ Ureq has serde support built in. The send_json() function will automatically convert your variable into JSON, create all of the HTTP requests and headers, and send it to your server.

❽ Ordinarily, unwrapping or expecting a value would lead to the program terminating if an error occurs. Inside a thread, it causes the thread to terminate—and emit a diagnostic to the console. In production code, you'd still want to handle the error gracefully.

And there you have it: a high-score submission system. When the player clicks the "Submit Score" button, the score is submitted to the server. The player can't submit the score again, and the submission is handled in a separate thread so the UI remains responsive.

Submission without a server isn't useful, so let's build a server. First, let's take a quick detour to talk about asynchronous Rust.

Understanding Asynchronous Rust

Rust has *two* types of concurrency built in: threads, which you've already used, and *async*. They're related but different.

Threads are an operating system construct. When you create a thread, the operating system creates an entry in its scheduler, and threads are scheduled to run on available CPUs. Threads are interrupted when the operating system decides to switch to another thread. When this happens, the CPU's registers are saved, and the registers of the new thread are loaded. This is a relatively expensive operation, and the operating system does it for you. This makes threads great for long-running tasks or CPU-intensive tasks.

Async is a different beast and can also be found in C#, Python, C++ (as co-routines), and JavaScript. You can run async code on a single CPU core or many CPUs. Rust provides the minimum required to make async work and leaves implementation details to libraries. Libraries provide an executor, which schedules task execution, and a reactor, which handles operating system events. Unlike threads, the operating system won't interrupt your async code. Instead, async code runs until it hits an "await point," allowing another async task to execute. This is similar to old-school cooperative multitasking on Windows 3.x, Mac OS prior to OS X, AmigaOS, and so on. Async is lightweight, and you can have thousands of tasks running on a single thread. Async is best for systems that spend a lot of time *waiting* on other systems: network requests, database access, and so on.

Async Rust has developed a bit of a reputation for being a minefield of complexity. Async was added after Rust's 1.0 release and sometimes feels like it was bolted on. Async Rust is, however, useful—and you won't run into most of the complexity unless you're writing libraries.

The most common complaints about Rust async include:

- Async "colors your code." You can't call an async function from a non-async function (you can go the other way). Adding async to an otherwise synchronous project becomes complicated.

- Rust doesn't have garbage collection, while most async languages do. You have to be a bit more careful about using references in async code because the order of execution isn't always clear. Tasks can be canceled, may switch to a different CPU, or may be delayed by the executor, so using references becomes difficult.

- Sometimes the async syntax can get a little verbose.

With that said, async Rust is great for high-performance servers. You can build a web server on a little MacBook Air that handles thousands of requests per second without breaking a sweat, or build tiny Docker containers that can handle a lot of traffic while consuming little memory.

Most web servers are written in async code, as they spend most of their time waiting for network requests. You'll be using async code to submit high scores to the server.

Building a Server

Rust is good for building small, fast, and reliable servers. You're going to build a small server that accepts high-score submissions from players, stores them in a file, serves them back to players, and displays them on a small web page. That sounds like a lot, but it's actually a small project.

Let's start by adding a new project:

```
cargo new highscore_server
cd highscore_server
```

You're going to need a few dependencies:

```
cargo add tokio -F full
cargo add axum -F json
cargo add serde -F derive
```

These dependencies are:

- Tokio is an async runtime for Rust. There are many to choose from, but Tokio has become the de facto standard, particularly in the web and Enterprise space. You're using the "full" feature flag to add all of its features.
- Axum is a web server that makes it easy to build web services. It's built on top of Tokio, and it's fast and pretty easy to use. The setup is similar to Express for nodejs if you've ever used it before. You're using the json feature to include automatic JSON serialization and deserialization.
- Serde is used for serialization and deserialization. You're using the derive feature to include the derive macros.

Let's start with a simple server and walk through what it's doing. Replace your main function with the following:

```
use axum::{routing::post, Json, Router};

#[tokio::main]
async fn main() {
    let app = Router::new()
        .route("/scoreSubmit", post(score_submit));

    // run it
    let listener = tokio::net::TcpListener::bind("127.0.0.1:3030")
        .await
        .unwrap();
    println!("listening on {}", listener.local_addr().unwrap());
    axum::serve(listener, app).await.unwrap();
}
```

❶ Routers are the heart of how Axum handles web requests. Routers map incoming requests to functions, typically by reading the requested URL and method (for example, POST to /scoreSubmit) and mapping them to a function that handles the request.

❷ Create your first route. This route listens for POST requests to "/scoreSubmit". When a request is received, it will call the score_submit function.

❸ Listen on localhost (127.0.0.1) on port 3030. This is a development setup: you aren't listening to any requests outside of your computer. If you want to take this live, change this to 0.0.0.0 (for IPv4) or :: (for IPv6).

❹ Async functions return a type called Future. Just running the function won't do anything at all—you have to use await. Await tells Tokio that it should execute the function and return control to your program when it completes. Listening to the network is an async function, so you hand control to Tokio until the network is available or an error occurs.

❺ Tell Axum to start and wait for it to return. It will only return if an error occurs—otherwise, your web server will sit and serve requests forever.

This won't compile yet because you still need to provide the actual score_submit function. Let's add that now:

```
#[derive(serde::Serialize, serde::Deserialize, Debug)]
struct HighScoreEntry {
    name: String,
    score: u32,
}

async fn score_submit(
    high_score: Json<HighScoreEntry>
) {
    println!("Received high score: {:?}", high_score);
}
```

❶ Axum is doing a little bit of magic here. Just like Bevy, your services can have a variable number of parameters, and Axum will try to match the incoming request to the parameters of your function. In this case, you're stating that you expect the POST body to include JSON and that JSON will match the schema of your HighScoreEntry structure. Axum will automatically deserialize the JSON into your structure and pass it to your function. If the JSON doesn't match the structure, Axum will return an error to the client and not call your function.

Those few lines of code are all you need to make a working web service. You can test it by running the server and then the game. When you submit your score, you'll see something like Received high score: HighScoreEntry { name: \"Herberticus\", score: 204352 } in the console.

Now that you can receive high scores, let's store and display them.

Displaying Scores

You're going to add one more dependency: serde_json. This is a library that provides JSON format support for Serde. Axum and ureq already use it internally, but don't reexport it for you, so you have to add it yourself. Add it to your Cargo.toml file with cargo add:

```
cargo add serde_json
```

You can now create JSON from your high-score entries and read JSON from the high-score file.

Server-Side State

Let's create a new type to hold the high-score table and persist it to disk:

MarsScore/highscore_server/src/main.rs
```
#[derive(serde::Serialize, serde::Deserialize, Debug, Clone)]
struct HighScoreTable {
❶   entries: Vec<HighScoreEntry>,
}

impl HighScoreTable {
  fn new() -> Self {
❷    if std::path::Path::new("high_scores.json").exists() {
❸      let file = std::fs::File::open("high_scores.json").unwrap();
❹      serde_json::from_reader(file).unwrap()
    } else {
      Self { entries: Vec::new() }
    }
  }

  fn add_entry(&mut self, entry: HighScoreEntry) {
```

```
      self.entries.push(entry);
⑤     self.entries.sort_by(|a, b| b.score.cmp(&a.score));
⑥     self.entries.truncate(10);
      self.save();
  }

  fn save(&self) {
⑦     let file = std::fs::File::create("high_scores.json").unwrap();
⑧     serde_json::to_writer(file, self).unwrap();
  }
}

#[derive(serde::Serialize, serde::Deserialize, Debug, Clone)]
struct HighScoreEntry {
  name: String,
  score: u32,
}
```

❶ Create a Vector in which to store the high-score table.

❷ Check if the high score file exists. If it doesn't, create a new high-score table.

❸ Open the high score file as a reader—a trait that can be read from.

❹ Read the high-score table from the reader, using Serde to deserialize the JSON into your high-score table.

❺ Sort the high-score table by score descending. You can use sort_by() to provide a custom comparator function to customize sorting.

❻ Truncate the high-score table to the top 10 scores.

❼ If the file doesn't exist, create a new high-score table. This creates a variable that implements the Writer trait, which can be written to.

❽ Write the high-score table to the writer, using Serde to serialize the high-score table into JSON.

You now have a type that can hold high scores, save them to disk, and load them from disk if they exist—or create a new high-score table if they don't. That's the bulk of the "business logic" for our high-score server. Now you need to add a few routes to the server to display the high scores.

At the top of your main.rs file, add an import for a *Tokio* Mutex:

```
use tokio::sync::Mutex;
```

Asynchronous Synchronization

In normal—synchronous—Rust, you would use a std::sync::Mutex to protect data from concurrent access. Regular Mutexes block the current thread and don't resume until the lock is available. This can be a problem in async code, especially with a multithreaded executor such as Tokio. It's possible to block the thread while waiting for a lock, but the lock is already held by an async task that happens to be running on the same thread. This deadlocks your program.

Tokio provides its own tokio::sync::Mutex that's designed to work with async code. It's designed to be used in async code, which will yield to other tasks while waiting for a lock.

Go back to your Router::new call and add a few more routes:

MarsScore/highscore_server/src/main.rs
```
let app = Router::new()
  .route("/scoreSubmit", post(score_submit))
❶ .route("/", get(high_scores_html))
❷ .route("/highScores", get(high_scores_json))
❸ .with_state(Arc::new(Mutex::new(HighScoreTable::new())));
```

❶ When a user opens http://localhost:3030/, display an HTML high-score table.

❷ When a user opens http://localhost:3030/highScores, return the high scores as JSON.

❸ Store the high-score table as global state, accessible to all route methods that request it. It's wrapped in a Mutex to ensure concurrent access is safe.

Adding the state to the router allows it to be injected into handler methods. Let's update the score_submit function to make use of the new state:

MarsScore/highscore_server/src/main.rs
```
async fn score_submit(
❶ State(table): State<Arc<Mutex<HighScoreTable>>>,
❷ high_score: Json<HighScoreEntry>,
) {
  let mut lock = table.lock().await;
❸ lock.add_entry(HighScoreEntry {
    name: high_score.name.clone(),
    score: high_score.score,
  });
}
```

❶ The left-hand side is pattern-matching—you can use pattern-matching in function parameters. The state is passed as a strong type, and this

---

Layers and State

Axum supports extension layers and states in routers, and they aren't the same. There can only be one State per router; it's a lot like Bevy's LocalState. You can have as many layers are you want, accessed by type. Layers are generally easier to work with and more flexible but offer slightly lower performance. Unless you're expecting a huge volume of data, you can use layers for most things.

Layers and states are cloned multiple times for each request. You almost always want to wrap your layers in an Arc. Atomic reference count (ARC) creates a single copy of the data on the heap and attaches an atomic "reference count." Cloning increments the reference count, and dropping decreases the reference count—deleting the data when the reference count reaches zero. Rust doesn't have garbage collection, but Arc is the same thing. It's thread-safe but read-only.

Arc can become read-write when you enclose a locking structure, such as a Mutex. Mutex ensures that only one thread or task can access the data at a time. This imposes a small performance penalty but guarantees that your data won't be corrupted by multiple threads accessing it at the same time.

---

extracts the contents of the state wrapper directly into a variable named table. The right-hand side of the expression lists the type, which will be matched at compile time to what you placed into the state table.

❷ As before, Axum will decode the JSON POST body and submit it to your function.

❸ Lock the state mutex—giving exclusive access. Call the add_entry() function you created in the state manager to store the score.

The injection is similar to Bevy's dependency injection; it's a powerful mechanism used by a few Rust frameworks.

When a score arrives, it's safely stored in the high scores table. Let's prove that by implementing the high_scores_html function to display the scores:

MarsScore/highscore_server/src/main.rs

```rust
async fn high_scores_html(
  State(table): State<Arc<Mutex<HighScoreTable>>>,
) -> Html<String> {
  let mut html = String::from("<h1>High Scores</h1>");
  html.push_str("<table>");
  html.push_str("<tr><th>Name</th><th>Score</th></tr>");
  for entry in &table.lock().await.entries {
    html.push_str("<tr>");
    html.push_str("<td>");
    html.push_str(&entry.name);
    html.push_str("</td>");
    html.push_str("<td>");
    html.push_str(&entry.score.to_string());
    html.push_str("</td>");
    html.push_str("</tr>");
    html.push_str("</table>");

  }
  Html(html)
}
```

The high_scores_html function uses the same dependency injection to obtain the
high scores. It then locks the mutex (notice the await—you're using a Tokio
async mutex) and iterates through the high scores. It emits some ugly but
workable HTML.

Finally, let's provide a function to retrieve the scores as JSON, allowing the
game to easily display a high-score table in the game:

MarsScore/highscore_server/src/main.rs

```rust
async fn high_scores_json(
  State(table): State<Arc<Mutex<HighScoreTable>>>,
) -> Json<HighScoreTable> {
  let lock = table.lock().await;
  let table = lock.clone();
  Json(table)
}
```

The only "magic" in this function is that you simply return Json(table). Axum
has built-in JSON serialization, so by returning data wrapped in a Json type,
Axum will automatically serialize it to JSON and return it to the client.

Congratulations! You have a working high-score server and have built your
first Rust web service. You can run the server and then run the game. When
you submit your score, you'll see it displayed in the HTML high-score table.

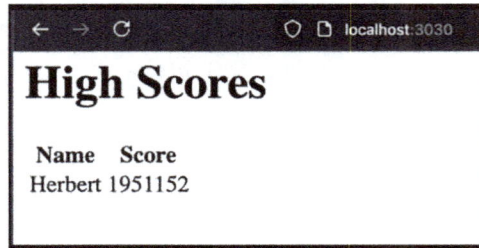

Let's go back to the game and add a system to display the high scores.

Displaying High Scores in the Game

All that remains for the game is to query the server for high scores and display them on the starting page. If the server isn't available, you want to make sure nothing bad happens, and the game continues as it was before. That allows for offline play, or simply forgetting to start the server.

To accomplish this, you're going to make use of another one of Rust's great features: channels. Channels provide a quick and easy way to send data between threads, with little overhead. You can send any type of data over a channel, and it's easy to use. You don't have to use spaghetti-style code with shared global variables everywhere. Channels make that a thing of the past for multithreaded Rust code.

Open your game's main.rs file. Start by defining two structures:

MarsScore/mars_base_one/src/main.rs
```
#[derive(Default)]
struct HighscoreTableState {
  entries: Option<HighScoreTable>,
  receiver: Option<std::sync::mpsc::Receiver<HighScoreTable>>,
}

#[derive(serde::Serialize, serde::Deserialize)]
struct HighScoreTable {
  entries: Vec<HighScoreEntry>,
}
```

This structure holds two optional fields: entries, which contains the high-score table, and an std::sync::mpsc::Receiver. This is the *receiving* half of a channel—it can be polled to see if a message is ready to be received.

The second structure simply holds a table of high-score entries.

Channels

MPSC stands for "multi-producer, single consumer." An MPSC channel may have as many "producers"—who submit messages to the channel—as needed. It may only have a single receiver, the recipient of the messages.

MPSC channels use Rust's Drop trait to automatically close themselves if the receiver is ever destroyed or there are no remaining producers. This avoids some of the difficulty that sometimes shows up with channels in languages like Go—but means that you have to be careful to never accidentally close your channel.

Now you're going to use these structures to create a system that queries the server for high scores in the background and only displays them when (or if) they become available. Add the following system to your game:

MarsScore/mars_base_one/src/main.rs

```rust
fn highscore_table(
❶  mut state: Local<HighscoreTableState>,
   mut egui_context: egui::EguiContexts,
) {
   if state.receiver.is_none() {
     // Create the channel
❷   let (tx, rx) = std::sync::mpsc::channel();
     state.receiver = Some(rx);

     // Request the table
❸   std::thread::spawn(move || {
       let table = ureq::get("http://localhost:3030/highScores")
         .timeout(std::time::Duration::from_secs(5))
         .call()
         .unwrap()
         .into_json::<HighScoreTable>()
         .unwrap();
❹    let _ = tx.send(table);
     });
   } else {
     // Receive the result
     if let Some(rx) = &state.receiver {
❺     if let Ok(table) = rx.try_recv() {
         state.entries = Some(table);
       }
     }
   }

   if let Some(table) = &state.entries {
     // Display the table
❻   egui::egui::Window::new("High Scores").show(
       egui_context.ctx_mut(),
       |ui| {
```

```
        for entry in table.entries.iter() {
          ui.label(format!("{}: {}", entry.name, entry.score));
        }
      });
    }
  }
}
```

❶ The Local allows for a system-local state. When the system starts, the state is initialized in its default state. When the system ends, the state is dropped. While the system runs, it can be accessed and modified by the system—and only the system. Local state provides a great way to isolate state management without the overhead of creating a new global resource.

❷ Initialize an MPSC channel. Rust will infer the message type from usage. Note that it returns a tuple containing the transmitter and receiver—you're destructuring the tuple to separate the variables in the assignment call.

❸ Spawn a thread that will manage calling the web service. Isolating it into a thread means that it won't cause any delays in the game, and errors won't crash the game.

❹ When (and if) the high-score table is received and has been parsed from JSON, submit the scores into the channel.

❺ Once the transmission thread has started, on each frame poll the receiver to see if a message is available. If there is, update the local state with the high-score table.

❻ Once high scores have been received, render a high-score table using egui.

Finally, in your application initialization, you need to add the new system to the "start" phase:

MarsScore/mars_base_one/src/main.rs
```
app.add_systems(Update, highscore_table.run_if(in_state(GamePhase::MainMenu)));
```

Now you can run your game and see the high scores displayed on the start screen:

Communicate State Instead of Storing It

When you learn about mutexes and shared data structures, it's easy to get excited and start storing the state in mutex-locked structures. This can work—but once your state starts being accessed all over your program, it can quickly turn into "spaghetti" code. Debugging programs in which the global state may change at any time can quickly become a nightmare.

Instead, consider using channels to communicate state changes. You can submit state changes to a channel and have a single system responsible for managing a global state structure. You can also include a channel sender—the oneshot inside your channel request. This allows you to send a message to the channel and wait for a response. This is a great way to manage state changes in a Rust program.

Wrapping Up

Congratulations! You've finished Mars Base One.

At this point, you have a complete physics-based game with objectives, failure modes, scores, and a networked high-score system. Along the way, you picked up key Rust concepts, including using channels for thread communication, Serde for data serialization, and Axum for web server development. You also gained insight into asynchronous Rust and how it differs from threading, and you used Arc for efficient state management in a web service.

In the final chapter, you'll learn about packaging your libraries into reusable crates and how to publish them to the Rust Cargo registry. You'll also learn more about the Rust ecosystem, open source, and how to contribute to the Rust community.

Part V

Library Curation

CHAPTER 15

Share Your Library

Libraries are great. You can share them between projects, with friends, and even with the rest of the world.

Rust includes a robust package management system as part of Cargo. You've benefited from it throughout this book. In this chapter, you'll learn how to share your libraries with others. You'll dive deep into the technical aspects of sharing your library, licensing considerations, and most importantly, the responsibilities and pitfalls that come with curating a public project.

Start by asking yourself two questions.

Is Your Library Worth Sharing?

One of the first complaints many C++ programmers have when they first start using Rust is "My goodness, where did all these dependencies come from?" The nervousness is understandable—"supply chain" attacks are a sneaky way to insert dangerous code into other people's programs, and many large companies insist on using audited dependencies. It can also lead to fragility. This inevitably leads to comparisons with the "left-pad" problem from Java-Script.[1] The "left-pad incident" occurred because a popular package was removed from the NPM repository (JavaScript's primary packaging source), breaking thousands of projects that depended on it. Further investigation showed a deeper problem: the package was only 11 lines of code, and many projects could easily have written their own version. JavaScript has a lot of micro-packages; the package "is odd" famously depends on "is even" and negates the function call.

Rust's crate repository doesn't have any rules against sharing one-line libraries, but the community has a strong preference for libraries that are

---

1.   https://en.wikipedia.org/wiki/Npm_left-pad_incident

"worth sharing." This is a subjective judgment, but you should always ask yourself if what you've created is worth sharing. Do this before you publish. If you're not sure, you can always ask in the Rust Discord server, Rust forums, or other Rust communities.

Is Your Library Ready to Share?

There are a lot of crates on crates.io that include the beginning of a project but not much else. It's frustrating when you track down a crate that looks perfect for your needs, only to find a helpful note about everything that the author hopes to accomplish in the future. Sometimes, if you check back later, more has appeared. But it's common for the content to never appear.

Crate Culture

The JavaScript and NodeJS communities encourage making packages for everything and sharing them immediately. The Rust community typically encourages you to start on GitHub (or equivalent) and only publish to Cargo when it's likely to be useful.

Please don't share your project until it's ready. This means that it should compile, do something useful, and have some tests. It should have some documentation and examples, so people know what to do with it and what it's for. It's surprisingly common to open a crate and find documented functions—and no description of what the crate actually *does*. Let's avoid that. The first paragraph in your README.md file should tell a visitor what your crate does and how it can help them.

Once you've decided that your library is worth sharing and is ready to share, you need to start thinking about licensing.

Choosing the Right License

If you commit a project to GitHub, you aren't automatically giving anyone else permission to use it. Without an explicit license, your code remains your property. Your code on GitHub—or another code-sharing service—must specify a license if you want to allow others to use it. And therein lies a problem: there are many licenses from which to choose, and unless you happen to be a lawyer with a lot of spare time, it can be difficult to evaluate them.

The most common license on crates.io is the MIT license.[2] The MIT license is extremely permissive; library users can copy, change, and redistribute your

---

2. https://en.wikipedia.org/wiki/MIT_License

Namespacing and Name Squatting

The crates.io system currently doesn't include *namespaceing*. There's only a single crate named Serde—and once taken, that name isn't available for anyone else. A namespaced system would allow bracket/Serde or similar—you could separate repositories by organization or user.

This means that if you were to publish your crate named my_library—nobody else can use that name. This is a good thing in that it prevents confusion and a bad thing because you could grab all the names you think you might use. Never fill them with anything useful—"squatting" the names until you get around to using them. Squatting on names is considered bad form—please don't do it.

The Rust community regularly considers namespacing, and this situation may change.

code as much as they want. They can sell it, profit from it, and don't have to share changes, profits, or anything else with you. The only requirement is that they include your copyright notice and the license text with the code. The MIT license is often a good choice for libraries: it's simple, it lets people enjoy your code, and it doesn't put any restrictions on your library users.

If unrestricted changes bother you, you might consider a "copyleft" license such as the GNU General Purpose License (GPL).[3] The GPL requires that any changes to your code be shared with the community. The GPL is also *viral*: if someone uses GPL code in your project, their project must also be GPL-licensed. This can be a good thing if you want to ensure that your code remains open source, but it can also heavily discourage the use of your library. Many corporate legal departments prohibit the inclusion of GPL code in their projects.

There are *many* other licenses. MIT is often a good place to start. If you're unsure, maybe try the Choose a License service.[4]

Bevy currently recommends dual-licensing your plugins to be both MIT licensed and Apache-2.0 licensed. This maximizes the number of people who can use your code. When you're integrating with existing projects, you'll often need to consult with the parent project on their licensing preferences.

3. https://en.wikipedia.org/wiki/GNU_General_Public_License
4. https://choosealicense.com/

Licensing and the Rust Ecosystem

The Rust ecosystem promotes open source. Rust itself is open source, and you can't publish a crate to crates.io without providing source code. If your library needs to remain proprietary, don't publish it to crates.io.

The Rust community is generally friendly and helpful. If you have questions about licensing, you can ask them in the Rust Discord server, Rust forums, or other Rust communities.

Keeping Your Secrets

If you have database connections, passwords, or anything else that you wouldn't share with a random person on the street, please be *very* careful about including it in your project. Git is the elephant that never forgets. Once you've accidentally committed a secret to your repository, it's no longer a secret. This is especially true with crates: you need to make sure you aren't sharing anything that you shouldn't be sharing with the world.

Don't Be Me

I was recently teaching a workshop in front of a large group of people. Someone asked a question, and I discovered that I didn't have the access I needed to a Git repository. So I opened up my secure notes file, grabbed my GitHub key, and realized that my screen was shared with the whole room. I quickly closed the file; nobody was recording, and as soon as I finished presenting, I changed my key. Fortunately, everyone laughed, and nobody tried to hack me. But it was a close call.

Collaborating with Others

If you haven't collaborated on open-source projects before, it's a good idea to open up your project on GitHub for a while before you take the leap to publishing on crates.io. Let people know that your project exists, and see how much interest there is. You'll get feedback, bug reports, and even some pull requests. That's great: "pull requests" are changes that people suggest you make to your project. You can review them and, *if* you like them, accept them. Don't feel like you have to accept every pull request—it's your project, and you get to decide what goes in.

Expect the Bizarre

You'll also receive some truly bizarre issues and comments. I once received a mysterious issue on bracket-lib asking that I remove the word "doctor" from the documentation, apparently because it was a "bad word." Since I use a tool named "RenderDoc" to help debug my graphics, I was a bit confused. The issue was deleted before I could respond, and I never figured out if there was an actual issue involved.

You may also find that you have no feedback at all. This is common: there are a lot of projects on GitHub, and it's possible that nobody noticed you. You should consider this a factor in whether you want to publish your project to crates.io. If nobody is interested in your project, it may not be as useful as you think—or more likely, you need to improve your documentation and project summary to make it clear what is on offer.

A secondary part of collaborating with others is personal responsibility. When you publish a project, you're effectively promising to maintain it forever. There isn't an expiration date on public projects, and requests don't stop arriving because you've moved on. If you're not willing to maintain a project, you should consider not publishing it. If you do publish it, you should make sure that you have a plan for what to do if you can't maintain it anymore.

Life Happens

My bracket-lib project and the Rust Roguelike Tutorial stopped receiving regular updates. This was partly because once Hands-on Rust shipped, changing anything in the library carried the strong risk of breaking code published in the book. It's hard to change printed, paper books after release! The lack of updates was partly because I'm now the proud father of a beautiful little girl—and she takes up a lot of my time. I also went through some burnout—too many things to do, and I just wanted to play games with the little one. Life happens, but it's good to have a plan for what to do when it does. Maybe try and find a co-maintainer, be honest about your availability, or just be prepared to archive the project if you can't maintain it anymore.

Now that you've decided your project is worth sharing, ensured it's ready, chosen a license, and prepared for the responsibilities of maintaining it and collaborating online, let's dive into the nuts and bolts of publishing it to crates.io.

Preparing Your Library for Sharing

The first step to publishing your library is to make sure that your GitHub repository is in good shape. Do you have a good README file? Does it clearly explain what your project does, and why it might be useful? Make sure you have a LICENSE file, too. It's a good idea to wait a little—maybe talking with the Rust community—and see if any GitHub users have anything to say about your project.

Once you're happy with your GitHub, you need to fill out Cargo.toml in detail, with the extra information needed by the crates infrastructure. Here's the Cargo.toml from bracket_lib:

```
[package]
❶ name = "bracket-lib"
❷ version = "0.8.7"
authors = ["Herbert Wolverson <herberticus@gmail.com>"]
edition = "2021"
❸ publish = true"0.8.7"
description = "Meta-crate holding the entirety of bracket-lib (and
❹ exposing it). Use this for the full roguelike toolkit experience."
❺ homepage = "https://github.com/thebracket/bracket-lib"
❻ repository = "https://github.com/thebracket/bracket-lib"
❼ readme = "README.md"
❽ keywords = ["roguelike", "gamedev", "terminal", "ascii", "cp437"]
❾ categories = ["game-engines"]
❿ license = "MIT"
```

❶ The name of your project. The project name must be unique on crates.io. Use "cargo search" to be sure.

❷ Start at 0.0.1, and increase the version for every release. You don't ever want to release a crate with the same version twice!

❸ If you don't include "publish = true" in your Cargo.toml file, Cargo will refuse to publish your crate.

❹ This is the description that will appear on crates.io and in the results of Cargo search. It's important that it accurately describes your project.

❺ This is optional, but it's a good idea to link to your website if you have one.

❻ It's important to publish a Git repository address. Cargo itself uses GitHub, and it's expected that crates provide a direct link to your source code.

❼ Include a README.md file in the base directory of your repository and link to it here. This is the body text people see if they click on your project

—either on GitHub or on crates.io. A good README will explain what the project is, why you might want to use it, and what it does. It should also signpost documentation and examples.

8 You can only list a few keywords, so choose them wisely. Browse crates.io for inspiration—find similar projects, and see what they use.

9 Just like keywords, browse existing crates to find appropriate categories.

10 Important: find the code that matches your license, and tag it here. Make sure it matches the LICENSE file in your repository. Many tools use this to determine if your crate may be used within the company policies—for example, excluding viral copyleft licenses. If you don't select a license, you aren't permitting anyone to use your code.

That's a fair amount of boilerplate, but with the exception of version, you only have to write it once. Please also read the Cargo Book's section on publishing to crates.io for more information.[5]

Once you're happy with your crate's meta-data, it's time to publish with a "dry-run". In the root directory of your crate, run:

```
cargo publish --dry-run
```

If everything goes smoothly, you'll see a message that your crate is ready to publish. If you get an error, you'll need to fix it before you can publish.

Now, take a deep breath. If you're ready to publish, run this:

```
cargo publish
```

And that's it! Your crate will appear on crates.io within a few minutes, and your documentation tags will appear on docs.rs. You can now share your crate with the world.

Wrapping Up

This chapter has covered the social and technical aspects of sharing your library. You've learned about the responsibilities of sharing a project, the importance of licensing, and the technical details of publishing to crates.io. You're now ready to share your library with the world.

---

5.   https://doc.rust-lang.org/cargo/commands/cargo-publish.html

Bibliography

[TH19]   David Thomas and Andrew Hunt. *The Pragmatic Programmer, 20th Anniversary Edition*. The Pragmatic Bookshelf, Dallas, TX, 2019.

[Wol21]   Herbert Wolverson. *Hands-on Rust*. The Pragmatic Bookshelf, Dallas, TX, 2021.

Index

Thank you!

We hope you enjoyed this book and that you're already thinking about what you want to learn next. To help make that decision easier, we're offering you this gift.

Head on over to https://pragprog.com right now, and use the coupon code BUYANOTHER2025 to save 30% on your next ebook. Offer is void where prohibited or restricted. This offer does not apply to any edition of *The Pragmatic Programmer* ebook.

And if you'd like to share your own expertise with the world, why not propose a writing idea to us? After all, many of our best authors started off as our readers, just like you. With up to a 50% royalty, world-class editorial services, and a name you trust, there's nothing to lose. Visit https://pragprog.com/become-an-author/ today to learn more and to get started.

Thank you for your continued support. We hope to hear from you again soon!

The Pragmatic Bookshelf

Pragmatic Bookshelf

SAVE 30%!
Use coupon code
BUYANOTHER2025

Rust Brain Teasers

The Rust programming language is consistent and does its best to avoid surprising the programmer. Like all languages, though, Rust still has its quirks. But these quirks present a teaching opportunity. In this book, you'll work through a series of brain teasers that will challenge your understanding of Rust. By understanding the gaps in your knowledge, you can become better at what you do and avoid mistakes. Many of the teasers in this book come from the author's own experience creating software. Others derive from commonly asked questions in the Rust community. Regardless of their origin, these brain teasers are fun, and let's face it: who doesn't love a good puzzle, right?

Herbert Wolverson
(138 pages) ISBN: 9781680509175. $18.95
https://pragprog.com/book/hwrustbrain

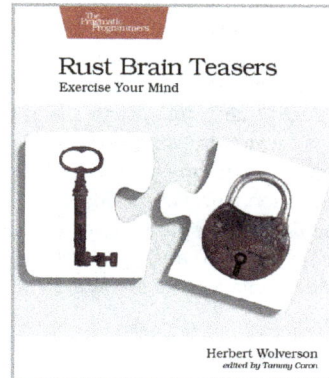

Programming WebAssembly with Rust

WebAssembly fulfills the long-awaited promise of web technologies: fast code, type-safe at compile time, execution in the browser, on embedded devices, or anywhere else. Rust delivers the power of C in a language that strictly enforces type safety. Combine both languages and you can write for the web like never before! Learn how to integrate with JavaScript, run code on platforms other than the browser, and take a step into IoT. Discover the easy way to build cross-platform applications without sacrificing power, and change the way you write code for the web.

Kevin Hoffman
(238 pages) ISBN: 9781680506365. $45.95
https://pragprog.com/book/khrust

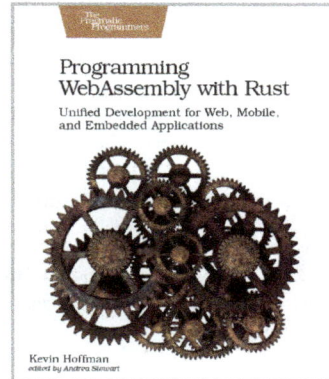

C Brain Teasers

You thought you knew C, but can you solve 25 puzzles
in this popular programming language? Noted C programmer and author Dan Gookin provides a series of
pointed questions, puzzles, and problems to keep your
C programming skills sharp. Each one will provide insight into various aspects of handling strings, numeric
operations, and other activities, giving you techniques
to take the best advantage of all C has to offer. Challenge yourself, and get to know some powerful tricks
and details for writing better, faster, more accurate C
code.

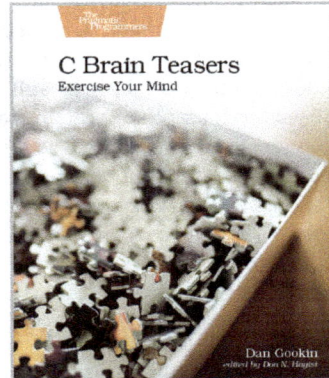

Dan Gookin
(118 pages) ISBN: 9798888650486. $32.95
https://pragprog.com/book/cbrain

C# Brain Teasers

C# is a deceptively easy language to learn, but you'll
soon discover that its underlying complexity conceals
many pitfalls for the unwary programmer. *C# Brain
Teasers* exposes some of those perils in the form of
puzzles to test and expand your knowledge of C#, and
shows how to avoid or defeat them using simple and
modern techniques. Whether you're fairly new to C#
or an experienced veteran, this book is sure to improve
your understanding of C#, and boost your productivity.

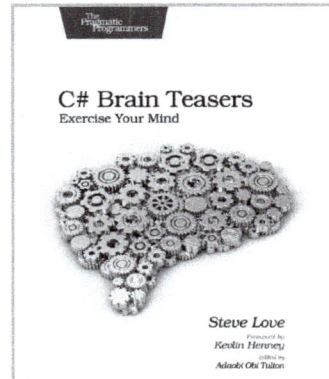

Steve Love
(142 pages) ISBN: 9798888651353. $32.95
https://pragprog.com/book/csharpbt

Vector Search with JavaScript

Make search results smarter and more useful for everyday users and deliver more relevant results with vector search. Go beyond keyword matching to build search experiences that understand meaning, context, and similarity. Use AI-powered techniques to create recommendation systems, personalized search, and content discovery tools. Implement vector search from the ground up with step-by-step guidance, real-world examples, and hands-on coding. Generate embeddings, construct vector indexes, and optimize search accuracy with practical methods that integrate seamlessly into JavaScript applications. Whether refining an existing project or developing a new one, unlock the power of AI-driven search to create smarter, more intuitive user experiences.

Ben Greenberg
(128 pages) ISBN: 9798888651735. $35.95
https://pragprog.com/book/bgvector

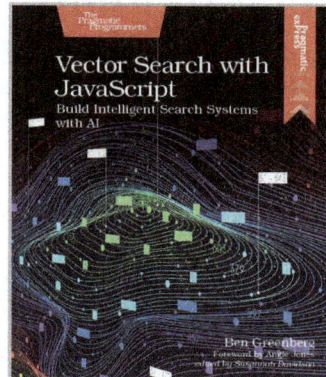

A Common-Sense Guide to Data Structures and Algorithms in Python, Volume 2

Want to write code that pushes the boundaries of speed, space savings, and scalability? Then you need more advanced data structures and algorithms. Go beyond Big O notation and evaluate the true efficiency of each algorithm you design. Pull out data structures such as B-trees, bit vectors, and Bloom filters to wrangle big data. Wield techniques like caching, randomization, and fingerprinting to tame even the most demanding applications. With simple language, clear diagrams, and practice exercises and solutions, this book makes these topics easy to grasp. Go beyond the basics and use these next-level concepts to build software that's ready to take on the challenges of the real world.

Jay Wengrow
(500 pages) ISBN: 9798888651322. $75.95
https://pragprog.com/book/jwpython2

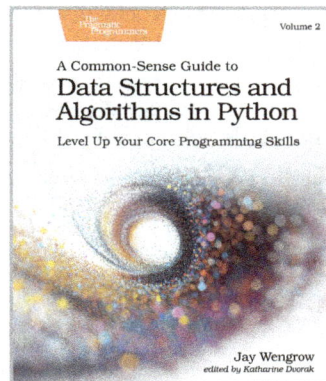

The Pragmatic Bookshelf

The Pragmatic Bookshelf features books written by professional developers for professional developers. The titles continue the well-known Pragmatic Programmer style and continue to garner awards and rave reviews. As development gets more and more difficult, the Pragmatic Programmers will be there with more titles and products to help you stay on top of your game.

Visit Us Online

This Book's Home Page
https://pragprog.com/book/hwmrust
Source code from this book, errata, and other resources. Come give us feedback, too!

Keep Up-to-Date
https://pragprog.com
Join our announcement mailing list (low volume) or follow us on Twitter @pragprog for new titles, sales, coupons, hot tips, and more.

New and Noteworthy
https://pragprog.com/news
Check out the latest Pragmatic developments, new titles, and other offerings.

Save on the ebook

Save on the ebook versions of this title. Owning the paper version of this book entitles you to purchase the electronic versions at a terrific discount.

PDFs are great for carrying around on your laptop—they are hyperlinked, have color, and are fully searchable. Most titles are also available for the iPhone and iPod touch, Amazon Kindle, and other popular e-book readers.

Send a copy of your receipt to support@pragprog.com and we'll provide you with a discount coupon.

Contact Us

Online Orders:	*https://pragprog.com/catalog*
Customer Service:	*support@pragprog.com*
International Rights:	*translations@pragprog.com*
Academic Use:	*academic@pragprog.com*
Write for Us:	*http://write-for-us.pragprog.com*

www.ingramcontent.com/pod-product-compliance
Lightning Source LLC
Chambersburg PA
CBHW081802200326

41597CB00023B/4117